CHALLENGING
THE ONE
BEST SYSTEM

CHALLENGING THE ONE BEST SYSTEM

THE PORTFOLIO MANAGEMENT MODEL AND URBAN SCHOOL GOVERNANCE

Katrina E. Bulkley
Julie A. Marsh
Katharine O. Strunk
Douglas N. Harris
Ayesha K. Hashim

HARVARD EDUCATION PRESS
CAMBRIDGE, MASSACHUSETTS

Paperback ISBN 978-1-68253-570-7
Library Edition ISBN 978-1-68253-571-4

Library of Congress Cataloging-in-Publication Data

Names: Bulkley, Katrina E., author. | Marsh, Julie A., author. | Strunk, Katharine O., author. | Harris, Douglas N., author. | Hashim, Ayesha K., author.
Title: Challenging the one best system : the portfolio management model and urban school governance / Katrina E. Bulkley, Julie A. Marsh, Katharine O. Strunk, Douglas N. Harris, Ayesha K. Hashim.
Other titles: Education politics and policy series.
Description: Cambridge, Massachusetts : Harvard Education Press, [2020] | Series: Education politics and policy | Includes index. | Summary: "In Challenging the One Best System, a team of leading education scholars offers a rich comparative analysis of the set of urban education governance reforms collectively known as the "portfolio management model.""— Provided by publisher.
Identifiers: LCCN 2020027728 | ISBN 9781682535707 (paperback) | ISBN 9781682535714 (library binding)
Subjects: LCSH: School improvement programs—United States. | School management and organization—United States. | Portfolio management—United States. | Education, Urban—Government policy—United States. | Urban schools—United States.
Classification: LCC LB2822.8 .B86 2020 | DDC 371.2/07—dc23
LC record available at https://lccn.loc.gov/2020027728

Published by Harvard Education Press,
an imprint of the Harvard Education Publishing Group

Harvard Education Press
8 Story Street
Cambridge, MA 02138

Cover Design: Wilcox Design
Cover Image: RobinOlimb/DigitalVision Vectors via Getty Images
The typefaces used in this book are Minion, Museo Sans, and Myriad Condensed

To our children:
Sarah, Talia, Ben, Eli, Bryce, Cole, Lyndsey,
Norah, Noor Claire, and Hany

CONTENTS

SECTION 1

THE PORTFOLIO MANAGEMENT MODEL

THE END OF THE
ONE BEST SYSTEM

In 1974, educational historian David Tyack observed that despite the decentralized nature of public schools in the US, school districts and schools across the country looked surprisingly similar. He argued that the American system of public education had taken on a standardized structure, which he coined the "One Best System." Over many decades, core aspects of that system have endured, with local school districts led by publicly elected school boards that hire education professionals and directly operate schools under standardized policies and governance. Over the last few decades, however, the edges of that one best system have begun to fracture, and, especially in large urban systems, major chunks have broken away.

One important manifestation of this reconceptualization of districts is the portfolio management model (PMM).[1] PMMs move away from exclusive, direct district management of schools toward a system of schools operating under varied types of governance and with varying degrees of autonomy. Portfolio managers decide which schools warrant public support, including independent charter schools, various forms of autonomous schools, and traditional district-run schools. In theory, this approach enables schools to adapt practices to better serve students and holds schools accountable for achieving results.[2] While we do not advocate for or against the PMM idea, we believe that examining the design and enactment of systems that embody this idea requires us to take seriously the theory of action suggested by its advocates.

At the heart of the PMM idea are five interlocking policy mechanisms: increased central office *planning* around what schools will operate within the system alongside performance-based *oversight* of those schools; broad-based *school choice*; an emphasis on increasing school-based *autonomy*; greater flexibility around *human capital* practices including hiring, reten-tion, and compensation; and a more extensive set of *school support* organi-zations, from which schools can select options that meet their needs.

In this book, we dive deeply into these five mechanisms in order to understand how they are both designed and enacted in the evolving school systems of three cities—New Orleans, Denver, and Los Angeles—that have adopted either elements of PMM, or PMM in its entirety. We selected these cities because of the important ways in which they vary both in context and in their interpretations of the PMM approach. Doing so allows us to consider two critical issues about system change and public education. First, are systems incrementally evolving or fundamentally restructuring, and why are these transformations happening? Second, are these system changes leading to meaningful changes in school practice and a new set of norms and structures?

Examining these two issues requires looking at systems and schools from multiple angles and considering the distinct and sometimes compet-ing goals being prioritized within them.[3] Scholars have long argued that education and education policy promote multiple values and goals that are often contested and can come into conflict. The PMM is no exception. Proponents argue that the PMM provides parents with greater freedom to select schools that match their children's needs and greater access to quality schools in ways that are no longer dependent on where they live—advancing goals of liberty and equity. The model also assumes that greater flexibility for educators and choice for parents (arguably both elements of liberty) will lead to innovation, improved quality, and efficiency. Yet, as one can imagine, these goals are not always in sync; nor do stakeholders always agree on what they mean. For example, although portfolio managers may define quality based on student achievement, parents may favor other as-pects of quality, such as the arts, or the value of building relationships with children and families in their local neighborhoods. Similarly, stakeholders may hold differing views of equity. Some may understand it as equal distribution of resources, while others view it as a fair distribution (not necessarily equal or uniform), while still others may have a transformative view of equity as challenging oppression.[4] And while the PMM could foster liberty, equity, and efficiency in complementary ways, too much autonomy could potentially threaten the rights and equitable access of students, or create inefficiencies previously avoided under the economies of scale of the traditional centralized system. While the portfolio model seeks to balance these competing values and tensions (for example, by providing centralized oversight to offer equity protections), achieving such balance is not guaranteed.

Given the historical stability of the "one best system," it is important to understand both why we are now seeing system transformations and whether these transformations are leading to a new common set of structures and practices at a system and school level. Indeed, the study's findings suggest different system trajectories that may lead away from a one best system altogether, with New Orleans largely abandoning the traditional central office, Denver seeking to balance autonomy and centralized authority, and Los Angeles splitting essentially into two distinct educational systems—one relying on traditional district authority and the other emphasizing school-based autonomy. While the study focuses on these cities, similar trajectories can be seen in high-profile districts such as New York City and Chicago, as well as less nationally recognized districts such as Spring Branch, Texas; Fulton County, Georgia; and Fullerton, California.

THE MORAL IMPERATIVE FOR IMPROVEMENT IN URBAN SYSTEMS

A variety of pressures may be contributing to the adoption of the portfolio approach. Urban districts educate a disproportionate share of students and particularly of students living in poverty in our country. The demographic profile of these students is also shifting, as more than half of all cities in the US are majority non-White, and the geographic reach of increasing diversity has spread.[5] The struggles of urban schools and districts to provide high-quality education for all students are well-documented, with many facing low academic achievement along with large achievement gaps tied to poverty and race/ethnicity, high levels of leader and teacher turnover, fewer certified teachers, and inequitable funding.[6]

The moral imperative for improving these systems has never been stronger. Yet years of budget cuts, declining enrollments, and dwindling public confidence have greatly complicated the task of reforming urban school systems. Critics argue that decades of education reforms have produced little in the way of concrete improvements for American students, particularly for those who have been the most traditionally underserved.[7] In response, contemporary education reformers have suggested that the only way to truly improve urban public education is to fundamentally restructure public education systems so that they incorporate all the publicly funded education within a geographic region such as a city.[8]

Many reformers emphasize the governance of public education—that is, the political and legal processes by which formal institutions and actors make decisions that determine "who is responsible and accountable for what in the system."[9] As a result, a variety of new types of school systems are emerging, including turnaround districts, state and mayoral takeover districts, networked improvement communities, charter school networks, and portfolio districts.[10] Often, these governance reforms aim to amend the traditional role of the school district by shifting management of schools away from locally elected school boards and the central offices they oversee and toward private organizations and charter schools. They fundamentally restructure practices commonly associated with the idea of a "best system," including standardized district policies and procedures, collective bargaining between unions and administrators, considerable job security for teachers and staff, and centralized control over school operations. They also target the perceived inefficiencies and dysfunction of the traditional centralized, bureaucratic structure and practices of district central offices, which are assumed to squelch school-level innovation, entrepreneurship, motivation, and capacity to improve.[11]

THE IDEA OF PORTFOLIO MANAGEMENT

While some school systems adopt the model comprehensively, others adopt particular PMM strategies more piecemeal. In many cases, the central authority (or authorities) overseeing a district is motivated to adopt some form of a PMM in response to an increasing number of students in the district attending charter schools. Growing enrollment in charter schools forces local officials to grapple with how to incorporate charters into traditional public education while ensuring equity, solvency, and quality. Advocates offer the PMM approach as a primary solution to meet this challenge because it can allow central district actors to shape the set of charter schools in the district.

For systems adopting portfolio strategies, the transformation is often ongoing. Systems continue to evolve in important ways in response to sometimes conflicting pressures. On the one hand, support from foundations and entities such as the City Fund (founded in 2018 in part by the Laura and John Arnold Foundation, with initial funding reported at $200 million) has brought substantial additional philanthropic support to school systems pursuing portfolio-type reforms.[12] On the other hand, pressures pushing back against portfolio management, especially as it involves charter schools, have led to protest and legislative change in some states. For example, teacher strikes in several California cities in 2019 coalesced around not only demands for better pay and working conditions, but also limits on charter school growth and portfolio management. Where these pressures will lead and whether they will shift systems toward being more similar or even more different are yet to be seen.

As a reform that is largely about governance, the PMM idea does not prescribe particular educational practices, such as curriculum or pedagogical strategies.[13] Instead, it builds on a set of interlocking policy mechanisms that local actors can shape to particular contexts. Paul Hill, Christine Campbell, and Betheny Gross describe the concept of a portfolio as grounded in a market metaphor that links the role of the portfolio manager to that of the manager of a stock portfolio: the financial manager's "diverse investments" are akin to a portfolio manager's "new and promising school options"; a financial portfolio requires "constant review of performance," while a portfolio of schools needs "sophisticated accountability systems"; and, as a result of these performance reviews, the financial manager makes "strategic investment[s] and divestment[s]," while the portfolio manager will "expand successful programs, [and] intervene in or close unsuccessful programs."[14] The central role of the portfolio manager makes the PMM distinct from a purely market system and retains a more substantial role for a government actor within the system.

In particular, the portfolio manager is charged with enacting and over-seeing the five key mechanisms described at the beginning of this chapter:

- A clear and rigorous approach to the intertwined roles of *planning* and *oversight*. The portfolio manager identifies and addresses the needs of the community, including decisions around school provid-ers' foci and location. Advocates see oversight as based on student and school performance against common metrics and on allowing portfolio managers to stay informed of schools' progress, to inter-vene quickly with struggling schools, and, if necessary, to take action such as closing schools, bringing in different school operators, or not renewing charter contracts.[15] In response, schools are expected to do their work differently and more effectively, so that students learn more and/or differently than they had in the past.
- Widespread student *choice*. A family's ability to select from more than one schooling option for their children is intended to drive quality improvement through both market- and nonmarket-based pressures.[16] On the market side, choice is expected to enhance competition for students, in turn creating incentives for schools to improve and decrease bureaucratic waste.[17] This development of competition, as a complement to the nonmarket side (that is, plan-ning by the portfolio manager), can give families better options to choose from, allow for stronger school-based communities with shared values, and increase parent satisfaction and engagement, and, in turn, student learning.[18]
- Increased *autonomy* to school sites and charter management orga-nizations (CMOs) over key domains such as staffing, budget, gover-nance, and curriculum and instruction. This autonomy is expected to foster the development of schools that are responsive to local contexts, staffed with committed personnel who share the schools' goals, and innovative in their practice.[19] Combined with choice for families, these locally driven operations are then expected to lead to greater alignment between educational programs and services on the one hand and student needs on the other.[20]
- The development of strong and appropriate *human capital*. The in-clusion of alternative pipelines for education professionals and the removal of the restrictions of union contracts and district policies

are expected to enhance recruitment and retention of teachers and administrators who are effective and well matched to their schools' needs, and to provide administrators with increased flexibility to manage schools' and districts' most valuable resources—teachers and leaders—in ways that best meet the needs of students.[21]

- *School supports* for school-determined needs from multiple providers, perhaps including but going beyond the portfolio manager. Such efforts are believed to enhance school-based personnel's ability to deliver high-quality education and to productively respond to the increased autonomy and accountability through building the capacity of schools and staff.[22]

As envisioned by advocates, such as Paul Hill at the Center on Reinventing Public Education and Neerav Kingsland of the City Fund, this comprehensive set of changes, used in concert and distinct from prior efforts, will yield more efficient and effective public education. In the ideal conception of a portfolio manager, systems adopt all five mechanisms. In practice, however, systems have moved in different ways along the path of each mechanism. For example, managers have sometimes provided autonomy for some schools but not others, or have increased choice but with limitations on what schools are available. Taken together, these variations render the portfolio model more of a set of ideas or strategies. When adopted in concert, these five mechanisms are intended to intersect to bring about improved outcomes for students. For example, the provision of enhanced autonomy for school operators, when combined with capacity-building supports and efforts to improve human capital, may lead to more substantive changes in practice—and thus to improvements in student outcomes—than the changes that emerge as a result of relying solely on autonomy.

These ideas, of course, are not entirely new. Some of these policy components are found in a range of approaches to reform, such as standards-based reform, performance-based accountability, charter schools, and efforts to improve the different aspects of human capital in schools by adopting new evaluation systems and changing the role of unions. Combining centralized planning with policy mechanisms used in other reforms creates not only the foundation for a different type of system but also the possibility that the interplay of all these moving parts may generate systems distinct from one another.

Above, we highlighted two big-picture questions we address throughout this book: Are systems incrementally evolving or fundamentally restructuring? Are these system changes leading to meaningful changes in school practice? In order to examine how school systems continue to evolve with the stated goal of better serving students, we must ask more specific questions about the nature of these systems:

- How are portfolio managers enacting these policy mechanisms? How are they balancing their responsibilities and multiple, potentially competing goals?
- Whose voices matter in these decisions? What are the roles of other actors, such as the community and organized labor?
- How do schools and families respond to and experience these policies? Are there differences based on school types, such as charter versus traditional public schools?
- How do the ways in which schools and systems operate connect to intermediate outcomes related to equity and achievement in schools?

While others have examined individual cities undergoing PMM-like change or the performance of students in portfolio districts, we know of no other effort to look both comparatively across multiple systems and deeply within such systems—from the central office to the classroom.[23]

THREE DISTINCT SYSTEMS: NEW ORLEANS, DENVER, AND LOS ANGELES

Although experiencing common system-level change, New Orleans, Denver, and Los Angeles have very different school systems in terms of their nature, size, and demographics. As table 1.1 illustrates, the Los Angeles school system is significantly larger than those of the other two cities, both in geographic size and in the number of students and schools. While all three systems serve diverse and high-needs populations, the racial/ethnic backgrounds differ. In New Orleans and Los Angeles, the majority of students were African American (83 percent) and Latinx (74 percent), respectively. Denver's student population was more heterogeneous: half of the students were Latinx (55 percent), less than a quarter were White (23 percent), and the remaining students were either African American (13 percent) or Asian (3 percent).

TABLE 1.1   Characteristics of the school systems (2016–17)

	NEW ORLEANS	DENVER	LOS ANGELES
Geographic Size	170 square miles	155 square miles	710 square miles
Number of Schools	86	211	1,028
Types of schools	Charter (92%) TPS* (7%) Independent (1%)	Charter (27%) TPS (45%) Innovation (27%)	Charter (22%) TPS (57%) Autonomous (17%)
Number of Students	48,375	92,331	633,621
Free/Reduced Price Lunch	88%	67%	81%
Student Race/ Ethnicity	83% African Am. 8% White 9% Latinx/Other	55% Latinx 23% White 13% African Am. 3% Asian	74% Latinx 10% White 8% African Am. 6% Asian/Other
English Language Learners (ELL)	4%	37%	25%
Special Education	11%	10%	14%

* Traditional Public School

Data sources: New Orleans: Kate Babineau, Dave Hand, and Vincent Rossmeier, *The State of Public Education in New Orleans, 2016–17* (New Orleans: Cowen Institute, 2017), https://tulane.app.box.com/s/ddngdxbtar9kkn21szyzi6gsplslwqn3.

Denver: "Facts & Figures: DPS by the Numbers," Denver Public Schools, 2020, https://www.dpsk12.org/about-dps/facts-figures; and other sources of publicly available data from Denver Public Schools (DPS) and the Colorado Department of Education.

Los Angeles: "Fingertip Facts, 2016–17," Los Angeles Unified School District, August 2016, https://achieve.lausd.net/cms/lib/CA01000043/Centricity/Domain/32/Fingertip%20Facts2016-17_FINAL.pdf; DataQuest, California Department of Education, dq.cde.ca.gov; and publicly available data from the California Department of Education.

Data come from the 2016–17 school year.

Note: These data are based on the years during which data were collected for this study. There have been some noteworthy changes since then, especially in New Orleans.

The types of schools operating in each city also differed considerably. Whereas almost all of New Orleans' schools were charter, the share of charter schools was considerably smaller in the other two cities. Nevertheless, at the time of this study, Los Angeles included more charter schools in sheer numbers than any other city in the nation.[24] Furthermore, both Denver and Los Angeles operated both traditional schools and a variety of school models managed by the district central office but granted greater autonomy, adding further diversity to their portfolios. Moreover, as we discuss below, differences in the nature of state charter school and accountability

policies, and in the strength of state and local labor associations, contributed to the variation in school types and governance arrangements across
the three sites. (See chapter 3 for more in-depth background information
on each city and school system.)

In order to analyze these systems at different levels, we gathered extensive qualitative, survey, and administrative data, along with relevant documents, in the 2016–17 school year (see appendix A for details). We surveyed
all school leaders in each system, receiving a total of 628 responses out
of 1,286 surveyed. We also received survey responses from 1,927 teachers
in 124 schools across the three systems, out of 3,590 surveys sent. At the
system level, the qualitative data included seventy-six interviews of central
office administrators, board members, civic organization leaders, state experts, and union representatives. School-level data centered on twenty-one
school case studies, and included interviews of forty-one individuals in
school leadership roles, ninety-three teachers, sixty-two parents, and four-
teen individuals who supervised school principals. We supplemented these
core data sources with documents such as media accounts, district and
school websites, and existing research.

Although they have undergone a common shift in the governance of
public schooling, the three cities at the center of the study differ in important ways. Distinct places, histories, and policies provide a critical backdrop, as they shape our understanding of how system change ultimately
affected school practices. As we describe in more detail later in the book,
the three cases underwent important transformations in the past two decades, and we characterize them as reflecting three distinct variations in
the portfolio approach:

- *Managed market (New Orleans)*: a system in which virtually all
  schools were highly autonomous charter schools, governed by the
  state-run Recovery School District (RSD) and the Orleans Parish School Board (OPSB). These central offices primarily served as
  gatekeepers in areas of enrollment and oversight of schools, as well
  as in areas needing centralization for policy or legal reasons, such as
  funding, expulsions, and special education.
- *Centralized portfolio (Denver)*: an integrated system overseeing
  traditional and nontraditional school options under a common
  policy framework, in which central office staff in Denver Public

Schools (DPS) took on a more expansive role while seeking to balance school-level autonomy with centralized control. Denver was notable for its explicit focus on developing a PMM that included autonomous "innovation" schools alongside charter and traditional schools, for its broad-scale shifts in union contracts, and for the overall collaborative and locally driven nature of the system.

• *Competing systems (Los Angeles)*: a centralized district that directly operated a set of district-run schools, including both traditional and autonomous schools, and oversaw a parallel system of charter schools, with little integration or interaction across the two sectors. Los Angeles had a polarized climate with sharp distinctions between those schools operated by the central office and charter schools. The district-managed schools were unionized, while most of the charter schools were not.

These varying demographic, organizational, and political conditions provided rich opportunities for exploring the implementation of portfolio reforms.

Later chapters dig deeply into the enactment of each of the five core PMM mechanisms at both the system and school levels. As an introduction, table 1.2 provides background on the design of these mechanisms and how they are intended to function at the system and school levels in each city.

TABLE 1.2   **Comparison of enactment of portfolio management mechanisms**

	NEW ORLEANS Managed Market	**DENVER** Centralized Portfolio	**LOS ANGELES** Competing Systems
Planning and Oversight	• Common expectations of all school types using performance framework with multiple measures in both RSD and OPSB • Extensive use of school closure by RSD • Annual review process to set priorities for charter applicants	• Common expectations of all school types using performance framework with multiple measures • Extensive use of school closure • Annual review process to set priorities for new schools—can be charter, innovation, or traditional public schools	• Varied expectations with multiple accountability frameworks based on school type • Less use of high-stakes accountability tools • Some planning within district-run school types, only reactive to applications in charter sector

(continues)

TABLE 1.2   **Comparison of enactment of portfolio management mechanisms,** *continued*

	NEW ORLEANS Managed Market	**DENVER** Centralized Portfolio	**LOS ANGELES** Competing Systems
Choice	• Overall broad access through portfolio managers' work with EnrollNOLA • Broad sharing of comparable information on schools • Some limits on access due to geographic preferences or admissions requirements • Access enabled because transportation required	• Generally broad access through OneApp • Broad sharing of comparable information on schools • Some limits on access due to geographic preferences • Access limited through partial transportation availability	• No common enrollment system; complex system within large district-run system; charters enroll on their own • Some common information for segments of district-run schools • Limited access as a result of complex processes, limited transportation, and geographic size
Autonomy	• Charters had extensive autonomy with some limits imposed by portfolio manager • Traditional public schools had charter-like autonomies	• Charters had extensive autonomy with some limits imposed by portfolio manager • Semiautonomous (Innovation) schools had extensive potential autonomy • Traditional public schools had guaranteed autonomy around educational programming	• Charters had extensive autonomy, minimal limits imposed by portfolio manager • Semiautonomous schools had a range of models with varied levels of autonomy • Traditional public schools had minimal formal autonomy
Human Capital	• School/network–based decisions for charters (except OPSB traditional public schools) • Outside organizations heavily involved on a school-by-school basis	• Partnership orientation: DPS, private organizations, and autonomous schools collaborate • School/network–based decisions for charter and innovation schools, but they can adapt/adopt the district's teacher evaluation system (Leading Effective Academic Practice)	• Charter sector: school/network–based decisions with teachers in some schools represented by unions • District-run sector: top-down
School Supports	• RSD and OPSB role in school capacity minimal (some OPSB supports for district-run schools) • Private organizations and charter networks are the central actors in providing capacity	• Range of DPS supports for all schools; more extensive and mandated supports for traditional public schools • Partnerships between DPS and private organizations for some supports • Private organizations and charter networks are engaged actors in providing capacity	• Extensive LAUSD supports for district-run schools including through outside partners; very minimal supports for charters • Private organizations and charter networks are the central actors in providing charter schools with supports

OVERVIEW OF THE BOOK

The chapters that follow first ground the study within the broader context and then turn to the five policy mechanisms, exploring them first individually and then in concert. Chapters 2 and 3 provide the foundation for our story. Chapter 2 delves into the empirical, theoretical, and conceptual foundations for the study, examining the role of school districts and central offices and change within those settings over time. The chapter connects this more historical view to the PMM theory of action, which connects the design of the policy changes to desired outcomes. Chapter 2 draws on principal-agent theory, which considers how those who determine organizational goals (the "principals") seek to ensure and motivate those doing the work on the ground (the "agents") through strategies such as monitoring and offering incentives.[25] Given the emphasis in this theory of action on structures and incentives for driving system change, the chapter also considers the value of research on policy implementation and organizational change. By highlighting the multitude of forces that can shape educational practices in both existing and new governance structures, such research challenges the assumptions of principal-agent theory that altering structures and incentives can lead to meaningful change.[26]

Chapter 3 digs more deeply into each of the three cities at the center of the study, providing an overview of each state and local context and system of schools. This chapter also lays the foundation for understanding change within each city by looking at trends over time in areas including the number and type of publicly funded schools (such as traditional, magnet, or charter), student performance, and student demographics. Through attention to history, context, and politics, the chapter examines not just what the systems look like, but why they look as they do and why they vary in substantial ways that ultimately influence how the PMM idea is locally enacted. In all three cities, a history of racial politics and desegregation provided a backdrop to ongoing tensions between those seeking reform and historically marginalized communities.

The second section of the book digs deeply into the design and enactment of the policy mechanisms described above. Chapters 4 through 8 look at the three cities through the lenses of the five policy mechanisms that are foundational to the PMM idea: planning and oversight, student choice, school autonomy, human capital, and school support. Extensive data allow us to trace each mechanism from the broad design of systems to the daily work of schools in each of the cities.

Chapter 4 examines planning and oversight of schools based on school performance, including decisions about what schools will operate and challenges involving issues of consistency, transparency, and fairness in high-stakes oversight. Chapter 5 explores issues of school choice, analyzing the different enrollment processes as well as school-level recruitment and marketing practices. Chapter 6 examines school-based autonomy, describing what autonomies were embedded in different school models and the level of reported autonomy for leaders and teachers between the different sectors. Chapter 7 considers issues of human capital, highlighting issues of retention and recruitment as well as the role of the teachers' unions in each system. Chapter 8 describes how schools received needed supports and the role of portfolio managers, CMOs, and outside organizations in providing those supports.

The final section steps back from the individual mechanisms to look at these systems as whole entities, revisiting the PMM theory of action and exploring how what we have learned can inform those who work within schools and systems as well as the policy makers who set the foundation for that work. Chapter 9 weaves together the different mechanisms in order to ask how, based on the theory of action, advocates of the PMM idea might expect systems to shape what happens in schools. The findings show that New Orleans, Denver, and (to a lesser extent) the charter system in Los Angeles are relatively well-aligned with the PMM mechanisms, while the district-run system in Los Angeles is less aligned. However, analysis of intermediate outcomes raises questions about the links between school improvement and the PMM mechanisms. Specifically, we identify two puzzling findings. First, despite the two systems being similarly aligned with the PMM ideal, teachers and leaders in New Orleans reported more positive intermediate outcomes on our surveys than those in Denver schools. Second, although the charter system in Los Angeles was far more aligned with the PMM ideal than the district-run system, reports from teachers and leaders in the two systems were relatively similar.

Finally, chapter 10 concludes the study by asking what we have learned about the PMM approach. We describe intersections of mechanisms within the model itself, and how one such intersection—between performance-based oversight, school-based autonomy, and varied school supports—resulted in systems prioritizing some mechanisms over others. Our analysis points us to ways in which competing ideas about equity and quality, both core values in education, sometimes led to challenges between stakeholders. And, most importantly, our analysis identifies critical conditions shaping system change, including institutional and political pressures as well as local educational capacity and context.

CHALLENGING THE ONE BEST SYSTEM

This book shares the findings of a rigorous mixed-method study based on rich interview data and extensive surveys of school leaders and teachers, along with administrative data sets and documents from 2016–17. It tells the story of these three changing systems—New Orleans, Los Angeles, and Denver—and how the systems and schools within them are grappling with changes in the five policy mechanisms noted above. While all three cities varied in the design of their policy mechanisms and the context in which these were implemented, they nonetheless faced common struggles spurred by decentralization. At times, schools within each city also adopted common practices that, while seemingly misaligned with the assumptions of the PMM, served to maintain a school's legitimacy in the current institutionalized context of public education, choice, and decentralization.

The challenge of how to govern schools to best develop high-quality, publicly funded education is one with which government has long grappled, and one which it will continue to face in years to come. By looking explicitly at the connections between governance and educational practice, this book sheds light on those linkages and helps illuminate the messy, complicated, and nuanced nature of educational system change. We find that the systems we studied are changing in fundamental ways, away from the one best system, and that these changes have resulted in important shifts in power and politics within the systems.

Yet, we also raise serious questions about the potential for this particular set of policy mechanisms—which emphasize incentives and structures over context and issues of the technical core of schooling (such as curriculum, pedagogy, and school organization)—to lead to sustained school improvement. Finally, we highlight implications for policy makers and system leaders interested in portfolio-style reform. These include: managing the tension between centralization and decentralization; explicitly focusing on the role of community voice; considering the trade-off between quality, as defined by a common performance framework, and the potential for a diverse set of school options; acknowledging the potential challenges related to local conditions, including educational capacity and institutional pressures; and investing in the relationships needed to make any educational reform successful.

2

THE DESIGN OF EDUCATIONAL SYSTEMS

Since the emergence of school districts in the early 1800s, policy makers have struggled with how to best design educational systems. What should be the role of a central office? What should happen in schools and classrooms? What other kinds of organizations should be involved and how? The portfolio management model (PMM) idea connects in important ways to this enduring set of questions, and efforts to understand its enactment must begin by examining how arguments in favor of a PMM approach intersect with previous efforts at system reform.

This chapter focuses especially on the structure of school districts as the foundational system in public education, and on the role of the district central office as the clearest analogue to the portfolio manager that oversees a PMM. This places the cities that are at the center of this study within the broader context of efforts to improve education through school system change. The following sections explore the different ways in which educational systems—especially school districts—have been seen as tools for or barriers to improvement.

In the context of that history, we examine the logic underlying the PMM idea and the ways in which it builds on—but is distinct from—prior efforts at system reform. The analysis incorporates the five policy mechanisms described in chapter 1 and studied in detail in chapters 4 through 8. Going beyond tinkering with one or two reforms—which leaves new practices vulnerable to leadership change and haphazard implementation—the PMM idea is meant to bring about lasting, deep, structural change in systems.

In economics and political science, the "principal-agent problem" posits that rational actors seek to meet their own goals, and that systems need to be designed in such a way that the *agents* doing the daily work are motivated and able to meet the goals set up by the *principals*—those in leadership roles in systems, not school leaders—who direct the work of the agents. Following this theory, PMM advocates believe that educational quality and equity can be improved by aligning system goals with incentives for those doing the daily work of education. But while principal-agent theory provides an intellectual framework for understanding this belief, research on policy implementation and organizational change in general, particularly that which draws on institutional and neo-institutional theory, challenges the assumptions of principal-agent theory. Contrary to the assumption that altering structures and incentives can lead to meaningful change, these theories identify a multitude of forces that can inhibit change and shape educational practices in both existing and new governance structures. In the case of PMMs, complex forces may push newer types of organizations, such as charter management organizations (CMOs), charter schools, and portfolio managers, toward practices similar to those of existing organizations rather than developing more effective educational approaches. These critical concerns will guide our analysis as we examine the relevant theoretical and empirical research.

THE ROLE OF SCHOOL DISTRICTS AND CENTRAL OFFICES IN EDUCATIONAL IMPROVEMENT

One of the enduring puzzles for policy makers seeking to improve educational practice has been how to structure a system of governance that promotes meaningful and positive improvement at the school and classroom levels. Changing educational structures and governance in order to improve the quality and equity of publicly funded education has a long history in the United States. Advocates of a broad range of reforms have consistently asserted that creating better structures would enable educational improvements and, implicitly, that existing structures functioned as barriers to such improvement. For example, advocates of community schools in the 1960s argued that decentralization would allow for greater local influence, while charter and voucher advocates have supported the idea that market structures would tap into competition in order to support school improvement.[1]

For the most part, governance changes have involved shifting authority between different levels of a fixed set of public entities, including federal, state, city, district, and district-run schools. These have included such changes as the consolidation of local schools into districts in the 1800s, but also more recent actions, such as devolving decision-making authority to schools through site-based management, moving responsibility to a single elected authority via mayoral control, and centralizing authority through state standards.[2] Despite those ongoing shifts of authority, certain aspects of public schooling have stayed relatively consistent, with an elected board overseeing a superintendent and central office that managed the day-to-day operations of schools. It was within this context, alongside an increasing skepticism about the effectiveness of governmental actors in managing large-scale challenges, that a growing chorus of reform advocates argued that public functions could be better served through "reinventing" government so as to better take advantage of entrepreneurialism and markets.[3]

Systems for running local publicly funded education, particularly in the form of school districts, have been a foundational element of American public schooling for well over a hundred years. Such systems, as described in Tyack's seminal work, emerged out of concerns that "community-dominated" education, with educators lacking in formal training and occupying tenuous positions alongside uneven and often minimal resources, would no longer meet the needs of a changing society.[4] Thus, educator organizations such as the then leader-dominated National Education Association and scholars such as Ellwood P. Cubberley, beginning in the late 1800s and through the 1920s, pushed for more professionalized and efficient school *systems*.[5]

The emergence of school districts—and their central offices—can be tied back to the Progressive Era and a focus on professionalizing education. Central offices were expected to bring a higher level of competence and consistency. They functioned as the primary governance structure within which public schools were created, located, and managed, while the superintendent—selected by the board—served as the professional leader of the office. These offices generally served a broad set of functions ranging from managing human resources, to building and maintaining facilities, to developing and providing curriculum, and so on.[6] Elected school boards served both as the oversight mechanism for districts and as the means for citizens to have a direct, democratic voice in decisions about education, at the same time separating elected board members from professional educators. While there have been tensions over the structure and role of such boards since they emerged as a central facet of public education in the US from the early days of the country, the basic idea of locally elected boards whose function is oversight of school districts has remained the clear norm.

The idea of central offices as playing a critical role in educational improvement has continually resurfaced, such as in scholarly work around the role of central offices in leading instructional change.[7] This research identifies conditions under which central offices engage in "fundamental shifts in the traditional systems and work practices" such that they can lead meaningful instructional improvement.[8]

This vision of the central office as a potentially powerful force in educational improvement stands in stark contrast to views that characterize those offices as either irrelevant or as barriers to change. During the 1980s and 1990s, in particular, the focus of educational reform shifted toward the individual school, as reflected in attention to issues such as the "effective schools" movement, site-based management, and small schools.[9] These reform efforts, which sit as one foundation of the PMM idea, largely sidelined the role of district central offices as significant actors in educational reform.[10] As Trujillo notes, "Implicit in the policies of [the early 1980s] was an assumption that seemingly impenetrable, cumbersome central offices were to be circumvented rather than embraced as potential contributors to educational reform."[11]

Since the 1990s, some researchers and advocates of charters and choice have gone beyond largely ignoring the role of district central offices to more explicitly centering this traditional structure as a barrier to substantial improvement, arguing for greater decentralization and increased influence of markets.[12] The seeds of the PMM approach are most often tied to this strand of thinking, which asserts that there are "organizationally and politically intractable problems inherent in district designs" (such as recalcitrant bureaucracies and political incentives that limit change), and that moving authority outside of the district structure will increase opportunities for innovation and accountability.[13] Indeed, the origins of the portfolio idea can be found in the work of Paul Hill, who wrote with colleagues in the 1990s about governance as a major barrier to reform in large urban districts and offered ideas such as "contracting" of school management as an alternative to hierarchical district governance.[14]

Enactment of the PMM idea involves significant rethinking of the roles of district offices, which, as portfolio managers, are situated as "key gatekeeper[s], mediating between local needs and demands, on the one hand, and external pressure and resources on the other."[15] PMM advocates do not subscribe to the idea that central offices (and districts more broadly) are irrelevant to change, but instead offer a distinct view of the role that such central offices might play. Such a distinct approach requires the reorientation of organizational cultures, norms, and practices in central offices.[16]

THE LOGIC AND DESIGN OF PORTFOLIO MANAGEMENT

Underpinning the PMM idea is a set of assumptions about the relationships among different parts of an educational system, especially between those who lead and oversee the system and those in schools doing the daily work of educating students. These assumptions incorporate ideas such as the need for "alignment" between the goals of the leaders and those in schools, on the one hand, and the nature of incentives believed to support such alignment, on the other. In many ways, these ideas are consistent with principal-agent theory, which suggests that principals should use varied incentives to align the goals of agents with their own.[17] This idea extends naturally to the portfolio model, in which portfolio managers build their portfolios through performance-based contracts with school-based agents such as school operators (such as CMOs), leaders, and teachers to meet expectations for schools.

Consistent with analyses of the principal-agent issue and critiques of traditional school districts, advocates for a shift toward PMMs assert that, because schools are "permanent" and will continue to operate regardless of whether they successfully educate students, there is little incentive for those in schools (agents) to attend directly to the quality of their outputs (the goals of principals).[18] Advocates argue that this permanence of schools, alongside the focus of traditional school districts on educational inputs such as fiscal resources, requirements around teacher certification, and extensive regulation, has enabled bureaucracies to become rigid and complex. In such bureaucracies, the goals of system principals are obscured and misaligned, thus inhibiting desired outcomes of educational efficiency, effectiveness, and equity.[19] Theoretically, a PMM would resolve this misalignment by establishing and closely monitoring performance contracts that delineate specific performance expectations to schools in the system, while giving schools significant school-based autonomy around the educational inputs necessary to achieve their goals. The consequence or disincentive of closure (for low performance) and the incentive in the form of increased autonomy (for high performance) are theorized to improve the motivation of agents to align their goals and efforts with those of the principals.[20]

The five policy mechanisms analyzed throughout this book are intended to enhance alignment between the goals of those governing a system and those doing the daily work of educating students. Performance-based *oversight* and *planning* linked to that oversight—including measurement of progress toward goals and accompanying decisions about who operates schools—are intended to motivate school and outside organization leaders to meet the goals of parents and portfolio managers. Also, performance-based contracts, in theory, allow principals to monitor the progress of agents and intervene as needed, and offer a means to determine access to desired incentives.[21] However, empirical research indicates that developing and maintaining a diverse range of school offerings for families can be challenging amid pressures that may encourage the emergence of new types of homogeneity or the retention of familiar forms.[22]

The market-based accountability that comes with school *choice* provides, in theory, further incentives for school-based agents to meet the goals of parents, who, when dissatisfied, can "vote with their feet" and take their children and the resources that accompany them to other schools. Research, however, has found limits to choice in practice. In the context of Denver specifically, for example, Denice and Gross examined school choice in Denver as part of the broader PMM there and found that the locations of high performing schools limited access for some families, while another report identified student access to schools of choice as shaped by school location.[23]

The remainder of the key PMM mechanisms enable agents in schools to meet the expectations of system principals. Granting school leaders *autonomy*, including flexibility around staffing and compensating their staff, allows them to structure instruction and operations in accordance with local needs. Studies that have focused on autonomy within broader PMM-style system changes have found that the availability of such autonomy can be used either as a reward for schools evaluated as successful or as a tool to enable such potential success.[24]

Ensuring that school leaders have options for *support* from the portfolio manager itself and from private organizations, including alternative education preparation organizations such as Teach for America (TFA), allows the leaders to develop the necessary capacity to achieve the lofty performance goals to which they are being held. However, studies indicate that decentralization of school management creates challenges due to more limited economies of scale, such as in addressing the needs of students with disabilities.[25]

Given the critical importance of professional educators, advocates of the PMM idea highlight *human capital* and suggest that teachers and leaders be given flexibility to do their work, and that having a range of different organizations preparing educators (not just traditional universities) will increase the breadth and depth of expertise brought by those educators to the challenges faced in schools. As we examine the enactment of PMM ideas in our three systems, principal-agent theory helps us to more deeply examine the intent of these policies and advocates' theory of action underlying these significant system changes.

ENACTING CHANGE IN THE PMM

The principal-agent assumptions infused in the PMM theory of action focus largely on the structures and overall design of a governance system. However, as seen in figure 2.1, other forces may shape the enactment of PMM ideas and their potential impact on schools and students in important ways. These include policy and political contexts at the federal, state, and local levels, as well as broader institutional norms within public education.

Political and Policy Influences

Politically, PMMs have included both national and local actors as supporters and critics, and they have often been tied closely to the politics of other governance changes including the introduction of mayoral control and the expansion of charter schools.[26] The potential for realignment around issues of power and changes in civic capacity through the enactment of PMMs is an important and sometimes neglected component of the story.[27]

FIGURE 2.1   **Understanding the portfolio management model**

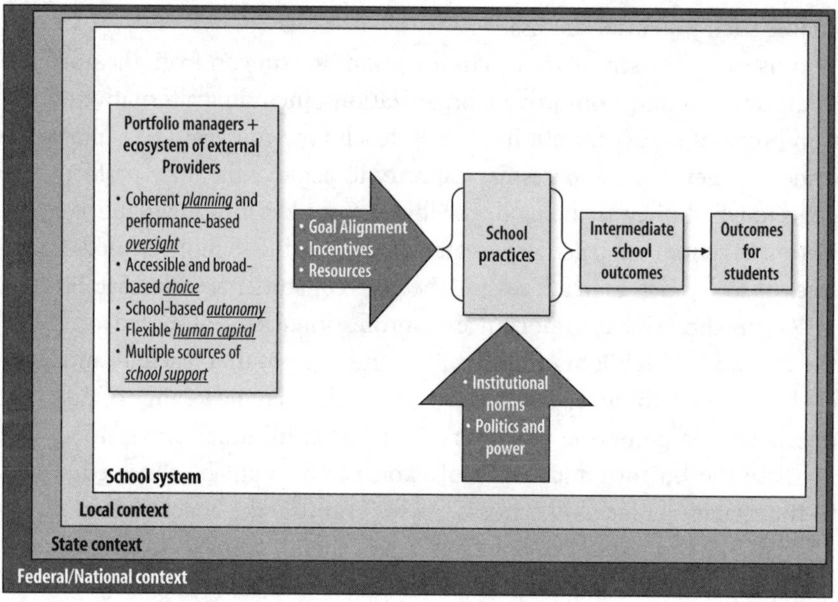

In cities with elected boards, political efforts have often focused on those boards, with both advocacy groups and funders pushing for their own candidates.[28]

Within these contexts are a number of national organizations that have played important roles advocating for and/or supporting PMM-style changes in both national and local conversations. These include funders such as the Walton Family Foundation, advocacy groups such as Democrats for Education Reform, and education providers such as TFA.[29] The emergence in 2018 of the $200 million City Fund, an organization with an explicit focus on portfolio ideas, with substantial funding from the Laura and John Arnold Foundation among others, created even more focused support for expanding PMMs.[30]

While claiming powerful supporters, the PMM idea has also engendered vocal skeptics, who have pushed back in regard to core components such as enhanced engagement of private actors, expansion of charter schools, a reduced role for unions, and the sometimes tenuous engagement of communities.[31] In particular, issues of race have inflamed tensions in places (including New Orleans) between those advocating for change and local communities that have felt both financially hurt and marginalized by such changes.[32] The idea of a PMM often draws the same concerns as those raised by the opponents who accuse charter schools of undertaking market-based reforms that seek to undermine public schools.[33]

Examining contexts in which PMMs are emerging leads one quickly to see an interaction between the presence of charter schools and the emergence of system change. On the one hand, as charter schools become a significant part of the educational landscape within a system, this change can increasingly place pressure on leaders to shape their approaches to this new reality. On the other hand, leaders interested in PMM-style reform can easily turn to charters—with their combination of performance-based oversight, student choice, and school-based autonomy—as a natural fit for such a system. The increase in systems associated with PMMs and the growth of systems with powerful charter sectors have been largely aligned. Figure 2.2 shows the expansion in the number of school districts in which a large percentage of students attend charter schools. For example, 214 districts had 10 percent or more of their public school students attending

FIGURE 2.2   **Charter school market share**

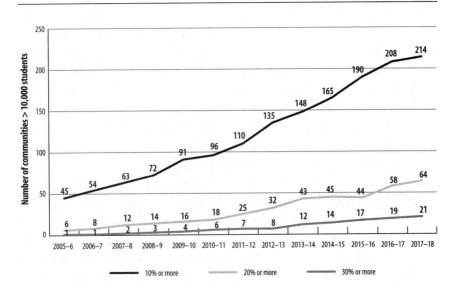

Note: Data are from annual reports produced by the National Association of Public Charter Schools. 2007–8 and 2008–9 are estimates, as no reports could be located for those years.

charter schools in 2017–18 (up from forty-five districts in 2005–6), while twenty-one had at least 30 percent of students in charters (up from one in 2005–6).[34]

The central role of charter schools in many large urban systems raises important questions about charter authorizing. Specifically, the extent to which a local district can act as an authorizer of charter schools within its boundaries, and particularly as the primary or sole such authorizer, influences that district's ability to act as a portfolio manager. The ability to control all or most decisions about which publicly funded schools operate within the district's boundaries was available to at least some extent in all three systems studied, although in distinct ways (see chapter 3). But it is not found in other cities, such as Detroit and Cleveland, that have large percentages of students attending charter schools, but also a wide array of authorizers who may not coordinate with one another.[35]

Institutional Pressures

While political and policy influences are important to shaping reform, research on institutional and neo-institutional theory highlights a different type of pressure that can shape educational practices in both existing and new governance structures.[36] This set of theories suggests that the role of institutions, which are "durable social structures made up of symbolic elements, social activities, and material resources," can subtly influence behavior.[37] These broader forces can potentially lead to resistance to change, the re-creation of existing structures, or other actions unaccounted for in straightforward applications of principal-agent theory. In so doing, they raise important questions about the PMM theory of action, potentially challenging the principal-agent logic that suggests that if incentives and principals' goals are well-aligned, then the behavior of school-based agents will change to meet the goals of system principals.

For years, scholars have documented the ways in which efforts to improve education via governance reform have met persistent challenges due to taken-for-granted ideas around what schools do.[38] Given these observations, creating meaningful change through altering structures and incentives in the ways that underlie the PMM theory of action may face these same challenges.[39] For example, institutional theorists have found that organizations seeking to change may revert to existing practices that bring new structures in line with preexisting ones, especially as new or altered organizations develop in the context of the norms and expectations that currently define legitimate forms of schooling.[40] Thus, new organizations, such as management organizations and charter schools, and theoretically distinct organizations, like portfolio managers, may seek to gain legitimacy through practices similar to those of existing organizations (such as authorizers or CMOs acting like school districts), while classroom teachers may return to or retain existing practices linked to historical professional norms rather than reform their practice in alignment with the expectations of these newer organizations.[41] In addition, alignment between principals and agents is complicated by the "loose coupling" between classrooms and the broader institutional environment, and the looseness of this relationship may make changes at higher levels in the system less likely to impact the day-to-day interactions of teachers and students.[42]

Institutional theory in political science, related to but distinct from that in sociology, has also long attended to institutional pressures when examining issues of politics and power. For example, this research identifies the potential for vested interests to exert power over policy actors in ways that work to protect the status quo of organizations and the connections between institutionalized structures and powerful elites.[43] As with institutionalized structures, such political forces can impede the influence of the incentives and clearly aligned goals that are central to the PMM approach. In particular, Moe argues that in many efforts at educational reform, the very actors tasked with changing have vested interests in maintaining education systems in their current form.[44] As a result, in the language of principal-agent theory, agents' incentives cannot be aligned with those of principals who wish to disrupt traditional institutions of public education because the agents' self-interest is preserved only by the maintenance of current organizational structures. This leads to resistance to reform both at its conception and during implementation. Thus, while PMM logic suggests that autonomy and goal alignment through performance contracts will lead to substantial changes in system- and school-level practices, institutional theory (as well as historical analysis) suggests that broader norms and logics may limit such changes in the "grammar of schooling."[45]

Nevertheless, recent research in neo-institutional theory highlights contexts in which institutional pressures may not hold sway. These studies examine the conditions under which organizations *do* change as a result of environmental factors and influential individual and organizational agents.[46] For example, clearly structured technical environments, consistent with the underlying precepts of principal-agent theory and the idea of performance contracts with measurable outcome indicators, as well as competitive markets that offer a different way of aligning the goals of consumers and producers, have led to organizations changing even in the context of strong institutional forces.[47]

Neo-institutionalists converge on the understanding that organizations are heavily influenced by their institutional environments but are also active participants within those environments.[48] In the context of PMMs, organizations such as CMOs and foundations may play critical roles in creating sustained pressures that push against institutional norms and in creating new institutions and institutionalized norms that alter ideas around "legitimacy."[49] While principal-agent theory suggests that the PMM will lead to beneficial practices and outcomes, institutional theory challenges this ideal picture and raises important questions for this study. These broader frameworks operate in the background throughout the analysis.

PORTFOLIO MANAGEMENT AND EDUCATIONAL IMPROVEMENT

Perhaps the most publicly desired but difficult to assess component of research on PMMs is the effects of such systems on student outcomes (both academic and otherwise) and school quality. Research specifically on student academic outcomes has shown some potential for test score improvement in New Orleans and Los Angeles but shown mixed results in Chicago.[50] Even in contexts with overall hints of improvement, school quality varied in important ways and thus limited the ability for all families to access higher-quality schools.[51] Some of the research suggests that charter schools may be favoring higher-achieving students while pushing out lower-performing ones.[52] Taken together, the existing research shows an uneven and uncertain intersection between PMM-style reforms and improvement in individual student outcomes.

In addition, studies of these emergent systems have suggested mixed effects on the nonacademic issues that are often central to questions of equity. These issues often get to the heart of the push/pull of centralization and decentralization within PMMs, as inequitable practices have generally (and, in many cases, legally) led to or required a centralized response. For example, portfolio managers in a number of cities have sought, with mixed results, to centralize/recentralize practices in the area of student suspensions and expulsions.[53] These attempts have at times sought to address issues of racial disproportionality in disciplinary actions. For example, Baker-Smith explored efforts in New York City to reduce out-of-school suspensions and found evidence that there was an overall success in reducing these suspensions, but "little evidence of reductions in the disproportionate likelihood of suspension by race or gender."[54] Questions of equitable access to schools and centralized responses to evidence of inequitable access show evidence of sustained or increased racial segregation in PMM systems, consistent with other research on the potentially segregating impacts of student choice.[55] Although data challenges limited our ability to look at such outcomes, chapter 9 explores a number of different intermediate outcomes that research suggests are good indicators of schools that are successful in supporting student learning. Other research has not sought to look inside schools at such outcomes in order to better understand questions of impact and quality.

CONCLUSION

Given the growth of PMMs nationwide and the significant resources being invested in these new systems, it is critical for scholars and policy makers focused on different levels of public education to better understand both what is shaping the substantial changes taking place under the umbrella of portfolio management and how those changes shape the practices of educators. In some systems, the shift toward PMM is already tied to dramatic changes, while in others, the movement is more incremental. By grounding the study in the research on district change, existing studies of PMMs, and distinct theoretical lenses, this book advances the conversation on how to best organize and govern high-quality, equitable public education systems. The scarcity of research on PMMs, however, leaves us unable to attest to the viability of the model and the assumptions embedded in its key mechanisms. Will the shift of systems toward a PMM lead to little change or to potentially fundamental improvements in the contexts for teaching and learning? How does the overall reorientation of systems away from direct management alter the work of central offices and address critical and traditionally centrally managed issues around equity, and how does this shape access and outcomes for historically marginalized students? These are the topics taken up in the chapters to follow. Before delving deeply into the enactment of PMM, the book provides background on the local context of the three cases.

SYSTEM TRANSFORMATION
IN THREE CITIES

*with Danica Robinson Brown
and Laura Steen Mulfinger**

W hile these three school systems have adopted some similar changes,
their histories and contexts are importantly distinct. This chapter examines the evolution of change in each city, highlighting the politics and
history of system transformation and concluding by comparing the systems, including a review of the key policy mechanisms discussed in chapter 2 that are intended to govern and drive improvements in schools. The
chapter generally anchors these descriptions to the time of the research
(2016–17) by drawing on extant literature, documents, and interviews
conducted with system leaders (see the appendixes for more information
on these interviews).

EARLY HISTORY

In all three systems, the structure and governance of the public schools
shifted significantly in the late 1990s and early in the first decade of this
century.[1] Prior to the turn of the century, these school systems looked quite
similar to one another and to the "one best system."[2] Elected school boards,

---

* Important contributions to this chapter were made by Tasminda K. Dhaliwal, Taylor Enoch-
Stevens, and Taylor N. Allbright.

often with a collective bargaining agreement between the district and a local teachers' union, oversaw a set of neighborhood schools assigned to families based on geographic residence. The majority of these schools were overseen by a central office with highly bureaucratized rules and procedures dictated by both district and collective bargaining policies. While a small minority of schools had discretion over aspects of their school programs (for example, magnet schools and a few charter schools operated in all three cities), district and union leaders retained control over the educational programs and staffing procedures for most schools.

During the late twentieth century, all three school systems changed incrementally, but the overall structures remained fairly stable. In Los Angeles, leaders responded to pressure from civic leaders by introducing new school options (such as semiautonomous school models) and by decentralizing power to some extent.[3] Although these models persisted, they were never adopted in a large share of the schools, and the overall reform initiatives did not last. In New Orleans, despite a long history of low performance, financial problems, and corruption, coupled with declining enrollment, the system changed very little. In Denver, a desegregation order led to shifts in school assignments via busing, a performance-based pay system influenced the approach to human capital, and periodic efforts at centralization created uncertainty.[4]

Starting in the 1980s and 1990s, all three cities began to face a similar set of increased performance- and market-based accountability pressures.[5] Federal and state policies promoting test-based accountability and school improvement were precursors to changes on the horizon. At this time, all three states also passed charter school laws (1992 in California, 1993 in Colorado, and 1995 in Louisiana). Although these laws were significant vehicles for future change, they were not immediately seized upon in the case cities. In Los Angeles, a handful of "conversion" charter schools opened up, primarily in White neighborhoods.[6] Denver leaders actively opposed the new charter law, denying petitions and legally challenging the law's constitutionality.[7] In New Orleans, a few charter schools opened, including some that were later taken over by the state's Recovery School District (RSD), discussed further below.

Toward the end of the 1990s and through the 2000s, however, significant changes emerged in all three contexts, with system-level changes in Denver and Los Angeles and state changes in all three locations. These changes were largely triggered by a set of interrelated crises (internal and external), new state policies, and new political leaders and actors. The combination of these forces led to the newly configured systems investigated in this book.

NEW ORLEANS: A MANAGED MARKET

Nicknamed the "Big Easy," New Orleans is known for its music, food, and nightlife, reflecting a rich history as a cross-cultural melting pot. The New Orleans public school system has gained considerable attention in recent years, having undergone one of the most dramatic transformations in the country. A simple internet search of "New Orleans schools" yields a bevy of headlines and articles, such as "What New Orleans Tells Us About the Perils of Putting Schools on the Free Market" (*New Yorker*) and "New Orleans Eyed as Clean Educational Slate" (*Education Week*).[8] How did this system come to be, and what makes it so different from other districts?

History

In the early 2000s, Orleans Parish School Board (OPSB) schools faced considerable internal crises: well-publicized corruption, mismanagement, and poor academic performance.[9] In 2004, the Federal Bureau of Investigation (FBI) indicted eleven district leaders and staff for a host of criminal offenses such as bribery.[10] As Douglas Harris reports, "The problems were so rampant that the FBI opened its own office within the Orleans Parish School Board buildings."[11] The US Department of Education, concerned about financial mismanagement, threatened to pull federal funding, forcing the state to assign an emergency financial manager. The district was also heavily in debt and ranked sixty-seventh out of sixty-eight Louisiana districts in reading and mathematics test scores.[12] This context fueled reformers' efforts to enact change systemwide. Changes in state law also set the stage for dramatic change. Passed in 2003, Act 9 created the RSD, enabling the state to take control of any school statewide with four consecutive years of "academically unacceptable" performance.

These changes in law had little practical impact until August 2005, when Hurricane Katrina hit New Orleans. Destroying 80 percent of its schools and displacing the majority of employees and families, the hurricane combined with subsequent state law changes to ignite the dramatic reform of

New Orleans public schools.[13] Politically, the aftermath of Katrina led to weakened local democratic control and left few individuals with the power to mobilize against the changes coming from the top. Soon after the hurricane, state-level leaders altered the definition of "academically unacceptable" so that the state RSD could take control of almost all schools in the city. The drastic post-Katrina transformation had begun.

Under the revised state law, the RSD, governed by the elected Louisiana Board of Elementary and Secondary Education (BESE), quickly took control of more than one hundred of the lowest performing schools in Orleans Parish, and eventually chartered almost all of them. A handful of higher performing schools remained under the governance of OPSB.[14] With so few students, OPSB was all but forced to dismiss most of its eighty-five hundred teachers, administrators, and staff and, in mid-2006, let the collective bargaining agreement expire.[15] Families now had the choice of either sending their children to RSD and OPSB charters or, if the children were eligible, sending them to a few direct-run OPSB schools.

Key leadership for this transformation came from Leslie Jacobs, a business executive, former OPSB board member, and BESE member. Widely cited as the visionary and architect of change in New Orleans, Jacobs recruited a "reform family" of charter, nonprofit, and RSD officials from within the system and nationally who worked mostly behind closed doors to advance poststorm reform through fundraising and the new state legislation described above.[16] By the 2009–10 school year, the New Orleans system had been transformed into a *managed market*.

Recent Fiscal Climate and School Funding

Post-Katrina New Orleans has experienced a boom of sorts, with major investments in infrastructure and housing, along with gentrification of some of its storied neighborhoods. While it is home to one of the world's largest and busiest ports and to a thriving tourist industry, the city nonetheless continues to experience large economic disparities and a high poverty rate, especially among its African American residents.[17]

The idealized portfolio management model (PMM) includes student-based funding—funding that is based on enrollment levels.[18] This is intended to create market accountability, as schools can only survive and thrive if they attract and retain a certain number of students. While we did not conduct original analyses of funding for this project, this chapter highlights some broad aspects of the funding context in each city. Louisiana is one of the most equitable states in the country when it comes to school funding. The state is well above average in its average funding level (given the state's low income); New Orleans school spending has generally hovered around the state average, or $13,000 per pupil in 2016.[19] Some charter schools also receive substantial philanthropic donations and charge nontrivial fees.

In most states, traditional public school funding is based substantially on local property tax funding, which is not directly dependent on enrollment levels, so traditional public schools do not lose funding when students exit to enroll in charter (or private) schools. In New Orleans, however, where essentially all schools are subject to choice, the combination of state and local policies provides almost the exact same per-pupil funding to traditional and charter schools. That funding formula is also weighted so that schools with more disadvantaged students receive more funding.

Funding in New Orleans is also unusually generous with regard to buildings. This is largely an artifact of the large infusion of funding from FEMA in the wake of Hurricane Katrina, which, a decade after the storm, allowed for substantial renovations in essentially all the schools, and the construction of many completely new buildings.

System Characteristics: Managed Market

Two primary portfolio managers assumed control: the state-run RSD oversaw the vast majority of schools, and the locally elected OPSB oversaw a small set of charter and less autonomous direct-run schools. A handful of schools were also overseen directly by the BESE. RSD and OPSB provided all types of schools with substantial autonomy. This flexibility extended to critical issues such as human capital, with charter management organizations (CMOs), nonprofit providers, and universities taking a more proactive role. The teachers' union was essentially decimated, as most teachers in charter schools were not union members.[20]

This newly granted autonomy was provided in exchange for oversight based on a strict performance-based accountability system that incorporated multiple measures of school and student success, and at times was connected with decisions around school closures. RSD and OPSB both used an annual review process to set priorities for new charter school applicants, and the agencies published a description of this process in a request for applications. The RSD was especially aggressive in closing low performing charter schools.[21]

The leanly staffed RSD and the increasingly "hands-off" OPSB played minimal roles in school support. This was partly by design. The old roles of the district, as well as the new roles necessitated by the portfolio model, were given to a new web of nonprofit organizations focused on everything from transportation, food, and afterschool activities to school improvement support, talent recruitment, and training. Major organizations included New Schools for New Orleans, Teach for America, the New Teacher Project, New Leaders for New Schools, and TeachNOLA.[22]

The initially decentralized PMM slowly became more recentralized in some areas. In 2012, the RSD adopted a centralized enrollment system, EnrollNOLA, which was used by the vast majority of the city's public schools, including, eventually, most OPSB schools.[23] In addition, new policies were adopted governing funding (a common formula is used across RSD and OPSB schools), expulsions (all schools adhere to the same code of conduct for expulsions), and special education services.[24] As RSD began to regulate its portfolio more through these changes, and as it engaged in more intentional planning around opening new schools, the system developed into more of a "managed," rather than free, market.

School Trends

As figure 3.1 illustrates, the changing nature of school types operating in New Orleans over time reflects the evolution just described. In 2004, there was one school (out of approximately 127) under the authority of the RSD, and there were only five charter schools. By 2011, the RSD oversaw sixty-five schools, while the OPSB, the original district, oversaw only eighteen. By 2012, sixty-eight out of the eighty-six schools were charters, and by 2016, 93 percent of public school students attended charter schools, representing the largest share of any district in the country.[25] In 2016–17, there were twenty-eight stand-alone charter schools (including five directly overseen by BESE), twenty-five charter schools that were managed by four larger CMOs (those with five or more schools), and another twenty-three charters managed by eight smaller CMOs.[26] It is worth noting that in 2016 the Louisiana legislature passed a "reunification" policy requiring all New Orleans RSD schools to return to OPSB oversight by 2018 (given the timing of this change, it was not a focus of our research).

System Leadership over Time

In New Orleans, from 2005 to 2018, four different superintendents took the helm of the state-run RSD. The first, a former Baton Rouge principal and assistant state superintendent, Robin Jarvis, faced the daunting task of reopening the district's flooded schools. She resigned in mid-2007, and the state superintendent of education recruited a high-profile urban superintendent, Paul Vallas, to lead the RSD as it recovered from Hurricane Katrina. Four years later, in 2011, another big-city public school leader, John White, arrived to lead the RSD. However, after less than a year, he was appointed state superintendent by the BESE. In 2012, a fourth superintendent—this time a New Orleans native, Patrick Dobard—was named to lead the RSD. In early 2017, a new leader, Kunjan Narechania, took over leadership of the RSD and was tasked with overseeing the "reunification" and shift of school oversight to the locally elected OPSB, which had appointed Henderson Lewis its superintendent in 2015.[27] Unlike the stable, long-term leadership in Denver (discussed below), the shifting figures in New Orleans were not as influential as many external figures and charter school leaders in the development and growth of this managed market over time.

Student Demographic and Performance Trends

As figure 3.2 indicates, the demographic profiles of students in district-run (recall, they make up a minority of schools in total) and charter schools in New Orleans are somewhat similar, with charter schools serving slightly lower percentages of underrepresented minority students than district-run public schools do. Both sets of schools have also experienced very little demographic change in the five years for which data were analyzed. (While not pictured, the pattern is similar for students eligible for the free and reduced-price lunch program across the school types.)

Student performance, however, differs considerably across the school types in New Orleans. Figure 3.3 illustrates the patterns among average standardized scale scores for underrepresented minority students. Their average performance is higher in charter schools from 2011 to 2013, but district-run schools have been making steady gains over time. Notably, traditional and charter schools converge to essentially the same average underrepresented minority student performance in 2014. The gap in performance between traditional and charter schools narrows over time due to an increase in the students' performance in traditional schools coupled with a slight decrease in their performance in charter schools. Overall, the gains made over time by traditional-school students results in an incremental increase in the district's overall average performance from 2012 to 2014. Though not depicted here, the average scale scores for students overall by school type map closely to the patterns illustrated in figure 3.3, but they are generally higher than the underrepresented minority figures.

FIGURE 3.1   **School models in New Orleans over time**

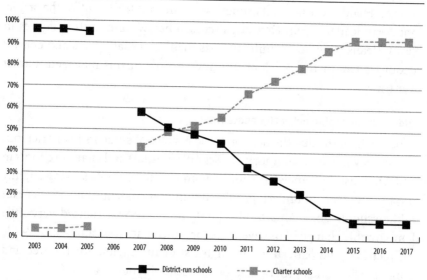

Source: Louisiana Department of Education.

Note: There are no publicly available data for 2005–6 due to the hurricane.

FIGURE 3.2   **Underrepresented minority student population by school type in New Orleans over time**

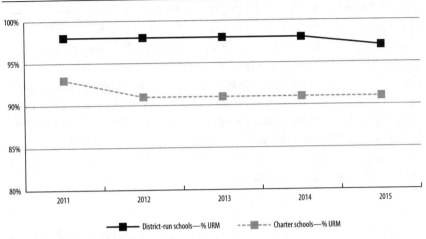

Source: Louisiana Department of Education.

FIGURE 3.3   **Average state standardized test scale scores for underrepresented minority students by school type in New Orleans over time**

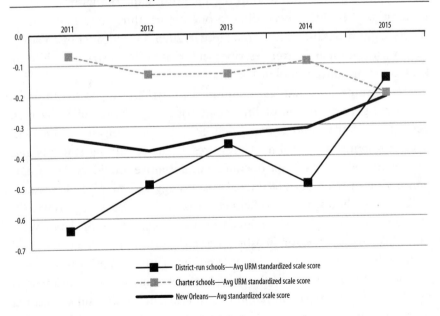

Source: Louisiana Department of Education.

DENVER: A CENTRALIZED PORTFOLIO

Denver, known as the "Mile High City," is one of the fastest growing cities in the United States. Recent census data indicate an 18.6 percent increase in the population from 1990 to 2000 and another 8.2 percent increase from 2000 to 2010.[28] Located at the foot of the Rocky Mountains, Denver is often ranked one of the "best places to live" based on affordability and quality of life.[29] The city's public school system also changed significantly between 2000 and 2016. Led by a stable set of reform-oriented leaders, Denver Public Schools (DPS) evolved into a centralized portfolio—coming perhaps closest, among the three study cases, to the idealized portfolio management model described in chapter 2.

History

Although less dramatic than the external crisis facilitating transformation in New Orleans, internal enrollment crises were one source of pressure for change in Denver. By 2005, the state's interdistrict choice policy resulted in significant underenrollment in Denver public schools, as students living within the city increasingly enrolled in neighboring districts. This mobility created serious financial concerns and left the district with numerous underutilized facilities. According to one report, thirty-one thousand of ninety-eight thousand seats were empty in 2005.[30] One leader of an advocacy organization in Denver described the crisis as "the district . . . bleeding kids to surrounding school districts."

At the same time, top leadership in the district changed significantly, providing perhaps the most important trigger of change in Denver. In 2005, businessman and lawyer Michael Bennet became superintendent and, in response to enrollment pressures, began recruiting students and seeking to open new schools operated by alternative providers. The abundance of empty campuses facilitated this strategy and minimized pressures on existing schools. In 2009, Bennet's deputy, Tom Boasberg, took over the superintendency (and remained in office at the time of data collection). Like his predecessor, Boasberg was an "education outsider" who had come to the district two years prior from the private and government sectors. Over time, Bennet and Boasberg brought consistent commitment to portfolio reform, marshaling support from external actors and advocating for state policy changes to apply pressure and enable systemic change. According to David Osborne, "DPS was so dysfunctional, Bennet concluded, that he could not fix it without significant outside pressure. So he asked several foundation leaders to create an organization of civic leaders, chaired by two former mayors, to push for change and support the board when it promoted reform. They called the initiative A+ Denver, and it has championed the portfolio strategy, along with the Piton, Donnell-Kay, and Gates Family foundations."[31] In the 2009 school board election, with the active engagement of the nonprofit Democrats for Education Reform (DFER) Colorado, supporters of portfolio reform gained a 4–3 majority and shifted power away from union-backed supporters of the traditional district model.[32] Subsequent elections cemented the pro-reform majority (7–0 majority in 2015; 5–2 majority in 2017), providing sustained political support for system transformation.[33]

Alterations in state policy also facilitated change. Passed in 2008, the state Innovation Schools Act gave districts authority to grant schools additional autonomy over personnel, calendar, and budget decisions. Along with a new state accountability policy (2009)—which gave the state board of education power to reconstitute and close low performing schools—and changes in teacher evaluation policy (2010), the Innovation Schools Act granted schools the opportunity to opt out of collective bargaining, a move that limited the power of the teachers' union and gave additional authority to reformers to provide schools with greater autonomy.[34] "The Innovation law itself passing was clearly a catalyst," said one state leader; "I think that was a huge game changer for districts like Denver Public Schools. We've seen that—they've increasingly used it." According to several interviewees, DPS leaders had lobbied for the passage of these policies, recognizing that they would provide useful cover and leverage for difficult reforms to the system.

From 2005 to 2012, Denver shifted significantly toward an integrated system overseeing a variety of school options, including direct-run schools (which have considerable freedom over educational programming, assessment, and professional development), semiautonomous innovation schools, and charter schools. For example, in 2010, the district reconstituted a set of schools in northeast Denver, replacing them with innovation and charter schools. The district later formalized a school-opening process through the "Call for Quality Schools," an annual request for new school proposals based on needs identified in the Strategic Regional Analysis. In the end, DPS had been transformed into a centralized portfolio.

Recent Fiscal Climate and School Funding

In recent years, enrollment has increased in Denver. While this has helped alleviate some fiscal pressures, statewide low funding of education, which dropped even lower during the recession, led to DPS having less funding per student in 2016 than it did in 2009–10.[35]

Colorado proudly operates as a local control state. The per pupil spending has traditionally been well below the national mean, with a state average of $9,809 in 2017. Like other states, the majority of the Colorado public school revenues are generated by state and local taxes. The state share of funding varies from district to district. In Denver, local property taxes still account for about 50 percent of the education revenues. DPS typically spends above the state average, spending $11,346 per pupil in 2017.[36]

Colorado's education funding structure is complicated by related fiscal legislation. Two major examples are the 1982 Gallagher Amendment, which reduces the assessment rate of residential property values, and the 1992 Taxpayer Bill of Rights (TABOR), which limits how much tax revenue the government can collect without voter approval. For districts such as Denver that rely heavily on property taxes, the convergence of these policies contributes to increased financial stress.

Colorado broadly, and DPS specifically, have several "charter friendly" fiscal policies. For example, charter schools are eligible for additional funds for at-risk students, and authorizing districts are required to give charters a chance to participate in ballot initiatives requesting capital facilities funding.[37]

System Characteristics: Centralized Portfolio

Those with formal authority and influence in the new system included a reform-oriented elected school board, a superintendent, and central office staff, as well as influential advocates outside the system, such as the individuals involved in A+ Denver. Charter operators—notably the two largest networks, DSST Public Schools and STRIVE Preparatory Schools—also gained influence, while the teachers' union saw a greatly diminished role.

The overall organization of the district included both a fairly traditional central office, with a hierarchy of offices and positions, and a formalized cross-sector collaboration established to ensure a voice for charters in district decisions. This was most clearly visible in the District-Charter

Collaborative Council (supported in part by a grant from the Bill and Melinda Gates Foundation). This committee was described by one advocacy leader as including "both district leaders and charter school leaders that are elected among their peers to be able to serve on a council to say, 'How do we continue to work together as one district even when we're a group of autonomous leaders?'" Several respondents argued that the influence and participation of CMO charter leaders often outweighed those of stand-alone leaders.

Overall, the new system included multiple school providers and a central office with a stated commitment to neutrality and equality in school oversight. District leaders sought to apply accountability policies equally to all school types through a uniform School Performance Framework. This oversight was conducted with an understanding that, in exchange for autonomy and the ability to innovate, schools had to meet performance expectations that included targets for test scores, academic growth, engagement, enrollment, and parent satisfaction. Not meeting those expectations could, and did, result in sometimes highly contentious school closure decisions that critics argued were made in ways that were not always consistent or transparent.

Alongside school closures, Denver developed criteria for portfolio planning decisions around school openings. Central office staff created an annual analysis of choice options and demand, and then the portfolio office issued a "Call for Quality Schools" that identified specific needs and locations. District-run and charter school applicants used the same process to apply for the opportunities noted in this call.

The central office embraced a management approach many described as "holding tight and letting loose." The district balanced school-level autonomy, including increasing autonomy for traditional public schools, with centralization around several core areas, leading to a relatively narrower range of autonomy for different school types (innovation, traditional, and charter) than found in other cities, such as Los Angeles. DPS included a common enrollment system intended to promote equitable access to schools by preventing schools from "cream skimming," and the system incorporated rules about setting aside seats for "late arrivals"—students who entered the system after official enrollment periods. Enrollment guides and the DPS online "schoolmatch" system provided consistent information about available choices across all types of schools, including multiple measures of school quality for all schools in the system and for families living in specific enrollment zones.

In terms of school support, the district offered available professional development spaces to charter schools as well as to traditional and innovation schools, and also provided support for special education. More intensive mandated supports for struggling schools were only available to (and required of) traditional public schools and innovation schools. For charters, the central office supports focused on leaders, boards, and providing information and resources—including what a former central office staff member described as "reflective feedback" and a charter advocate called "shining a light" on challenges facing schools. Charters were also able to adopt or adapt systems that the district created, such as DPS's teacher evaluation system (called Leading Effective Academic Practice, or LEAP).

While the central office was less engaged with charters than with district-run schools, central office staff were in regular contact with charters. For example, central office staff often attended charter school board meetings. A growing ecosystem of outside organizations that supported schools was also central, with DPS directly partnering with some organizations (such as the Relay Graduate School of Education) that worked with both charter and district-run schools. Many charter schools were located in district-run facilities; these required an agreement to operate under several centralized policies and to take all children. At times, they were required to offer specific programs for students with disabilities that were needed by the district overall.

School Trends

Once again, changes in school types over time illustrate the evolution of this centralized portfolio in Denver. As figure 3.4 illustrates, from 2003 to 2017 the number of innovation and charter schools increased dramatically, and the number of traditional public schools declined. This shift occurred right after the passage of major state reform legislation and the emergence of the new superintendent, Boasberg, and the reform-oriented school board. In 2004, there were just nine charter schools and no innovation schools (out of 152 total). By 2015, there were fifty-one charter and fifty innovation schools, representing 48 percent of the 212 total schools in Denver. During this period, traditional public schools decreased from 136 to 99. In 2016–17, there were twenty-four stand-alone charter schools, twenty-nine charters that were managed by three larger CMOs, and another four managed by two smaller CMOs.

System Leadership over Time

DPS has had remarkable leadership stability in recent years. Following a period of rapid turnover in superintendents from the mid-1980s to 2005, DPS hired Michael Bennet in 2005 and then his deputy, Tom Boasberg, in 2009. Boasberg went on to serve for nearly a decade. In 2018, after data collection for this study ended, Boasberg announced his decision to step down. Overall, the consistency of leadership played a critical role in perpetuating a common understanding and commitment to a centralized portfolio that balanced autonomy with limitations advancing equity.

Student Demographic and Performance Trends

As figure 3.5 illustrates, the demographic profiles of students differed across school types in Denver, particularly in the case of magnet schools, which serve considerably lower percentages of underrepresented minority students than all other school types. (These differences are likely driven in part by the integration goals and requirements tied to the magnet schools program.) All other schools enrolled similar proportions of underrepresented minority students (approximately 75 to 85 percent), with traditional public schools enrolling slightly smaller percentages than charter and innovation schools. While the underrepresented minority student population was quite stable in charter schools over the period of 2011–15, there were slight decreases in magnet, traditional, and innovation schools (indicating overall increases in the White student population during this period). While not pictured, the population of students eligible for the free and reduced-price lunch program seemed to increase slightly for all schools in 2010–11 and 2011–12, and then to stagnate, with very small decreases for all three school types.

Student performance varies considerably across the school types in Denver. Figure 3.6 illustrates the patterns among average standardized scale scores for underrepresented minority students. Notably, average performance of underrepresented minority students is substantially higher in magnet schools than in all other schools, and higher than the district average, followed by charter schools, then traditional schools, then innovation schools. Innovation schools demonstrate the lowest performance of underrepresented minority students over time, with notable decreases from 2011 to 2014 and a slight upward tick in 2015. Overall trends over time indicate slight decreases for magnet and traditional schools and slight increases in the aggregate for charter schools. While not depicted here, the average scale scores for students overall by school type map closely to the patterns illustrated in figure 3.6, but are always higher than the underrepresented minority figures.

FIGURE 3.4   **School models in Denver over time**

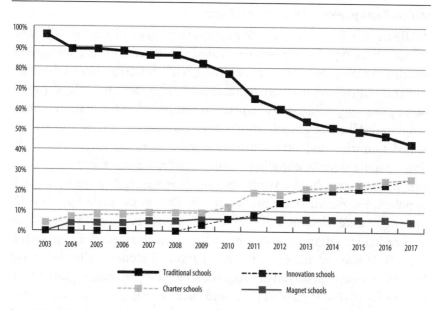

Sources: Colorado Department of Education and Denver Public Schools.

FIGURE 3.5   **Underrepresented minority student population by school type in Denver over time**

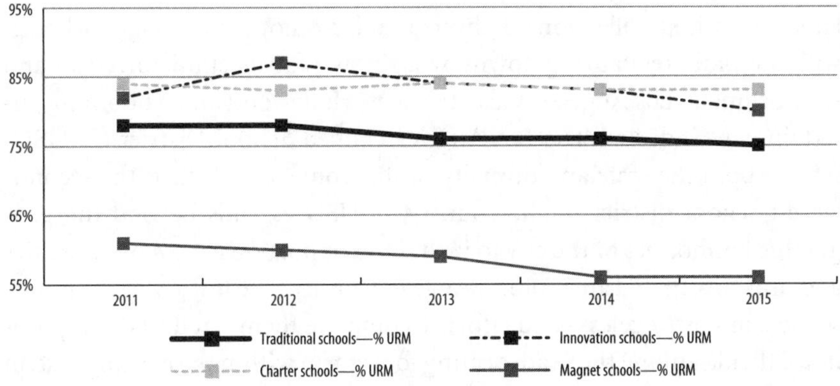

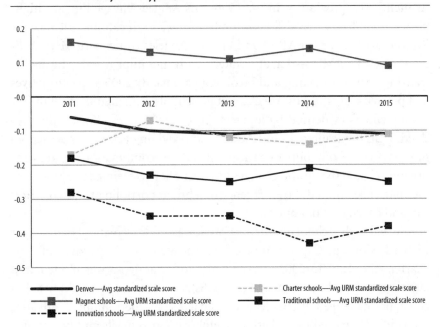

Traditional schools—% URM

Innovation schools—% URM

Charter schools—% URM

Magnet schools—% URM

Sources: Colorado Department of Education and Denver Public Schools.

FIGURE 3.6   **Average state standardized test scale scores for underrepresented minority students by school type in Denver over time**

Denver—Avg standardized scale score

Charter schools—Avg URM standardized scale score

Magnet schools—Avg URM standardized scale score

Traditional schools—Avg URM standardized scale score

Innovation schools—Avg URM standardized scale score

Sources: Colorado Department of Education and Denver Public Schools.

LOS ANGELES: COMPETING SYSTEMS

The city of Los Angeles, with a population of close to four million, is a large, sprawling collection of diverse and cosmopolitan neighborhoods with a rapidly revitalizing downtown. Known for its ethnic diversity and warm climate, Los Angeles is also home to Hollywood and a booming entertainment industry. The Los Angeles Unified School District (LAUSD) reflects both the scale and diversity of this context. In fact, as the second-largest school district in the country, LAUSD extends beyond the geographic boundaries of the city to include all or portions of twenty-six cities and unincorporated areas of Los Angeles County. The history of the public schools in Los Angeles—and efforts to improve them—reflects a deep political divide among those advocating for reform within the existing system and those asserting that the best hope for change lies outside of the traditional system in the charter sector.

History

As mentioned previously, in the 1990s Los Angeles engaged in two high-profile, civic-led reform efforts—the Los Angeles Educational Alliance for Restructuring Now (LEARN) and the Los Angeles Annenberg Metropolitan Project (LAAMP)—that attempted to advance improvement by decentralizing decision-making and involving parents. By 2000, these initiatives had petered out, and Los Angeles public schools remained in need of improvement, as evidenced by low test scores. Reformers' efforts shifted to shaking up the leadership of LAUSD and providing access to new school models freed from bureaucratic control.[38] A combination of reform-oriented civic activism and changes in state policy accelerated the growth of the charter sector and the emergence of a broad portfolio of both district-run and charter school options.

Elected to the school board in 1999 with the endorsement of then mayor Richard Riordan, Caprice Young "spearheaded rapid approval of new charter schools."[39] In 2005, Mayor Antonio Villaraigosa was elected, and although his attempts to take over the district were ultimately thwarted in court, he challenged district leaders such as the teachers' union to advance reform.[40] "He would unite Latino neighborhood activists and big-money Democrats to accelerate the spread of charter schools and create dozens of largely autonomous pilot schools," observed Bruce Fuller.[41] Modeled after schools in Boston with greater freedom from the union-district collective bargaining agreement, these pilot schools provided another in-district school option to the growing portfolio of schools.

New leaders also began to emerge in the charter sector itself. In 2004, many of the former leaders of LEARN and LAAMP formed a CMO named Alliance, with the goal of opening one hundred new schools in the city and pressuring the district for change.[42] As one such activist and current board member explained, "L.A. Unified has back-doored itself into a portfolio model. It has not done it through policy. . . . It did it through the fact that the outside was pushing in. Charter operators like myself said, 'We want difference for our kids in our neighborhood, so we're going to do something different.'"

Changes to the state charter school law also contributed to the expansion of charter schools in Los Angeles. In 1998 and 1999, state legislators increased the number of charter schools allowed statewide, created clear parameters around when school boards could deny charter petitions (making it more difficult to do so), and strengthened schools' accountability and independence (including expanded authorizing and appeals power).[43] Instead of being required to seek approval from district school boards, charter petitioners could now approach the state or county for approval, greatly increasing growth opportunities. At the same time, the voter-approved Proposition 39 created opportunities for charters to "co-locate" on traditional public school campuses with unused space, providing another avenue for charter expansion.[44] While the early wave of charter schools prior to this period opened as conversions of existing schools (often in wealthier communities), new civic leaders organized around the opening of start-up charter schools particularly in low-income communities.[45]

Toward the end of this transition period, in 2009, LAUSD experimented with a short-lived reform reflecting a more centralized and proactive portfolio approach. The Public School Choice Initiative (PSCI) allowed internal (teams of teachers and/or administrators) and external (nonprofits or charter managers) teams to apply to operate the lowest performing schools and a set of newly constructed schools under a variety of governance models.[46] At this time, a reform-oriented board and superintendent John Deasy explicitly used the language of "portfolio management" and reorganized schools into regional networks to provide more targeted support and facilitate learning across semiautonomous and traditional schools. Yet, after two years and mounting political push-back, the initiative was dramatically altered by an agreement with the teachers' union. Unlike in the early years, all employees of schools participating in the PSCI were now required to work within the collective bargaining agreement—thus curtailing the growth of externally operated schools. Despite Superintendent Deasy's efforts to expand a more formal PMM, the parallel systems of an independent charter sector and a traditional school district remained intact.

By around 2007, Los Angeles had developed into competing systems of schools with those schools directly run by LAUSD in competition with the independent charter sector.

Recent Fiscal Climate and School Funding

The Los Angeles economy is largely driven by international trade, entertainment, aerospace, technology, apparel, manufacturing, and tourism. In the years following the economic downturn, real estate prices have soared, and affordable housing has been scarce. While sectors of the city have prospered and grown economically, public schools have struggled financially. LAUSD has operated in a state fiscal context that provides some of the lowest levels of per-pupil funding in the nation.

California public schools, primarily funded by the state, receive funding from three sources: 58 percent from the state, 32 percent from property taxes and other local sources, and 9 percent from the federal government.[47] In 2013–14, California adopted the Local Control Funding Formula, a new education funding formula that allocates base funding to school districts and independent charter schools, along with additional funds for high-needs students, including foster youth, English language learners, and economically disadvantaged students. Despite these changes in how the state allocates funding, California per pupil spending continues to be below the national average. In 2017, California spent $12,143 in per pupil expenditures. LAUSD typically spends above the state average, spending $13,549 per pupil in 2017.[48]

These low levels of funding, alongside declining student enrollment in LAUSD and rising pension and health benefit obligations for teachers, created an important backdrop to the decisions and practices observed during this study.[49]

System Characteristics: Competing Systems of Schools

By 2007, traditional district actors, including school board and union leaders, retained significant influence over LAUSD by setting district and collective bargaining policy. Over time, the school board elections became heated political battles with significant influxes of funding from prounion and procharter forces.[50] At the same time, a new set of civic leaders tied to the charter sector emerged as powerful actors in the city.

During this time, a highly centralized bureaucratic district oversaw one system of traditional and semiautonomous public schools. LAUSD's central office organized schools into regional configurations known as local districts, each with a local district superintendent and a set of middle-level administrators overseeing and supporting district-run schools. To compete with the growing charter sector and fend off occasional threats of mayoral takeover, the district introduced some more autonomous school models, including pilot schools (introduced in 2006 and expanded over time), partnership schools (started in 2008 with Mayor Villaraigosa's Partnership for Los Angeles Schools), and magnet schools. Although they had started in the 1970s and 80s, magnet schools expanded in times of intense competition and threat from the charter sector. A second distinct system was the charter sector, which included both network-managed and individual schools, authorized primarily by the local school board. Most respondents in interviews agreed that there was little to no integration or interaction across these two sectors.

Consistent with these distinct systems and the vast scope of the district, multiple accountability frameworks and rubrics were used, based on the type of school. Consequences for not meeting expectations also varied both by type of school and, for district-run schools, by the practices of local districts. In the charter sector, charter revocation or nonrenewal was relatively rare, and consequences typically centered on corrective actions. The LAUSD central office's role in analyzing and guiding decisions about the portfolio of school options was minimal. Rather, the central office took an organic approach, allowing new school proposals to come from the bottom up, with different LAUSD entities serving to review applications. LAUSD did not view itself as a portfolio manager, and thus did not seek a unified portfolio vision that incorporated a set of consistent criteria to examine school openings, interventions, or closures.

School-based autonomy, including around human capital practices, also varied across sectors. Within the district-run sector, traditional public schools had no real formal autonomy, while six semiautonomous types of schools operated with formal autonomy in narrowly defined areas of school management. Traditional top-down human capital management dominated in district-run schools, although LAUSD did invest in building coherence across human capital programs and provided some flexibility to semiautonomous schools. In contrast, charter schools operated with extensive autonomy, not being bound by the state education code, district policies, or collective bargaining agreements, and retaining primary control over their internal operations, including hiring and other human capital functions, budget, curriculum, and so on.

While families in LAUSD potentially had access to a broad range of schools, they largely needed to identify schools individually or within zones, with neither enrollment processes nor information provided consistently across district-run and charter schools. This diffuse approach to choice in an already highly complex system was shaped in part by the geographic scope of the district, but also by a lack of trust between charters and the district. Efforts to create a unified enrollment system in this low-trust environment gained little traction.

The provision of supports for schools was decentralized to local districts, but it was relatively top-down from the perspective of district-run schools. Local districts were expected to be the main source of ongoing support for these school models, while LAUSD provided district-developed assessments and a data tracking system. The complexity of school models, district reorganization, and the varied capacity of local district instructional directors created challenges for the district in supporting all the schools in need of assistance. Some struggling traditional public schools received support through contracts between LAUSD and nonprofit partner organizations. The district did not view support as part of their responsibility to independent charters, although small efforts at sharing ideas across the sector were supported. Instead, charters received supports through the wide array of private organizations and CMO networks found in Los Angeles.

School Trends

As figure 3.7 indicates, trends in the number and types of schools over time mirror the emergence of these competing systems in Los Angeles. Starting in 2001, when the state charter school law revisions took effect and early internal reforms ended, the number of charter schools and other school types operating under varying levels of autonomy steadily increased. By 2016, 230 charter schools operated, representing 23 percent of the more than 1,000 public schools in Los Angeles, with an additional 178 within-district semiautonomous schools (18 percent). At the same time, the number of traditional public schools remained fairly steady (with a slight decline at the end of this period) due to a massive school construction program that built 130 new facilities from 2000 to 2015. Thus, while the number of schools in the district increased overall, the percentage of students in traditional public schools (not including semiautonomous and magnet) decreased from 70 percent in 2003–4 to 57 percent in 2015–16. In 2016–17, there were 47 stand-alone charter schools and 178 CMO charter schools.

System Leadership over Time

LAUSD has experienced many changes in senior leadership in recent years. From 2000 to 2018, the district employed seven superintendents, including a mix of insiders, with extensive experience in the district, and individuals from outside the district, both educators and noneducators (including a former governor and a former navy admiral).[51] During this same period, the district witnessed several highly competitive and well-financed school board elections. Backing from the teachers' union, elected officials, charter school advocates, and wealthy donors in and outside of Los Angeles featured prominently in these races. In fact, the election of 2017 was deemed the "the most expensive school board election in US history," involving more than $14 million in campaign spending.[52] The highly politicized nature of Los Angeles educational governance and the instability of leadership contributed to the fractured nature of the system of public schooling.

Student Demographic and Performance Trends

As figure 3.8 indicates, the demographic profiles of students in the different school models in Los Angeles differed somewhat and changed only slightly from 2011 to 2015. All schools enrolled a majority of students classified as underrepresented minorities, but independent charter schools served the highest percentage of underrepresented minority students, followed by traditional public schools, then semiautonomous schools and magnet schools. While not pictured, the pattern is similar for students eligible for the free and reduced-price lunch program across the school types.

Student performance also varied across the school types in Los Angeles, as illustrated by the average standardized scale scores for underrepresented minority students by school type from 2011 to 2015 (figure 3.9). Average performance was highest in magnet schools, yet those scores were steadily decreasing in the last years of this analysis—a trend mirrored by the decline in performance for traditional public schools (and overall district averages). Notably, average scores increased over time in independent charter and semiautonomous schools, surpassing district averages in 2015 (just slightly for semiautonomous schools). While not depicted here, the average scale scores for students overall by school type map closely to the patterns illustrated in figure 3.9, but were always higher than the underrepresented minority figures.

FIGURE 3.7   **School models in Los Angeles over time**

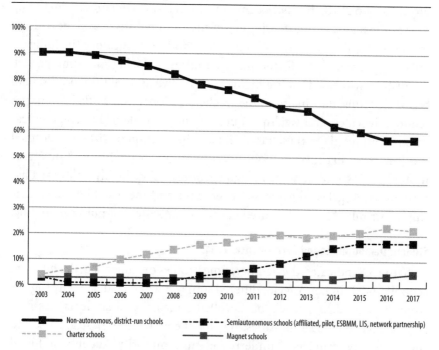

Sources: California Department of Education and Los Angeles Unified School District.

FIGURE 3.8   **Underrepresented minority student population by school type in Los Angeles over time**

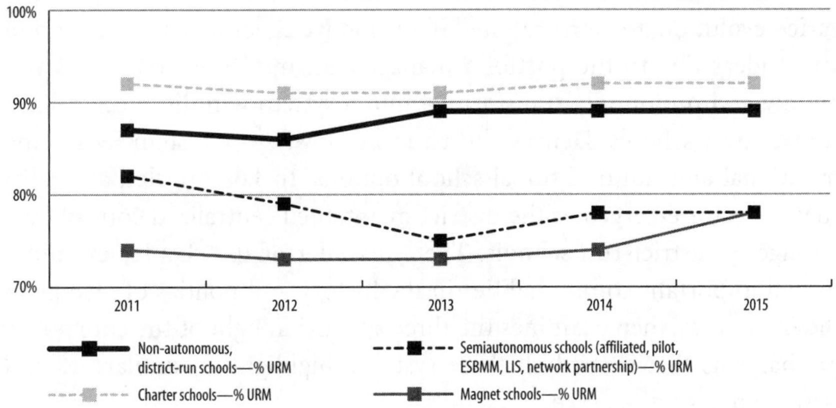

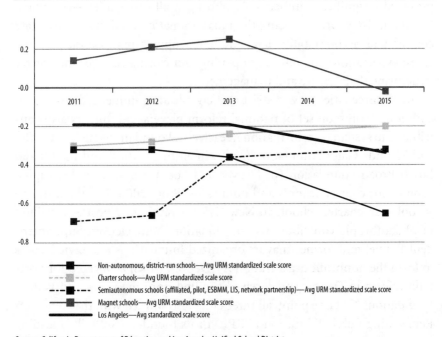

Sources: California Department of Education and Los Angeles Unified School District.

FIGURE 3.9   **Average state standardized test scale scores for underrepresented minority students by school type in Los Angeles over time**

Sources: California Department of Education and Los Angeles Unified School District.

CROSS-CUTTING COMPARISONS

As described above, the three cities evolved differently over time, and their varied evolutionary paths resulted in distinctive enactments of a common set of ideas tied to the portfolio management model. New Orleans was rapidly and profoundly transformed into a system with little centralized control over schools. Denver shifted more slowly to a system overseeing traditional and nontraditional school options. In Los Angeles, a parallel charter sector emerged as the district maintained centralized control over a range of district-run schools. The remainder of the chapter examines several important commonalities in the history and politics of change in the three cases, then examines the three systems in light of the core policy mechanisms that shaped all three systems, highlighting similarities and critical areas of difference.

Commonalities in the History of Change

As the above case descriptions illustrate, a set of common forces or "triggers" facilitated change in all three cities. Internal and external pressures provided a significant impetus for reform in all three cities—Hurricane Katrina in New Orleans being the most dramatic. In addition, new state charter and accountability laws presented opportunities and, in some cases, expectations surrounding opening and closing schools and for restructuring their nature and management.

In all three cities, new district and civic leaders influenced change. In addition, a common set of national reform players and funders also contributed to system transformation in each city. Foundations such as the Bill and Melinda Gates Foundation (active in all three cities) and the Eli and Edyth Broad Foundation (in Denver and Los Angeles) provided capital support for charter schools and nonprofits. From 2006–7 to the 2012–13 school year, charter schools in New Orleans received almost $77 million in philanthropic contributions and donations.[53] In Denver, Superintendent Bennet and former mayors organized foundations and civic leaders to form the nonprofit organization A+ Denver, which advocated for portfolio reform in Denver and received funding from the Gates and Walton Foundations.[54] At one point, all three cities also worked with the Center on Reinventing Public Education (CRPE) or its founder, Paul Hill, a leading advocate for the portfolio model. In addition, New Orleans and Los Angeles received federal Investing in Innovation funds that supported their portfolio reforms.

A second common feature of the change process was that it sparked considerable pushback in all three locations, especially from traditionally marginalized communities, who saw the new systems as not reflecting their needs and interests. These tensions were evident in the study's interviews, conducted years later. Respondents in New Orleans and Denver, in particular, expressed concerns that new system leaders were from privileged social groups (that is, primarily White men) and minimized the voices of communities of color and local leaders in decision-making. The displacement of Black administrators and teachers by the mostly White reformers in New Orleans post-Katrina was perhaps the most widely cited example of this perceived injustice.[55] "There are people that had dedicated their professional careers to education in New Orleans," commented one White leader of an organization that generally supported the reforms. "They feel they were completely disrespected." Similarly, observers in Denver noted that new policy leaders—including central office leadership and the heads of large charter networks—were predominantly White men. One nonprofit leader described Denver as "a kind of guys' club" in which the predominantly White and male leaders of large charter networks "box everyone else out."

In all three cities, interviewees also expressed concerns that the new actors and system structures and strategies were exacerbating racial and socioeconomic inequities in students' educational experiences. Some observers in New Orleans, for example, argued that the predominantly White, nonlocal educators who dominated the new system—and came to the city via new recruitment and training programs run by nonprofit organizations—lacked the cultural competency needed to support Black students. One Black community advocate noted the importance of "young people seeing folks from their communities who understand when they walk in the school door . . . what they're experiencing at home, what's happening in the local context, [and] what their history is." In Denver and Los Angeles, people criticized PMM-oriented change for unfairly burdening low-income communities of color and the educators serving them. One observer pointed out the inequities of choice in Los Angeles, noting that barriers of transportation, information, and language limited traditionally disenfranchised parents' access to school options. "There are still a number of issues out there that make it a lot easier for me, upper middle class, White woman, to get my child into a great program, than an unemployed, single mother of four who has no car, choice wise," she said. "There's still a lot more that could be done on the equity front to give her choices."[56] These early tensions foreshadow some of the lingering issues that emerged in the study's investigation of implementation of portfolio reforms; the same tensions will be examined throughout upcoming chapters.

Important Differences

While all three cases reflect the spirit of portfolio reform, the contexts and policy mechanisms are quite different. As table 3.1 illustrates, the contexts—key actors, organizational structure, overarching strategy, and other contextual conditions—differ in important ways across the three cases.

TABLE 3.1   Comparison of contexts in the three case studies

	NEW ORLEANS: MANAGED MARKET	DENVER: CENTRALIZED PORTFOLIO	LOS ANGELES: COMPETING SYSTEMS
Key actors	RSD & OPSB; portfolio managers; new nonprofits	Reform-friendly district leaders (union leaders are less central); CMO operators	• District & union leaders; charter operators
Organizational structure	RSD: lean; OPSB: traditional; charter: some networks	Central office and cross-sector collaborative; CMO and other networks	Two subsystems with little collaboration: • LAUSD: vertical, bureaucratic • Charter: some networks
Strategy	Free market with some centralized regulations regarding equity & access	"[H]olding tight & letting loose"; balance centralization & decentralization	• LAUSD: Diverse within-district options to compete with charters
Other contextual conditions	No union presence	Leadership stability; weak union presence	• Leadership instability; • fiscal challenges; • strong union presence

Looking Ahead

The remainder of the book digs deeply into the enactment of each of the five core PMM mechanisms—*planning and oversight, choice, autonomy, human capital,* and *school support*—at both the system and school levels. It analyzes how these policies and structures played out in daily practice, the challenges that were encountered, the patterns that emerged across and within the case cities, and the conditions accounting for these findings.

SECTION 2

FIVE MECHANISMS
FOR CHANGE

PLANNING
AND OVERSIGHT

Building System Accountability

*with A. Chris Torres and Sarah M. Woodward**

The idea of accountability in education is central to much of current educational reform. In the context of an idealized portfolio management model (PMM), we consider accountability to have two separate but intertwined components: 1) how portfolio managers plan which schools will be part of the portfolio, including decisions about new and existing school operators, and 2) the oversight of schools by the portfolio manager, which includes rewards or consequences based on performance.

This chapter explores several related questions around planning and oversight, and considers how our understanding of these issues varies when we look from the perspectives of the various system actors. The chapter considers planning largely at the level of the system. Planning is an important consideration for portfolio managers because it raises questions about whether the kinds of options available to families throughout the school system reflect the needs and preferences of the communities that schools serve. Therefore, it's important to understand *how* schools are selected and whose perspectives are valued or considered in the process.

---

* Important contributions to this chapter were made by Danica Robinson Brown.

Decisions about which schools would operate, replicate, and expand were made differently in each city. Denver and New Orleans tried deliberately to establish consistent and transparent processes for planning decisions, but concerns were raised about the fairness of these processes. In the vast and complex system in Los Angeles, planning decisions were less clearly coordinated and were mostly driven by the initiative of those seeking to operate schools. Across the three cities, charter management organizations (CMOs) were favored by portfolio managers because of their perceived success in creating school models that were able to meet academic goals. CMOs were also seen as having an advantage because, relative to other applicants, they could bring efficiency and resources to the application process.

Efforts at consistency in oversight paralleled those in planning, with portfolio managers in New Orleans and Denver emphasizing common performance expectations while the Los Angeles Unified School District (LAUSD) had multiple approaches to oversight and expectations. Schools' responses to these systems reflected, in many ways, the pressures and expectations placed upon them, with schools in New Orleans and Denver attending more directly to the high-stakes performance-based nature of their systems. Student performance, however, wasn't the only focus of oversight efforts. Tensions around compliance as well as parental and community oversight emerged from the analysis. Across all three cities, there were concerns about the extent to which communities and families, especially those from historically marginalized populations, had an authentic voice in system decisions that directly impacted schools. Finally—as explored in chapter 8 as well—we found that portfolio managers faced struggles with balancing their responsibilities for oversight with their efforts to support school improvement.

REDEFINING ACCOUNTABILITY: PLANNING AND OVERSIGHT

Although accountability for student performance has been increasingly emphasized in the US education system generally, over the last three decades student outcomes, in particular, have been emphasized. This trend was pushed nationally by the 2001 passage of the federal No Child Left Behind Act, whereby states were required to measure student achievement in specific subjects and grade levels. While the stated consequences for failure have been things like public shaming, reconstitution, or school turnaround, in reality, many of the more severe consequences available in these systems, such as school closure, have not been imposed in traditional districts and schools. A PMM takes this idea of performance-based accountability and connects it both to high-stakes consequences through formalized oversight processes and to planning processes that attempt to increase the availability of high performing schools as lower performing schools are reformed or taken out of the system altogether.

As we noted, portfolio managers take on a critical planning role: making decisions such as which new schools to open, which schools should be restructured or have their operators replaced, who should operate new schools and what should those schools focus on, what grade levels they should serve, and where particular schools should be located based on community needs and preferences—all while considering the facilities available in any given location. The idealized planning role of the portfolio manager involves taking proactive steps to stitch a set of autonomous schools into a cohesive system by balancing issues such as operators' records of success, enrollment patterns, and community needs and preferences. In contrast to a traditional central office simply reacting to school applications via approvals or denials, this vision of a portfolio manager actively managing the set of schools through planning processes is an important aspect of a broader vision that is proactive rather than simply reacting to the free market.

Consistent with more conventional ideas of accountability, portfolio managers also serve an oversight function, developing assessment and data systems to measure student proficiency and growth. Oversight in a PMM also involves creating clear and transparent consequences based on student performance. Such consequences can include closure, but they also might involve school reorganization (such as leadership and staffing changes or a takeover) or the provision of additional supports to struggling schools. These systems can also serve a support purpose by providing schools with formative data to assess their own performance and guide school planning for improvement.

Research is both scarce and mixed on whether high-stakes consequences tied to performance-based oversight will produce desirable outcomes and continuous improvement in public school systems, with scholars raising questions about how high-stakes decisions, such as charter approvals by authorizers, are made.[1] Research on school closures and charter takeovers demonstrates that closure can adversely affect the performance of students who must change schools. But it also has the potential to eventually improve outcomes for students leaving poorly performing schools, if their new schools are higher performing.[2] This suggests that a PMM system could be successful if it is able to provide students from closed schools with higher performing schooling options. However, there is no clear evidence that portfolio managers can enable access to such schools for all students.

Other forms of accountability, not just oversight and planning, also influence PMM systems. Market-based accountability through choice can also shape school-level student enrollment and influence whether certain schools close due to insufficient demand or expand due to strong enrollment. However, unlike in a purely market-based system, in a PMM the portfolio manager plays an important role in addressing issues of school quality, attending to community needs, and monitoring factors such as student enrollment, availability, and location of facilities in a given area when making decisions about opening or closing schools. In addition, PMMs still contend with bureaucratic accountability to other levels of government around issues ranging from teacher certification to facilities, special education, student discipline, and questions of due process.[3]

SYSTEM PLANNING

When describing their planning processes, system-level actors across the three cities identified several challenges: balancing the preferences of multiple actors, including the portfolio manager itself, families, and the community; determining what types of schools and operators are desirable and should be allowed to operate or replicate; and having clear and transparent criteria for making high-stakes decisions about schools.

The three systems reflected varied approaches to planning, but also faced some similar challenges. Overall, portfolio managers in both Denver and New Orleans approached planning proactively, with an increasing effort over time to use data to guide the seeking of applications and to provide transparency around portfolio decisions. This was not as much the case in Los Angeles, where there was little evidence that the central office was actively shepherding the creation of new schools. This may be a result of the competing systems structure, but the sheer size and scope of the district, the many subunits within the overall district, and the varied available models of schools may have also contributed to a less centralized approach and pushed the central office toward a more reactive stance.

Finally, in all three cities, participants noted that processes to select new school operators advantaged CMOs, as they could bring resources and evidence of past work to new applications. Combined with hints about the political influence of CMOs in Denver and New Orleans, these preferences raise important questions about charters as a path for innovation (as opposed to replication), and about schools with strong community ties.

Planning from the Center (Denver)

In terms of managing its portfolio, Denver Public Schools' (DPS) centralized approach included central office staff who sought to provide a relatively clear set of criteria for decisions about opening new schools or changing operators, although concerns were regularly raised about inadequate community voice in these decisions. Moreover, there were concerns about equity and access for the most marginalized students even as DPS worked to institute fail-safes to ensure these students had opportunities to access high-quality schooling options.

DPS administrators collaborated with the Denver Board of Education to strategically identify annual needs for school openings through a Strategic Regional Analysis. Every year, the portfolio manager sent out the "Call for New Quality Schools," which identified district priorities such as the location and/or grade levels of new schools. Applicants who responded to the call could propose a district-run school, a new campus for an existing charter school, or a completely new charter school. Applicants to the call needed to demonstrate potential for success on the School Performance Framework (SPF), which was the main tool used for oversight of all publicly funded schools in the district. In addition, applicants, at times, needed to demonstrate their willingness and preparation to offer specific programs within the district, such as specialized programs for students with special needs. While the district accepted applicants for new charter schools outside of the call for schools process, those applicants who were selected to meet the district's priorities gained access to what many told us was one of the most valuable resources within Denver's PMM—school facilities.

In terms of being strategic about planning, DPS sought to use data from the open enrollment system to better understand who was using choice options with an eye toward using the call for new schools to prioritize the opening of schools that might be in more demand by historically marginalized students.

In practice, this meant prioritizing those operators who had, as one DPS employee put it, a "track record of success." Yet many noted that DPS faced a tension between providing a diverse supply of school choices and giving preference to those operators that might be most successful in promoting measurable academic growth, which favored the expansion of CMOs. As a staff member from DPS reflected, "Part of the reason CMOs have an easier time opening new schools, it is not just scale, but they also have a track record. It is tough as an individual school site to handle all of this." Asked about this push to expand CMOs, a leader of an advocacy organization that supported the PMM argued that it would not be equitable to provide underserved students other options that were not as likely to be academically high performing as some of the well-known CMOs in Denver: "Look, we can't experiment with these kids. We can't test models with these kids."

DPS leaders and others grappled with whether to involve the wider community in decisions about which schools to open as part of the planning process as well as which ones to close in response to oversight issues. And if the community was to be involved, then how? Regarding the process of opening a new school, one CMO leader noted that "you have to demonstrate community demand—it's not really clear what that means but you have to do that." He described how community events designed to solicit input sometimes became a "shouting match" between the schools that wanted to open in a specific location and the community members who were opposed to removing the existing program and staff. A representative of the state's charter school association raised questions about how well community voices were being heard, focusing on how the processes for determining school operators were not necessarily responsive to the desires of historically marginalized communities. She reported:

> I have an African American friend who said, "Why is it that my community needs to have one more no-excuses model?" She said, "I would like a dual-language Montessori in my community. I would like an expeditionary learning school in my community. Why is it that these external adults are making the decision about what's best for my kids?"

Despite efforts to use intentional planning processes to enhance access to schools for historically marginalized students, some of the most desired schools remained difficult to access. As one central office representative familiar with planning and enrollment stated: "If you live in the neighborhood and the school has a neighborhood preference, that is a guarantee. You don't even have to submit a form. . . . I think most schools have some geographic priority." A leader of an advocacy organization in Denver pointed out that because of this, "you just won't find a seat" in the highest performing schools in the district unless you "happen to buy a million-dollar house in the neighborhood."

Coordinating Planning and the Market (New Orleans)

The New Orleans portfolio managers—the Recovery School District (RSD) and the Orleans Parish School Board (OPSB)—also worked to set clear criteria for school openings that were centered on academic performance. As in Denver, these efforts were sometimes challenged by concerns about equity and community influence on decision-making, especially for the city's more marginalized populations. New Orleans' process was distinct from that used in Denver, however, in that New Orleans included external actors in strategic decisions around portfolio planning, including the influential and well-funded nonprofit New Schools for New Orleans (NSNO).

In New Orleans, staff working for the two portfolio managers believed that planning should be based on data, identifying portfolio priorities using enrollment and performance data, with a special emphasis on specific student populations in need (such as special education or English language learners). The RSD and OPSB both used an annual review process to set priorities for new charter school applicants, which were communicated through a request for applications (RFA), and described making decisions about school options based on those strategic priorities. For example, the RFA for a new operator to take over McDonogh 35 Senior High School specified a preference for applicants who would seek socioeconomic diversity, work to attract students from private schools, and maintain the "long standing tradition and identity [of McDonogh] in the New Orleans Community."[4]

Nonetheless, critics of the system raised concerns about the extent to which attention was paid to determining community needs and setting strategic priorities in portfolio planning, especially in the early years of the PMM approach. One nonprofit leader argued that the community voice was largely "tossed aside" by the RSD and OPSB. The RFA process for schools was intended in part to bring greater public transparency to the selection of school operators. Indeed, an OPSB staff member described an informal process, saying, "We talk to people all the time about the schools and the work that we do. All of it is relevant. We did a series of community meetings last fall and were not—everything counts towards building those strategic priorities." Despite these efforts, community advocates continued to raise concerns in our interviews for a more inclusive process that prioritized community needs.

The focus on performance-based oversight and high-stakes consequences, discussed at greater length below, also shaped planning decisions and led to concerns that the emphasis on student outcomes would stifle the support for and approval of innovative and diverse options for students. One RSD staff member noted that the portfolio strategy has created "a sense of urgency around performance" and that "how the school leaders view the world, absolutely, is shaped by the accountability system." As a result, others argued, portfolio managers as well as school operators and school leaders were not looking more broadly at school offerings, pointing to potentially valuable but unmeasured programs such as mentoring or music.

Another noteworthy challenge for the RSD and OPSB in making portfolio decisions was the limited availability of facilities in post-Katrina New Orleans and the varied quality of those facilities. The minimal availability of facilities, as well as the portfolio managers' commitment to citywide open enrollment, made it difficult for portfolio managers to make decisions about where to locate schools based on geography and community needs and preferences. In other words, even if they identified demand for a particular type of school in one area, facilities might not have been available to create a new school there. In addition, consistent with the idea of a managed market, there was some philosophical hesitation about the portfolio manager driving location; one former RSD staff member argued that the RSD should "let the entrepreneurs [such as CMO leaders] figure out where they want to locate their schools; trust them to not be totally stupid in terms of thinking about supply and demand and just focus on identifying the needs and catalyzing them and don't be prescriptive with people on where the schools go because that was never our unit of measure in the first place."

Finally, unlike in Denver and Los Angeles, outside organizations played important roles in portfolio-shaping decisions. The National Association of Charter School Authorizers (NACSA) aided in the review of charter applications, while NSNO was directly involved in discussions about portfolio needs. One former RSD staff member described how staff from the OPSB and the RSD "would meet with our teams and look, and within NSNO also, and review data together and say, 'Based on the data and based on other things, what do we think are the big pockets of need?'" The inclusion of NSNO and NACSA brought additional supports and expertise to planning processes through NSNO's capacity-building work with charter applicants and experiences with school reviews and NACSA's development of standards and processes for review of applications. However, the involvement of these organizations also raised questions about democratic influence, local control, and community voice in major decisions with critical community impact. For example, a former RSD staff member described how, in the earlier years of the reform, OPSB and NSNO collaborated: "We worked regularly with NSNO and other partners, but they weren't representative of community for sure." There was also concern that NSNO did not assist community members with writing applications as they assisted others, making it difficult for community members to open charter schools. According to one nonprofit leader: "Where those community entities, individuals, really got active, there was a lack of direct support from the infrastructure in the city. When we talk about that time, NSNO was providing training for boards, and incubating schools, and had resources to do that. Those resources were not provided for community. They weren't accessible to community groups during that time."

This perception that the emerging system in New Orleans was not always well connected to the community itself is an oft-raised critique.[5]

Building a Portfolio from the Bottom and the Top (Los Angeles)

Within both the charter and district-run sectors of the LAUSD's competing systems, we found that, for the most part, the central office did less than portfolio managers in Denver and New Orleans to actively manage the district's portfolio of school options. They neither explicitly located schools, nor consistently captured relevant data on school enrollment and choice patterns across geographic locations. Instead, the central office largely followed a bottom-up process for new school and program openings, in which potential school operators and/or teams of educators and community members initiated applications with support from local district offices (subunits of LAUSD) and central office divisional units (such as the charter school or magnet offices) as needed. As one staff member put it, "This is an organic process. We don't tell the schools, for the most part, we need this [school] here, because we want it to come from the community, but we counsel them. We steer them to different paths."

However, there were hints within the vast system about some more intentional and data-driven planning efforts. For example, a board member described how the board decided to close two specific schools. Those schools, the member said, "were powerful leaders in bringing about change." However, they ran into issues around enrollment and questions about the comprehensiveness of their educational program. In light of this, "We had to make a choice that there was a better solution for those children, and it wasn't those two small schools. That was a very difficult decision, but we made it."

While the portfolio itself was less centrally managed in terms of which schools opened and where, starting or opening new schools within LAUSD required working through specific (and sometimes unclear) application procedures for each of the different types of district-run autonomous schools. There was general consensus among participants that the district set a high bar for opening a new district-run school or converting a school to a different model; the criteria included providing evidence of student demand, with different school types focusing on different processes and purposes. For example, applications to open pilot schools, Local Initiative Schools (LIS), and schools based on the Expanded School-Based Management Model were managed by the Local Options Oversight Committee—a supervisory council consisting of a representative from the district central office, one from the teachers' union, and one from the administrators' union—and each application involved different requirements, rubrics, and committee approvals (for example, approval from the Pilot Steering Committee for pilot schools, or 60 percent approval from staff on requested waivers for LIS). Network partnership schools were approved through a process resulting in a memorandum of understanding between the district central office and the school operators on a case-by-case basis, with limited oversight from a dedicated administrative team within the central office. Magnet school applications were reviewed by the Student Integration

Services division of the central office, which focused on opening schools with distinct thematic offerings desired by the community, in part alongside efforts to attract students for racial integration. Finally, the Charter Schools Division reviewed charter school applications, a process that was generally described as rigorous and extensive, and that included criteria specific to charter policies, charter board requirements, and state priorities for all new local education agencies. These distinct and largely disconnected processes potentially enabled greater community voice to direct school openings and options than in the other two cities, such as through requirements for community input, but they also contributed to a lack of consistent attention to the sets of schools available in different communities and how those sets of schools as a group met community needs.

For both district-run autonomous schools and charter schools, we heard from multiple interviewees that approval processes for the different forms of autonomous and charter schools were cumbersome to navigate despite district-sponsored public orientation meetings on the school authorization process for charter schools and technical assistance to internal teams submitting applications for semiautonomous and magnet schools. In recent years, the district had rejected more than half of proposed magnet school applications, and there was minimal activity around opening other forms of semiautonomous schools. Declining enrollment was one factor affecting this hesitation to open additional schools, as a central office member explained: "To open a new district school, I would say the bar is really high right now because of just the cost of opening new schools, the tightness of the facilities, the number of options that are available. It is becoming increasingly harder to open a pilot school. It is easier if you want to convert your governance model than to actually start a school from scratch. The bar is really high."

These challenges were also apparent among charter school applicants. The complexity of the application process and the resources needed in order to navigate the process and open a new charter school, alongside increasing expectations that applicants be able to demonstrate prior success in educating children, resulted in both a perceived preference for applications for CMO-managed schools and a decrease in applications for stand-alone charters. One central office staff person described how the district approved a larger number of charter schools from "CMOs or networks that already had existing schools or have resources [to operate such as] . . .

facilities, teachers, and leaders." While those interested in opening schools had opportunities to explore different options within the system, including appealing rejected decisions on charter school applications to potential county or state authorizers (state authorizers were removed in 2019), there was not a centralized effort to shape the portfolio so as to meet the needs of particular locations and communities.

THE COMPLEXITY OF OVERSIGHT

Oversight in the idealized PMM is relatively simple, with clear performance standards for schools and explicit consequences for not meeting those standards; the expectation is that this combination of clear expectations and high stakes will create incentives for schools to align their internal practices in order to meet performance standards. In all three cities, portfolio managers established accountability expectations and gathered and analyzed data from multiple measures to inform their oversight of schools. These measures were then used to a greater or lesser extent in decisions about the future and direction of individual schools. In many ways, the design of Denver's centralized portfolio and that of New Orleans' managed market more explicitly link to this idealized system, while the more complex and diffuse nature of LAUSD is less clearly aligned. However, in practice, enacting this seemingly simple idea was challenging and contentious in all three cities.

In theory, the potential consequences for failing to meet accountability expectations were similar in terms of the possibility of closure, reconstitution, revocation, or nonrenewal in each city. In practice, cities differed significantly in the extent to which and how they enacted these consequences. In addition, the public played potentially significant, but distinct, roles in shaping oversight responses in each city. In this section, we explore how schools experienced oversight within these systems, with attention to how the combination of performance-based accountability and high-stakes consequences was enacted, how compliance and other aspects of oversight came into play alongside student performance, how tensions developed between high-stakes accountability and supporting schools, and how parents, the community, and the media actually shaped the systems.

While we focus here on variations in the experiences of those in different school contexts, it is also important to note that there are commonalities in the experiences across schools. For example, school leaders in all three cities, across all school models, felt strong pressure to improve from system school boards, school-based boards, and (if different) authorizers. On the other hand, they felt less pressure overall from teachers and parents and the least pressure from unions. In addition, leaders had similar perceptions of what they were being held accountable for. When asked about the objectives for which they were held accountable, leaders in all three systems were most focused on student achievement, budget, and, for charter schools, their school mission. Enrollment and community relations issues were not perceived as important. Only in Denver, which had the most explicit system-level focus on equity, was there substantial attention to school diversity as an explicit objective. (See figure 4.1.)

FIGURE 4.1   **For what are schools accountable?**

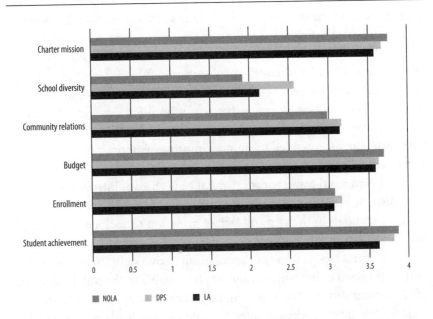

Note: School leaders were asked, "To what extent did your CMO or district hold your school accountable for the following objectives?" They were given the following response options from which to select: increase our student achievement, increase enrollment, effectively manage school budget, improve relations with community, increase the diversity of our school's student body, and, for charter schools, fulfill our mission and charter petition. Items were asked on a four-point Likert scale that ranged from "not at all" to "to a great extent."

Test Scores and Consequences as Drivers of Change

Focus on Testing

At the core of oversight in Denver and New Orleans were the frameworks for school performance used in these cities. These frameworks formed the basis for ratings of schools (by color in Denver, with "Blue" being the best, and by letter grade in New Orleans), which were intended to quickly convey information about school quality to families and others. The framework in Denver consisted of multiple measures, including academic growth, academic proficiency, college and career readiness, student engagement, enrollment rates, and parent satisfaction. The accountability framework in New Orleans included academic proficiency, financial measures (fund balance, audits, debt-to-asset ratio), and organizational measures (enrollment rates, special education and at-risk student populations, facilities, governance, discipline, health and safety, compliance, and reporting).

While incorporating multiple metrics, each framework centered on the importance of student performance on state assessments. Academic growth received the most weight in Denver's SPF calculation. In New Orleans, academic proficiency was the most significant component of the annual performance framework, and one RSD staff member suggested that other aspects of the framework didn't meaningfully differentiate schools, as "almost everyone gets 100" on the organizational and financial measures. In these two cities, our surveys of school leaders and school case studies found commensurate attention to state testing and, often, to interim assessments intended to support improvement on state assessments. The heavy reliance on academic proficiency was a clear source of tension in both Denver and New Orleans. Several New Orleans interviewees shared their distrust of testing as the primary measure of student learning, citing cheating scandals in the city and lack of attention to socioemotional well-being as their primary concerns.

Los Angeles lacked some of the cohesion in oversight that we witnessed in the other two cities, which could be attributable to the much larger size of the school district and the competing systems approach. Multiple accountability frameworks operated at different levels of the system. This was in part due to uncertainty because of shifting state and federal policies at the time of data collection (the state accountability system was in flux as the California plan for the federal Every Student Succeeds Act was not complete, and state metrics and a data dashboard were in development).

The LAUSD central office administrators described the incoherence of the accountability system as a "holding pattern," a "void," like "Play-Doh," and "in flux," making it very difficult for schools to balance multiple accountability demands and requirements. Variation in accountability measures was particularly evident across different types of schools in LAUSD.

Despite myriad accountability frameworks, school report cards were used more coherently and consistently across the district-run schools for monitoring performance and providing parents with information, at least to some degree. According to the LAUSD website, independent charter schools also had school report cards, but "they [we]re missing data on several metrics due to lack of overlapping data systems and differing metrics between traditional schools and independent charter schools."[6]

While test scores were considered important in Los Angeles, they were not as central to oversight as they were in New Orleans and Denver. Other potential objectives, such as graduation and dropout rates, were identified as comparably important, and school case studies raised more explicit discussion of oversight around issues of compliance than we saw in the other cities. For district-run schools, one central office staff member described a long-standing focus on five goals, including proficiency on assessments, but also graduation and attendance rates, parent and student engagement, and safety, saying that "those five goals have kind of been in place for probably the last eight years. That's been pretty consistent."

Connecting School Performance to Consequences

Multiple means of seeking to measure school quality have been common in public education over the last several decades, and the PMM idea ties those measures to consequences enacted by portfolio managers. In Denver and New Orleans, in particular, school leaders reported pervasive concerns about high-stakes consequences (including closure, takeover, or loss of autonomy) and placed substantial weight on test scores as a result. For example, a principal supervisor at an RSD stand-alone charter in New Orleans commented: "Test scores are not everything, but certainly they're somewhat of an indication . . . of how kids are doing. We all [have] got to live by the test scores, because if you don't, you'll be out of business. You [have] got to consider the test scores, and make sure that you make improvements." Similarly, in Denver, a school leader at a traditional public school said: "That's the big accountability piece, our school performance framework rating. Just on the district-state level, there's our school performance framework, where every school is rated on a very robust number of indicators having to do with standardized testing, like the PARCC test, the ACCESS test."

Denver used reconstitution and closure, and New Orleans used closure, more often than Los Angeles, and both experienced intense pushback from the community, especially parents whose children attended schools slated for closure. The process of school closures was acknowledged to be contentious by those more directly involved in portfolio management—for instance, staff within the DPS central office—but they believed that it could be alleviated by the setting of clearer criteria for decisions to close schools and identify new operators. In effect, stakeholders generally perceived decisions about management and access to schools—both which to close and which to open—as being made without the community's input and as a problem to be managed by better communication about the efficacy and accuracy of decisions rather than by changing criteria for closure and selecting new operators. As one DPS staff member put it, when closure was used, it needed to be based on highly visible "bright lines."

As figures 4.2A and 4.2B show, leaders across all types of Denver schools were concerned about both school closure and potentially seeing their own position in the school jeopardized. Interestingly, in Denver, it was not school leaders in charter schools—for which nonrenewal was a formal opportunity for closure—but those in traditional and innovation schools that were most concerned about closure. This is consistent both with the history of DPS, which saw many district-run schools closed early in the development of the PMM, and with the centralized portfolio and SPF process, in which all schools are potentially subject to closure and other negative consequences. It could also reflect the fact that closure is a relatively new possibility for traditional public schools, whereas charter schools, by nature of the authorizing process, were always subject to the possibility of closure and thus potentially more comfortable with the idea.

Compared to other cities, Denver also embraced a wider range of consequences, such as the potential for loss of autonomy from the central office. For example, innovation schools could lose their innovation status as a consequence for low performance on the SPF. Others saw scaling back autonomy as an intermediate step taken before the portfolio manager decides to close a school. In addition to decisions about autonomy, Denver made other strategic school-by-school decisions, such as varying the length

FIGURE 4.2   **High-stakes consequences**

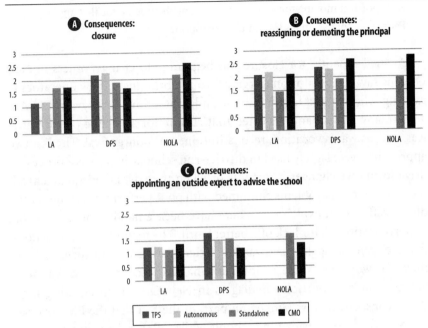

Note: School leaders were asked, "If a school does not meet the expectations of your district administration and/or school board, how likely are the following consequences?" They were given the following response options, each of which was answered on a three-point Likert scale (not at all likely, somewhat likely, very likely): takeover by another leader or organization, decreasing management authority at the school level, appointing an outside expert to advise the school, restructuring the internal organization of the school, reassigning or demoting the principal, replacing all or most of the school staff, entering into a contract with a private management company to operate the school, and closure.

of charter school renewals from one to five years based on the school's performance on the SPF.

Political and community pressure after the initial years of the PMM made continuing to regularly close schools increasingly unappealing in both Denver and New Orleans, with one stakeholder describing closure as "undercutting" the portfolio managers' own strategy in the sense that it undermined public trust in the system overall. One RSD staff member explained:

> If we close schools every year and we do it too often, then we're sort of eroding the confidence of consumers in the thing that we're building. We're undercutting our own strategy by having too much turmoil, too much churn—I guess is the right word—in the system. I think we went through a

period over the last ten years [where system leaders thought school closure] was cool, but moving forward, there's not much appetite for that any more. People see that as, that's too much disruption.

As the "appetite" for closure was beginning to change, others in New Orleans saw reconstitution (largely through bringing in new operators to existing schools) as a less disruptive and contentious strategy. In Los Angeles, many participants reported that closure for academic performance was rare, as was revocation, reconstitution, and nonrenewal. The last two approaches were largely used in district-run schools, in part as a process to drive formative changes in schools or when there was inadequate enrollment or financial problems combined with poor performance. One central office staff person explained: "There have been a handful of schools that have reconstituted, for lack of a better word. The majority of these schools that are really struggling get warning letters that give them suggestions of things to work on. There is not heavy-handed accountability." Variation between the two portfolio managers in New Orleans in enacting high-stakes consequences was linked, in part, to the fact that the RSD oversaw many of the lower performing schools while OPSB primarily oversaw the historically higher performing schools in the district.

While the charter context is distinct in terms of potential consequences, including the fact that state law builds the possibility of closure directly into charter school renewal, LAUSD central office staff described rarely using such tools: "For revocation, in the last two years, I think there probably have been about three cases [of potential charter closure], and I think in all three, maybe there was one that went all the way through. The others fixed [the issues]."

Responses to High-Stakes Consequences

Schools in all three cities incorporated practices designed to improve test scores. Yet these practices varied in important ways both among and within cities. As shown in the three graphs in figure 4.3, school leaders in New Orleans particularly emphasized strategies directly tied to improving test scores, including the use of test preparation materials and encouraging teachers to spend more time on tested subjects. Denver and Los Angeles schools used these strategies less often, with CMO-run schools in both cities the heaviest users.

FIGURE 4.3   **Strategies to increase student achievement**

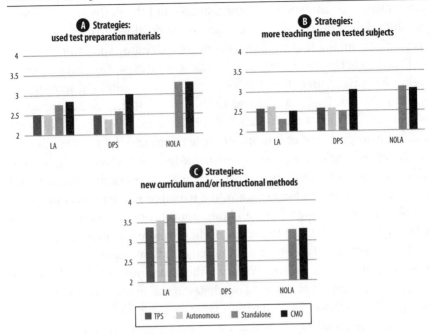

Note: School leaders were asked, "To what extent has your school employed the following strategies to increase student achievement during the 2015–16 school year?" and were asked to rate each strategy on a four-point Likert scale ranging from "not at all" to "to a great extent." Respondents were also given a "not applicable" option. The strategies listed were: used student achievement data to inform instruction, used test preparation materials, discussed methods for preparing students for the state test at staff meetings, encouraged or required teachers to spend more time on tested subjects, helped teachers identify content likely to appear on the state test so they can cover it adequately in their instruction, focused on improving the academic performance of students on the cusp of state proficiency levels, focused on the academic performance of special populations of students, focused attention on the lowest performing students, implemented new curriculum and/or instructional methods, provided professional development aligned to identified educational needs, built in time for teachers to collaborate with one another, and provided incentives to students for high performance and/or participation.

Alongside variations by type of city and type of school, we also noticed differences in responses to the strong testing focus based on the performance level of the school. Specifically, in all three cities, school leaders from higher performing schools reported being less likely to engage in practices that could be narrowly conceived as emphasizing score improvement, such as spending more time on tested subjects or focusing attention on students who were close to performance-level cusps (this analysis is based on examining the survey responses shown in figure 4.3 by performance tertiles in each city).[7]

The combination of pressures around testing and potential high-stakes consequences tied to student performance—and the perception that testing outweighed other evidence of success for portfolio managers—led to frustrations among leaders, especially in New Orleans. The principal at an RSD CMO charter, for example, longed for a more expansive focus for oversight: "Essentially, they [the authorizer] say you are really held accountable for three things. Really, at the end of the day, what they most care about is scores. . . . Again, I think there's absolutely a place for that. I think it's extremely important, but it is one of those things that does not tell the tale of the school. Just one number by itself, one test date." Concerns about test scores sometimes outweighed other potentially important objectives and metrics for schools. In New Orleans, the managed market was designed to enable variation among schools and thus opportunities for families to select schools that best matched the needs of their children. However, a leader at an OPSB-authorized charter school raised questions about the idea of distinct school missions, saying, "We all got the same mission as everybody else to try to maintain a B or A school or whatever, not go into corrective action, being a failing school. That's basically what we strive on."

While the specifics of Denver and New Orleans differ in important ways, the overall combination of performance-based metrics and high-stakes consequences driving the focus of schools was consistent with the PMM theory of action. However, some of these responses might challenge the notion of success, including strategies aimed at improving scores (such as the use of packaged test preparation materials) without improving things like student engagement or rigor of learning, as well as the possible minimization of variation among school practices and thus the lessening of meaningful choices for parents.[8]

Interestingly, the strategies for responding to lower student achievement in Los Angeles also appeared to differ from other cities. This was especially clear in contrast to New Orleans, as all school types in Los Angeles reported that they focused less on using test preparation materials and shifting teaching time toward tested subjects, and paid more attention to adopting new curriculum and/or instructional methods (see figures 4.3A–4.3C). Overall, while there were many similarities across the systems, the more complex and sometimes uncertain oversight environment found in Los Angeles did appear to produce less pressure in ways that connected with a more formative orientation toward improving student achievement. For example, one

CMO staff member in Los Angeles described what might occur if a specific school were not performing well: "I would meet with my Chief Learning Officer and we would brainstorm next steps with that school leader. I would then meet with that school leader and reflect on what had happened and the areas that they had successes and the areas that they need to grow in. Then we would create a plan for that to happen."

In the abstract, charter schools, with their need to have charter contracts periodically renewed in order to continue to operate, are particularly likely to attend to performance-based accountability. Survey findings supported the idea that charters were more concerned about school closure, but, in general, worries about a range of high-stakes consequences in Los Angeles were not as high as in the other cities. In contrast, leaders in at least one school type in Denver and New Orleans were concerned about school takeover, change of management, reassigning of leaders, or replacing staff. These survey data, taken together with evidence from interviews, suggest that accountability was felt to be lower-stakes in Los Angeles, possibly as a consequence of the relatively decentralized planning and oversight approach of that portfolio manager.

Compliance as Oversight

Although the PMM theory of action emphasizes oversight of performance, public schools still have to comply with a host of state and federal laws and regulations, and portfolio managers maintain responsibilities in overseeing that compliance. While the surveys asked few questions related to oversight around compliance, system and school-based interviews found more attention to such issues in Los Angeles than in the other cities. Charter schools, in particular, focused strongly on oversight in areas including governance, leadership, and fiscal operations. One central office staff person who worked with charter schools described how, during annual visits, they would ask: "Do you have structures in place to review academics, finances, et cetera? Do you evaluate your principals or your leadership?" They continued: "If compliance is not in order, well, it's hard to do other great things for youth if you don't deal with some of those foundational pieces of compliance like safety, making sure the adults there are appropriate to work with youth, et cetera. Those are types of expectations that are laid out."

A charter advocate took a more critical perspective, arguing that oversight by the LAUSD was not constructive and was overly compliance focused, saying that the Charter School Division "is basically a compliance unit and—that's it. I don't believe that they—they don't have a theory, they don't have enough autonomy, they don't have a mission." Another charter advocate sharply criticized oversight as a "compliance bluff" and "jumping through the hoops." From the district's perspective, charters were considered fully autonomous but still needed to comply with the law; as one central office staff member put it: "[If charters] make sure that all your things are in order, we don't have to spend the majority of our time on compliance." By contrast, with schools that the district felt they had more responsibility for, they took a more hands-on approach of looking at instructional programs, operations, and stakeholder input for autonomous schools and focused on racial integration for magnet schools.

Finally, New Orleans portfolio managers specifically identified special education compliance as an area of emphasis. This was the direct result of the state of Louisiana and OPSB operating under a consent decree due to past violations of special education students' rights in the earlier years of the PMM reforms, illustrating why monitoring issues of compliance in charter schools (as the LAUSD was doing) is important. In comparison to Denver, the focus on special education can be understood as a reactive approach to oversight that was in line with the relatively more hands-off role of portfolio managers within the managed market of New Orleans.

Oversight tied to compliance was not solely the purview of portfolio managers. In Denver and New Orleans, the local media and community members also played a role in monitoring issues around compliance, particularly through open records requests about student enrollment (Denver) and media attendance at charter board meetings (New Orleans). For example, in New Orleans, local media played an important role in holding accountable charter boards that were sometimes seen as lacking in transparency. According to one charter advocacy representative:

> I would also say here it's been interesting when I pointed to a lot of nonprofits and other support organizations, you have some media outlets here that have made charter board meetings a part of their coverage. That's really helped—some would tell you, "They're a pain. I don't wanna see them in my board meetings." I frankly am like, "Good. I'm glad they're there. It brings some transparency."

Parental Oversight

In restructuring systems of public education, PMM ideas have the potential to reconfigure the relationships between schools and those who are served by schools, including parents. One of the underlying assumptions of the PMM idea, and, more broadly, of school choice and market-based logics, is that the ability of parents to enroll and potentially unenroll their children (and the associated funding) from a school will increase schools' responsiveness and sense of accountability to families.

Our findings, however, suggest that perceived pressure from parents was less associated with the "choice" status of a school than with the socioeconomic status and performance level of schools. Figure 4.4 shows these patterns. Figure 4.4A demonstrates that charter school leaders in DPS and Los Angeles were not consistently more likely than traditional public school leaders and autonomous school leaders to report perceiving pressure from parents. In some ways, this is not surprising; since all schools in these systems are operating within a choice environment, concerns about losing enrollment may be spread across school types. However, in the relationship between parental pressure and school performance, for example (figure 4.4B), leaders in higher performing schools consistently reported experiencing the greatest pressure from parents in all three cities. And in Los Angeles and Denver, leaders of higher socioeconomic status schools reported experiencing greater pressure from parents than leaders of lower SES schools (see figure 4.4C).

These findings echoed in the school case studies, during which we heard much more from school staff about feeling accountable to parents in higher performing and higher SES schools. For example, when the school leader at a higher SES stand-alone Denver charter was asked about sources of pressures, she responded that "on the day-to-day families, without question, that's—and that's the pressure, and the privilege that I feel every day in interacting. It's my job to make sure that this place feels good for people."

Various factors may explain these differences. For example, lower performing schools generally reported feeling greater pressure around test scores, especially if they were at risk of closure, and thus may have focused their attention more on raising scores than on responding to families. While parental pressure was not clearly tied to school governance type, we did identify hints that the managed market nature of the New Orleans

FIGURE 4.4   **School leader–reported pressure by school type, school performance, and school socioeconomic status**

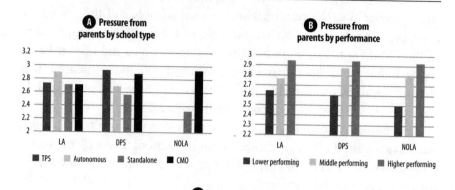

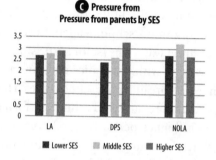

Note: School leaders were asked, "To what extent do the following groups place pressure on your school to improve?" They were asked to rate the following groups on a four-point Likert scale, ranging from "not at all" to "to a great extent," and were given a "not applicable" option. The groups were as follows: parents, teachers, district school board, district leadership, teachers' associations or unions, administrators' associations or unions, and the community as a whole.

PMM was enabling one group to potentially have greater influence—teachers. Specifically, school leaders in New Orleans, especially those in CMOs and in lower performing schools, reported particularly high levels of pressure from teachers. For example, leaders in New Orleans reported feeling very strong pressure from teachers, a 3.7 on the 4-point Likert scale, whereas leaders in both Los Angeles and Denver rated teacher pressure a 2.9. As described in chapter 7, issues of high turnover have been a significant struggle in New Orleans and have, at times, led to school leaders and CMOs emphasizing strategies for teacher retention. The high level of pressure from teachers on school leaders may reflect leaders' need to attend more directly to the concerns of teachers in order to minimize turnover.

Community Oversight

In addition to changing the relationship between parents and schools, PMM-style changes may also alter the role of communities in schools. As noted earlier, leaders in all three cities pointed to system-level school boards as an important source of oversight. However, participants raised other areas in which community actors sought—and sometimes failed— to be involved in oversight.

Stakeholders in all three cities expressed concerns about limited community voice in decision-making, especially in the context of equity. In New Orleans and Denver, specifically, interviews brought to the surface tensions around limited community input tied to school closures and the selection of school operators, and in both systems, participants identified this tension as a particular concern in the Black community (a concern echoed by research, particularly in New Orleans).[9] Indeed, in New Orleans, it was Black system-level actors who were most likely to raise such concerns.

The potential for more community oversight via charter school boards, with their smaller and more focused charge, was seen as a problematic option in New Orleans. Several interviewees, including staff of the portfolio managers themselves, expressed concerns about the ability and capacity of charter school boards to hold school leaders accountable. An OPSB staff member described the issue of charter school board governance as a "hot potato issue" that both the portfolio manager and other supporting nonprofits had yet to "own." Another OPSB staff member described the problem as an existential threat to the PMM: "It is unbelievably frightening. We have moved from a corrupt publicly elected school board to a potential now of forty corrupt charter school boards. No one is checking that." The lack of faith in charter board governance raised questions about New Orleans portfolio managers' ability to forge pathways for democratic engagement.

Tensions Between Support and Oversight

Finally, one of the most notable differences between DPS and the other PMM cities we studied was that DPS characterized itself as a portfolio manager that both engaged in rigorous and high-stakes oversight and was willing to play a proactive role in supporting struggling schools (see chapter 8 on school supports). This blurring of lines between authorizing schools, supporting them, and holding them accountable enabled DPS to negotiate with struggling schools to close on their own when necessary.

While sanctions such as closure were the most commonly perceived consequences of not meeting expectations, school leaders also saw possibilities that placed more emphasis on supporting schools (figure 4.2C). Leaders in DPS and Los Angeles stand-alone charters, which by their nature do not have an organization directly managing them (such as a district or CMO central office), were less likely than leaders in other school models to report receiving additional supports. In New Orleans, however, that was not the case when it came to the potential support of an outside expert; instead, stand-alone charter leaders were more likely to identify this possibility. Given the context of New Orleans, it may be that the supports provided by NSNO were of significance in this area (see also chapter 8).

The capacity of the LAUSD as a portfolio manager also created challenges. Given growing fiscal pressures, loss of revenue, and resulting mandates to cut administrative staff, the size of the central office had dramatically decreased over time. One participant from the teachers' union specifically tied these fiscal pressures and loss of revenue to the LAUSD to the expansion of charter schools. Various reorganizations over time had also deliberately shifted responsibility for direct oversight and support to local districts. Within the local districts, each school was matched with an instructional director, who had a caseload of approximately twenty schools. There were divergent beliefs about the efficacy and capacity of the local districts, with one central office representative describing their services as "excellent," and others reporting that the directors are "shuffled around" and that the local district system "breaks down." Data suggested that the structure of accountability and the distinction between central office and local district office roles were at times unclear. One central office staff member described it as:

> an ongoing challenge, because you have the vision of the . . . superintendent and the board and not necessarily in one sentence. Then you have the various offices that have oversight responsibilities. . . . All of those things are not necessarily [consistent] with one another. . . . Each one of those programs does have its own accountability and demands and requirements. Then you have the local district that is rolling out its own initiative independent of the superintendent and board vision and all of the

accountability categorical programs. Things like that. It's hard for schools to balance these things.

Adding to the complexity of oversight in LAUSD, different autonomous school types were accountable to different entities in the authorizing and renewal process, each with different requirements and rubrics used for reviewing operations and outcomes.

The LAUSD Charter Schools Division, with its staff of more than fifty personnel, was not seen as having the same capacity challenges. In addition to annual visits, the Charter Schools Division continually monitored charter schools, including through situations that may be prompted by parent calls. Notably, in Los Angeles we witnessed the same debate about the appropriate balance between the portfolio manager's role as a charter school authorizer and its role as a supporter that we observed in Denver and New Orleans. One charter division staff member felt that the LAUSD's role was to keep an "appropriate distance" and that the "onus" was on schools to improve in response to accountability reviews.

SUMMARIZING THE CHALLENGES OF OVERSIGHT AND PLANNING

After initial critiques around lack of transparency, portfolio managers in both New Orleans and Denver worked toward more proactive and transparent planning processes based on common performance frameworks largely used for all school types. Consistent with expectations around test-based accountability and high-stakes consequences, schools in these two cities focused efforts on test score improvement. In the larger and more complex context of Los Angeles, there was less centralized planning around the closing of schools, opening of new schools, or changing of operators in existing schools, and instead the closing or conversion of schools to different autonomous models was largely driven by the decisions of potential operators submitting applications. Los Angeles schools also saw less consistent oversight expectations and high-stakes actions such as school closure, which may explain why school-level leaders were less concerned about high-stakes consequences. In this environment, school leaders focused more on compliance, and we saw hints that Los Angeles charter schools were less likely to report using strategies that were immediately focused on raising test scores.

In all three cities, we saw common challenges and concerns. Of particular note were the repeated questions raised about the role of community voice and parental influence on decisions around both planning and oversight. As described above, those with close ties to communities sometimes felt sidelined in planning decisions about what schools would be located where, an issue exacerbated by ongoing challenges around the availability of facilities. The potential for these weaker ties between portfolio managers and local communities raises questions about the long-term sustainability of PMM-style reforms.

The theory of action underlying the PMM idea assumes that those in schools will respond rationally to pressures and expectations placed on them by performance-based oversight and high-stakes consequences. The observed responses to oversight pressures, however, revealed hints of the challenges experienced by those in schools who face high-stakes consequences and yet may be unclear as to what, exactly, they should do in order to meet the performance goals of portfolio managers. In this context of uncertainty, school leaders may respond in ways that they see as legitimate even if they aren't clear that those responses will lead to desired outcomes. In the high-stakes environment of New Orleans, for example, adoption of school practices such as using test preparation materials and interim assessments may help school leaders conclude that they are responding to uncertainty in ways that are perceived as legitimate.

SCHOOL CHOICE

Expanded Options, Increased Competition

with Tasminda K. Dhaliwal and Taylor N. Allbright*

Traditionally, families have had relatively little choice over their children's K–12 schooling. School districts assign students to schools based on where they live, so that "educational choice" means choice of neighborhood location or choice of a private school option. For many, especially low-income families, this means that options are limited. Advocates of the portfolio management model (PMM), and choice policy more broadly, assert that all families and students should have access to expanded options. Yet how do PMMs make options available to families, and what are the tensions and trade-offs entailed? What factors shape these policy decisions? How do schools and families experience these processes? This chapter examines the design and implementation of choice systems in the three case cities, especially the enrollment systems and other processes and practices used to communicate and make options available to families.

School choice could help families and educational outcomes in various ways: allowing families to exit low performing schools and pressure schools to close or improve, allowing parents to match the needs of their

---

*Important contributions to this chapter were made by Kate E. Kennedy, Eupha Jeanne Daramola, and Catherine Balfe.

children to schools that are diverse in their programs and cultures, and increasing parent engagement in the educational process.[1] The PMM is designed specifically to facilitate these potential benefits. Giving schools autonomy so that they can control their budgets, personnel, and other elements allows educators to define their school missions in order to compete and differentiate themselves from other schools. Planning and oversight also shape the options available to families, as the portfolio manager is supposed to keep out low-quality schools.

However, schooling is an unusual market, and these theories may not hold, at least not in the simple way described above. This means that the PMM has to address a wide variety of policies in order to create real choices. For example, schools have incentives to choose students, and have at least twenty different ways to do so; this suggests the importance of enrollment systems that give students a choice of schools instead of giving schools a choice of students.[2] Also, information about schooling tends to be poor, and families cannot make wise decisions if good information about their options is unavailable. Further, even when they choose and gain admission to a school that is best for them, the fact that students have to physically get to school each day makes transportation policy important. More generally, the conditions of well-functioning markets generally do not hold in schooling, and creating choice therefore involves more than changing enrollment systems.[3]

This chapter starts by outlining the various options for enrolling students in schools—attendance zones, decentralized choice, and centralized choice. Each of the three cities created its own hybrid versions of enrollment systems and changed them over time as they saw how each system worked and, in some cases, failed to work. Each city had its own reasons for adopting choice, shaped by its own political, geographic, and demographic circumstances.

The decisions about these and other aspects of the choice systems created tensions among competing values and priorities, especially tensions between the value of choice and the value of neighborhood schools, and between school autonomy and active centralized management of a portfolio of schools in order to increase equity. The chapter also shows how school-level choice practices such as recruitment and marketing in the three cities varied by school type, especially where charter schools were governed by charter management organizations (CMOs).

DESIGN OF CHOICE MECHANISMS

The enrollment system is the first policy decision to make regarding school choice. There are three main designs of enrollment systems—attendance zones, decentralized choice, and centralized choice—and the three cities made very different choices. This was partly because they had different goals and differing levels of trust among key actors.

Enrollment System Designs

Attendance zones have been a mainstay in traditional public schools. Assigning students to schools based on where they live means that parents know the schools their children will attend well in advance of the time when the students enter them. Zone-based enrollment also keeps transportation costs low and may encourage positive neighborhood relations and a sense of community. On the other hand, attendance zones mean that families can only choose alternative schools at the considerable cost that comes with leaving neighborhoods. This obstacle may result in mismatches between student needs and school programs and reduce accountability of schools for meeting student needs. The zone-based approach also means schools will reflect, and perhaps accentuate, segregation in the housing market, as low-income families lack the means to move into affluent areas.[4]

Two other approaches seem to give families more options and, in theory, allow families to break the link between the housing and schooling decisions. With *decentralized enrollment*, parents apply separately to every school they are interested in. Each school manages its own enrollment process, and families choose from among those to which they gain admission. Most charter-based policies require schools to use lotteries when there are too many applicants and ban discrimination against students on the basis of race, ethnicity, income, or other factors.

However, decentralized choice creates a lot of work for families, requiring them to visit schools and manage the rules of different application procedures and forms; families without cars and without experience in other decentralized choice processes, such as college applications, may be at a particular disadvantage. Also, the outcome is unpredictable for families. They do not know where their children will attend school until just a few months before school starts; in contrast, with attendance zones, they know years in advance. This uncertainty also extends to school leaders who may not know how many students will show up until the first day of school. Since enrollments drive school revenues, this also means schools are unsure of how many teachers they can hire and how much money they can spend. Also, schools have incentives to bypass lottery rules and instead choose their preferred students. It is difficult for districts and other agencies to monitor decentralized school enrollment practices, so that "school choice" can mean that schools are the ones doing some of the choosing.

Centralized enrollment, the third option, is less frequently used nationally, but gaining in popularity. Sometimes called unified or coordinated enrollment, this approach allows families to submit their preferred schooling options to the school district, which assigns each student to a school while taking into account families' most preferred options. Some of these systems, specifically, allow families to rank their preferred schooling options on a single form, and a computer algorithm assigns each student to a single school. Compared with decentralized choice, these centralized processes are meant to better account for parent preferences and to reduce the administrative burden on families and schools.[5] They may also yield more equitable access, preventing schools from bypassing lotteries and otherwise selecting advantaged students. However, the computer algorithm that assigns students to schools is complex and difficult for families to understand or trust.

With both centralized and decentralized enrollment, it is common for schools to use priority categories, or point systems, in conjunction with lotteries. Common considerations that give some students a leg up in the admissions to any given school include having siblings attending the school, having parents working in the school, and/or having strong academic backgrounds. Distance to school is also commonly factored in. While choice means that students are never guaranteed seats in any school as they are in traditional school districts with attendance zones, it is still possible to give students living nearby greater odds of admission.

In many cities, enrollment systems have evolved over time, resulting in some combination of these three forms of enrollment processes. In particular, as charter schools begin to enter school districts, they create a mix of attendance zones (for traditional public schools) and decentralized choice (for charter schools). As the number of choice options expands, so does the complexity and unfairness, and these consequences frequently drive local leaders to consider centralizing the process.

Other Policies Shaping Choice

The enrollment system, however, is only part of school choice. Even before parents apply, schools make decisions about school design, location, and admission processes. Schools offer particular curricular programs and then market themselves and recruit interested families. Some also have admission requirements that restrict enrollment and have admission processes that, more subtly, attract some families and dissuade others. In these ways, schools can shape both the number and types of students they attract, even before anyone sets foot in those schools.[6]

Location is also important, and, consequently, so is transportation. Students have to get to school every day, and parents have to get there themselves sometimes. For this reason, school leaders pay a lot of attention to where schools are located—sometimes called the "siting decision"—and what kinds of transportation they offer. Practically speaking, if a school is located far away from home and parents' work, and no transportation is offered, then students will not be able to attend that school in practice, even if they can in theory.

Schools can also shape their enrollments after students enter. Even if students can get into desirable schools, schools can push them out indirectly (such as by regularly calling parents to pick up their children when they misbehave) or directly (by expelling them).[7]

Given these potential ways in which choice and autonomy can lead to unhealthy school reactions, and given the principle that the PMM is supposed to make schools accessible to all families, portfolio managers can and do create rules that help ensure access. Therefore, in addition to enrollment systems, the discussion below focuses on two factors that are also likely to affect the choice process: information and transportation.

Varied Approaches

Each of the three cities designed its choice infrastructure differently, which in turn influenced how local leaders and educators talked about school choice. Los Angeles overlays all three enrollment system designs in a somewhat uncoordinated fashion—another example of the city's competing systems. Denver's centralized portfolio also combines these enrollment systems, but with much more centralized coordination. Finally, New Orleans relies almost completely on centralized enrollment. New Orleans also has more uniform information and transportation, in keeping with the characterization of this city as a managed market.

New Orleans

Enrollment System   Before Hurricane Katrina, like almost every other city, New Orleans relied on attendance zones, albeit with many avenues for exceptions, constituting a form of decentralized choice. Partly to address the unpredictable return of families after Katrina, New Orleans shifted to a more formalized decentralized choice system. The problems with that were predictable: schools could freely choose which students they wanted, and they did so. Special education students, in particular, were often excluded, and the Southern Poverty Law Center eventually sued on their behalf. The lawsuit, public pressure, and other factors eventually pushed the state Recovery School District (RSD) toward centralized enrollment and related policies.

All charter schools were required by law to choose students by lottery. Beginning in 2012, all the state-governed schools and, over time, most of the district schools used a system called the OneApp that incorporated, in varying ways, sibling and geographic priorities. Geographic zones played a minimal role, however, as the zones were quite large. Some schools also used testing or other performance requirements, mostly continuing the city's prereform tradition of magnet schools. The shift to centralized enrollment was coupled with requirements that schools allow midyear transfers and accept additional students when existing students depart (also known as "backfilling"), though the details and enforcement of these policies varied over time.

Transportation and Information   State law in Louisiana required bus transportation for families residing more than one mile from their school. After some schools simply provided bus tokens for the city's (largely dysfunctional) public transportation, the state changed the rules to require charter schools to provide yellow bus service that picked students up near their homes.

Nonprofits were important in providing families with information, such as the widely used *New Orleans Parents Guide*, which provides detailed and standardized information for every publicly funded school. While the information is self-reported by schools and is therefore largely seen as a marketing tool, there is some auditing of the data in the guide, and it is still widely used, in print and online. Among other things, the guide includes specific academic outcomes and the A–F letter grades given by the state to all public schools in Louisiana. Other nonprofits offered additional information, such as an online "equity index," and also held school fairs. Eventually, the RSD created publicly funded "family resource centers" to help families in the choice process.

As we will see, of the three cities, New Orleans made the heaviest use of centralized enrollment during the period of data collection, though the information function was largely deregulated and taken on by nonprofits.

Denver

Enrollment System   Denver, like New Orleans, shifted from attendance zones to decentralized enrollment to more centralized enrollment and choice policies. The district's centralized enrollment system, SchoolChoice, started in the 2011–12 school year. Designed with the input of school leaders, parents, and advocates, the system was intended to address concerns that individual schools might manipulate enrollment to accept only privileged and high performing students. All publicly funded schools in Denver were required to participate in the system, to hold vacant seats for late arrivals, and to backfill vacant seats when a student left the school midyear. The system incorporated sibling priorities, allowed schools to set geographic priorities, and also allowed some charter schools to set aside spots for students from marginalized backgrounds, such as low-income or English language learner students. Using an online system that included all types of publicly funded schools—traditional public, innovation, magnet, and charter—families ranked schools in order of their preference.

A key difference between Denver and New Orleans is that in Denver students maintain guaranteed access to a particular neighborhood school or, if living within a district-designated "enrollment zone," a subset of schools. Some district leaders described enrollment zones as designed to promote racial and socioeconomic integration, though they expressed mixed views over whether such integration was actually taking place.

Transportation and Information   The district provided transportation to K–8 students attending their assigned neighborhood school and, in five of the twelve K–8 enrollment zones, transportation for all students attending schools identified as part of the zone. Outside of these options, families were largely responsible for transporting their children.

Consistent with its centralized portfolio, Denver Public Schools (DPS) directly provided information about all schools (traditional public schools, innovation, magnet, and charter) rather than relying on nonprofits. This information often did not identify which schools were charters, emphasizing a commitment to treating different school models equally. The enrollment guides, available in multiple languages and both for the overall system and for each enrollment zone, provide basic enrollment information and measures of school quality. DPS also holds multiple "school expos" each year, where families can gather information about schools in person. District- and school-level participants and parents spoke positively about how enrollment information was communicated to families.

Overall, the portfolio manager–driven Denver system was as coordinated as that in New Orleans, but also more complex and multifaceted—with its combination of traditional attendance zones, enrollment zones, and citywide choice.

Los Angeles

Enrollment System   Los Angeles, a far larger system than New Orleans or Denver in terms of both population and geography, has easily the most complex choice environment. The city used all three enrollment systems simultaneously. Unlike Denver, Los Angeles had different school types (such as traditional public schools, pilot, magnet, and independent charter) operating under different sets of rules. As a result, while families had choices, they faced a convoluted process of accessing information and enrolling their children in schools and, once enrolled, were subject to different policies and opportunities affecting access.

For example, independent charter schools in Los Angeles operate under lottery-based decentralized choice as well as district policy requiring backfilling from their waiting lists when students leave midyear. The Los Angeles Unified School District (LAUSD) also operates a "zones of choice program" within limited geographic areas for district-run high schools in the same or similar locations (about half of eighth graders districtwide participate). While this program is similar in concept to the enrollment zones in Denver, its purpose is not racial and income-based integration, and charter schools do not participate. The district website describes the choice zones as "a strategy to increase the number of personalized educational options available to students."[8]

Like most other cities (including Denver and New Orleans), Los Angeles also offered some degree of choice through magnet schools, though they seem to play an outsized role in LA. Initiated in the 1970s in response to court-ordered desegregation, the magnet schools program relies on centralized enrollment and a complex point system (unlike other aspects of choice in the city, magnet schools are intended to promote racial integration). Widely viewed as a highly competitive process, the system awards points to students for any of the following actions or circumstances: applying to the same magnet where a sibling attends; living within the neighborhood boundaries of an overcrowded school; living within the boundaries of a predominantly Hispanic, black, Asian, or other non-Anglo school; being on a waiting list for a magnet; and having completed the highest grade level in a magnet program and applying to another magnet. Explaining the system, one local newspaper headline read "Magnet Schools: How to Navigate One of L.A.'s Most Complex Mazes."[9]

The district also has Schools for Advanced Studies, using a separate centralized enrollment process, and, rather than integration, these schools prioritize students identified as gifted. There are also more than 130 bilingual and dual-language programs that require separate applications and often lotteries.

Finally, the LAUSD has a basic open enrollment policy that allows families at all levels (K–12) to apply directly to district-run schools outside of their neighborhood attendance boundaries. If space allows, families are granted admission under the agreement that they provide their own transportation. Many of these programs operate on different application deadlines, which is also seen as fueling the competitive environment in Los Angeles.

Given so many distinct sets of schools, each with its own approach to enrollment, each family could conceivably access traditional attendance zones, decentralized choice, and centralized choice simultaneously. They could have a traditional public school as a guarantee, but then pursue multiple avenues for choosing out of it. System leaders said they supported a potential move to a more centralized choice system that encompassed all schools, partly so that traditional public schools could better compete with charter schools. At the time of data collection, central office leaders were developing a new online enrollment system to simplify the application process for district-operated schools.

Transportation and Information   As with enrollment processes, different Los Angeles schools operated under different rules with respect to transportation and information. For example, the magnet program provides limited transportation to some students who reside beyond a specific distance, but families wanting to access other school types outside their attendance zone, including charter schools, have to find their own transportation. Because of low population density in some areas, limited public transportation options, and long commute times, exercising choice often requires considerable time and financial resources.

Unlike families in the other two cities, Los Angeles families do not have a one-stop option for accessing information about all of the available schooling options. The district provides a *Choices* brochure and information on its website describing all district-run choice options, but charters are not included. Much of the outreach is conducted by a school, regional district, or central office department (such as the magnet schools office). Regional districts that operate zones of choice help coordinate communication about high school options (via school fairs, zone of choice brochures, and other methods describing school options in a given area). The magnet schools office runs magnet fairs in collaboration with regional local districts and also conducts outreach and advertising. In recent years, the central office has also provided support to in-district schools in marketing their schools.

Table 5.1 summarizes the key elements of the enrollment, information, and transportation policies in the three cities. This reinforces just how differently policies can be designed and the varying degrees of centralization that are possible within the PMM label.

TABLE 5.1. **Summary of school choice policies**

	NEW ORLEANS (MANAGED MARKET)	DENVER (CENTRALIZED PORTFOLIO)	LOS ANGELES (COMPETING SYSTEMS)
Enrollment Systems			
Attendance Zones	None	All families; some schools	All families; some schools
Decentralized Choice	A few remaining schools	None	All independent charters
Centralized Choice	Citywide choice: Nearly all schools in citywide choice (soon to be all)	Citywide choice: All schools in citywide choice (all grade levels), including schools with attendance zones	Citywide choice: None
	Broad priority zones: Broad geographic zones for priority categories, but they play a very small role	Enrollment zones: Exist in some parts of the city, usually with 3–4 schools to choose from	Choice zones: About half of district-managed high schools in choice zones
Other Choice-Related Policies			
Transportation	All schools required to provide transportation beyond 1 mile	District-provided transportation for attendance zone schools (beyond 1 mile for grades K–5, beyond 2.5 miles for grades 6–8)	Available for some traditional public school students; required for magnet schools and students participating in the integration program
		District-provided transportation for some K–8 enrollment zones (including charters in enrollment zone)	
Information	*Parents Guide* includes all publicly funded schools; citywide fairs and family resource centers	District website includes all publicly funded options	Centralized information about district-governed schools; no centralized source for independent charters; some guides for some neighborhoods and other schools

Note: All three cities have magnet schools, which are not reflected in the above table. "Attendance zones" refers only to traditional neighborhood-based zones where students are guaranteed enrollment based on residence (see discussion of other types of zones in the other rows). "Decentralized choice" means families apply to each school separately and schools manage the enrollment process. All the "centralized choice" in these cities is based on parent rankings of their preferences unless otherwise noted. Other than magnet schools, all forms of choice in all cities officially require lottery enrollment when there are more applications than seats.

CHOICE IN PRACTICE

The infrastructure of choice in each city is just the starting point, however. This section describes some key findings—from system leader interviews, school case studies, and school leader self-reports—regarding the design, experiences, and perspectives of key stakeholders. What factors have shaped the design and implementation of choice policies in these three cities? How are schools responding to choice? What concerns have emerged?

Factors Shaping the Design and Implementation of Choice Policies

The design of choice policies in all three cities was shaped by the degree of trust and collaboration among system and school leaders, as well as by the goals that key leaders embraced. Trust in system-level leaders varied across cities, and this translated into different levels of centralization. The degree to which equity was a key goal of school reform, versus other goals such as providing more choice and options, also varied across cities.

Trust and Collaboration

PMMs necessitate new relationships between government officials and school leaders. The success of these individuals' relationships, and therefore the success of their collaboration and joint decision-making in the three cities, depended on the degree to which they trusted one another.

Denver system leaders, for example, were intentional in their efforts to codesign enrollment processes with leaders in traditional and charter schools, and they attributed widespread buy-in to this collaborative approach. One central office leader explained:

> It's something we all went into with some fear and trepidation of how would this work. We worked really hard with the charters in designing it. Again, it wasn't we designed it and then we said, "Here it is. Take it or leave it." It was . . . "isn't this a worthwhile goal? Yes? Okay, let's design it together. Let's think through those policy choices together and really reach consensus on the key policy decisions within that enrollment system."

DPS also created an oversight board for those first few years, a board that included a charter representative "to make them feel comfortable with the [enrollment] system," said another district leader. Trust was further built through ongoing collaboration and opportunities for input, by way of a "compact" codeveloped with the charters. According to a DPS leader, the compact established a set of principles or "equities of opportunity":

> That all schools get the exact same access to resources, including facilities, including grants. Second to equity is access and opportunity, which is, charters have to serve all kids. There can't be any difference in enrollment and access to charters that there is with district-run schools. Third was the equity of accountability that will have the exact same rules for and processes for new schools to open, whether they be district-run or charter.

While trust was not a topic of frequent discussion in New Orleans—in general or in interviews—other research on New Orleans suggests that relationships and trust among system and school leaders have evolved. In the early years of the reform effort, decisions were top down, being made by a handful of leaders.[10] Over time, system leaders (especially in the RSD) began to meet more often with school and CMO leaders and gave them more of a voice in discussing problems and developing solutions, such as the centralized enrollment system.

In contrast, a climate of trust was lacking in Los Angeles, where many leaders doubted that the district could effectively run a citywide centralized system or provide information that would be trusted. "I don't know that I would want LAUSD to run the system," said one Los Angeles reform leader, "especially because of their track record in large technology projects. And it wouldn't be trusted by the charters." This concern was partly rooted in historical missteps by the district, such as an incident when the student information system malfunctioned at the beginning of the school year, forcing schools to create handwritten rosters. The lack of trust may also have been related to the much larger size of the LAUSD, which made coordination more difficult and meant that the district office was more remote from schools, as compared with the smaller districts in Denver and New Orleans. A few individuals also doubted the district's interest in including charter schools in the enrollment system, speculating that district leaders believed district-operated schools would lose out in the competition, exacerbating enrollment declines. Overall, findings suggest relatively high levels of trust in Denver and relatively low levels in Los Angeles, while trust has improved in New Orleans over time.

Equity Goals

In Los Angeles, district leaders spoke mostly about the value of choice as a means to offer more options for students. One LAUSD central office administrator explained the rationale for the choice zones this way: "It provides choice that is relevant to a student interest, because within zones and depending on the number of choices, you can have anything from a visual and performing arts school to a STEAM school or a STEM school or a visual animation school. It's providing those relevant instructional experiences that students will be excited of attending [sic]."

System-level leaders in Denver and New Orleans, in contrast, articulated a clear intent to design choice policies in the pursuit of equity. In New Orleans, most system-level leaders were quite complimentary of the enrollment policy and the way it has "been a greater leveler" of the playing field for families. A city leader explained:

> There's a clear theory in literature around charter schools that are No Excuses, can push kids out. They can figure out how to recruit kids who are more likely to succeed than average and disrupt the equitable flow of kids into schools so that they're really homogenous student bodies, and in fact they're not. What we've decided in New Orleans is that actually there are certain things that you have to do at a districtwide level to ensure equity and fairness . . . and the OneApp being the key one of those items.

A New Orleans charter advocacy leader echoed this sentiment:

> I think what OneApp ensures us is it still gives schools freedom to do their programming and do kind of what their vision of their school is, but One-App ensures that anybody has equal access and opportunity to get into that school. . . . Generally, it's saying, "You're going to be a public school. You're going to participate in OneApp. Go after it. Go after all of those things that you have control of, but you're not going to determine who you're gonna serve. You're gonna get to determine how you serve them."

DPS leaders also emphasized the fairness of centralization. They were adamant that Denver charters and noncharters follow the same rules regarding enrollment. Advocating for consistency and citing equity as their "North Star" in developing these systems, a Denver central office leader explained:

We spent a lot of time together saying as a community of public schools, "What should our systems look like so that it is equitable in the school and the schools do drive greater equities?" For example, we have a common enrollment system where we run the enrollment system for every school in the district. District-run and charter. We run the wait list for everyone. . . . Increasingly now, charters are . . . part of enrollment zones and they have all the same obligations around late-arrival kids and middle-of-the-year kids. Having to serve all kids in the boundary. There are no screening mechanisms, right? All of these where enrollment conditions are exactly the same among district-run schools and charters.

This central office leader also boasted that Denver's charters and district-run schools serve similar proportions of students with disabilities, due to common expectations as well as the provision of extra funding to support these students: "The traditional stalemate has been, charters have said, 'You don't give us the money,' the districts have said, 'You don't serve the kids.' We said let's do both, right?"

Other Denver system-level respondents similarly attested to the fairness of the system. An advocacy leader explained, "For the most part, it's working really, really well." One district partner contrasted the new system to what existed prior: "Parents who were in the know and who had the time and the resources can game the system. They're at the front desk every day bringing cookies to the secretary, who's like, 'I can get you in.' All right. That's how it worked. . . . A lot of that's been sort of taken out of the equation."

DPS leaders further articulated an intent to promote racial and economic integration in the development of enrollment zones. Not only did the drawing of broader boundaries provide families with greater choice for schools matching student need, but the boundaries also provided greater opportunities for students from different backgrounds and neighborhoods to attend schools together. As one DPS leader explained:

We, like many cities, have primarily neighborhood-based school systems in an environment where you have intense neighborhood segregation along racial and economic lines. That's true for many cities across the country. It's one of the reasons we've taken steps like these enrollment zones to cross traditional boundaries. Where you had two neighborhoods next to each other and one was really affluent white and one was primarily low-income kids of color, to say we're going to have one common enrollment zone. . . . It's a way to get greater integration at the different schools within that enrollment zone.

While the LAUSD also had choice zones, Los Angeles participants in the study spoke less about integration as a goal for this structure (except for the magnet schools program, where integration is a legally mandated goal). This highlights the fact that the same policy can be used to pursue different objectives at the same time. As discussed later, efforts to achieve equity were not always successful, and in all three cities the enactment of choice policies raised concerns about equitable access for *all* families and students.

Implementation: School-Level Recruiting and Marketing Practices

The survey data provide a detailed look at how schools responded to system-level choice policies, particularly efforts to market themselves and recruit students. These data also indicate how much pressure school leaders felt to increase enrollment—reflecting the potential accountability created by choice. As noted above, different types of schools might respond differently to the competition created by choice; those with more autonomy or perhaps greater support from a central office could be expected to engage in recruitment and marketing differently from those with less autonomy or less support. The theory underlying choice also suggests that competition would potentially drive schools—especially those in relatively high demand—to recruit the most desirable students and push out those who had special needs, low test scores, and/or discipline problems that disrupted the schooling environment. For the study, we surveyed school and district leaders to understand how the choice system was working and how schools responded to it.

Marketing and Recruitment

School leader survey responses suggest that the design of enrollment and extent of choice affected school recruitment and marketing practices. Schools in New Orleans reported the highest average number of recruiting and marketing activities, followed closely by Denver, and then by Los Angeles. This is partly reflected in the box plots in figure 5.1.[11]

FIGURE 5.1   **Sum of recruiting and marketing activities by city**

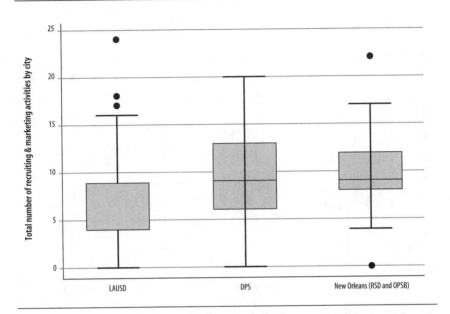

These results are in line with the choice infrastructure in the three cities; the fact that New Orleans engaged in the most recruiting and marketing activities fits with the complete absence of attendance zones, as schools did not have any guaranteed students. This pattern also appears to be partly driven by the larger share of schools in New Orleans that were managed by CMOs, which engaged in more recruiting activities than the managers of other school types.

Somewhat surprisingly, however, schools in New Orleans did not report higher levels of pressure for increasing enrollment. Also, the extent of marketing was unrelated to parental demand for schools reflected in the choice process. This could be because the total number of seats in the system was in line with the total number of students, so that schools were indirectly guaranteed sufficient enrollments (though this could not be tested with the available data).

School-Level Choice Practices

As figure 5.2 illustrates, across the three cities, CMO schools consistently engaged in more recruiting activities than traditional public schools in

FIGURE 5.2   **Sum of recruiting and marketing activities by school model across cities**

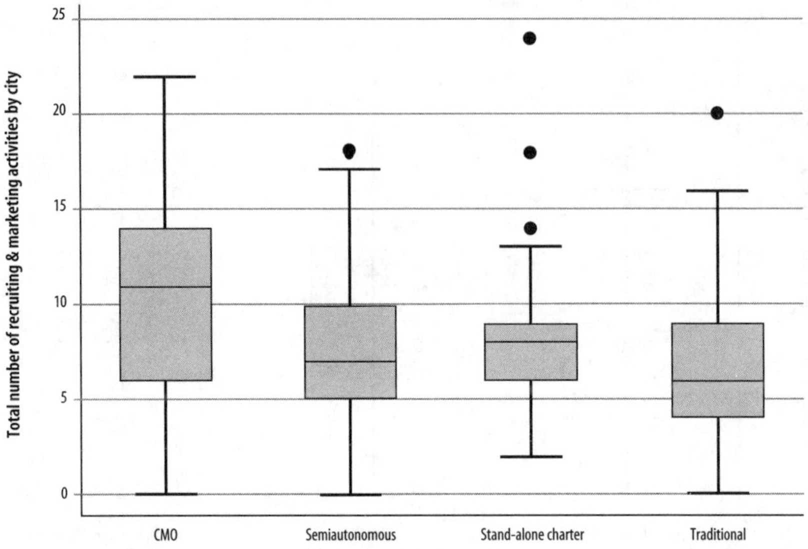

Note: Since the number of schools and the number of school categories differ across the three cities, we also created the same box plots (and t-tests of means) in each city individually. The pattern in all three cities looks similar to the pattern reflected in figure 5.2.

Denver and Los Angeles, and more than stand-alone charter schools in New Orleans (though the New Orleans results were not statistically significant).[12] This could be because marketing was simply too far outside the institutional norms of traditional public schools and the districts that govern them, or because they felt less financial pressure than might be expected, since funding for traditional public schools is more loosely related to individual school enrollment levels than it is with charters. Finally, economies of scale might be at work, as someone in the CMO office would manage this activity across all schools and would purchase advertising materials and space in bulk.

This finding was reinforced by case study interviews. When asked about recruiting, a principal at a CMO charter in Denver described how CMO staff managed these processes, saying that one specific staff member "would have a much better idea of . . . all of that stuff, which is one of the things that I think is nice about our organization, is that I don't have to think about that. She owns that." Another principal, at a CMO charter in Los Angeles, described how the CMO and dedicated school site staff worked together: "This year they've [the CMO home office] really done a great job of streamlining the whole recruiting process. They've been a lot more hands-on this year in terms of providing the resources and providing the distributables [marketing materials]." A New Orleans principal commented similarly: "A lot of the marketing and the branding is actually network-based. There are roles of the [CMO] network designed to develop a branding strategy and a marketing strategy. Then there are specific liaisons at each site. We've got one person here, in particular, who, in addition to having a full-time job here, also spends a lot of his time going to school fairs." The strong role of CMOs is perhaps not surprising as they are designed to take some burdens and responsibility out of the hands of school leaders. However, this is some of the first concrete evidence that the phenomenon extends to recruiting and marketing.

School Demand

Based on the survey data, we found no differences in recruiting and marketing between low- and high-demand schools in Denver and New Orleans.[13] However, interviews support the idea that recruitment activities may have been driven by *perceptions* of pressure to enroll students, rather than by actual demand. Several educators in high-demand schools reported strong external pressures to reach enrollment targets, even though these schools had sizable waiting lists. For example, one principal of a high-demand CMO school in Denver reported, "There is always pressure for enrollment. I mean . . . enrollment drives our funding, funding drives our paychecks and programming and what we offer kids. So, absolutely there is pressure for enrollment." Such pressure—emerging from a broader policy context in which enrollment is tied to funding— might help explain why high-demand schools continued to engage in marketing activities.

There are several other potential explanations for the lack of relationship between demand and recruiting activities. First, high-demand schools benefit from their exclusivity, giving them an incentive to select the best students to maintain their market status (in the same way that even top colleges market themselves). Second, school leaders might have believed that they were in high demand because of prior marketing and recruitment efforts, and that they needed to continue those efforts to maintain demand. Third, if the total number of students roughly equaled the total number of seats available, almost all schools were guaranteed a sufficient number of students, so the school application numbers we used did not actually reflect the pressure schools faced. Fourth, and finally, it could be that engaging in marketing and recruitment activities provides other benefits, such as conferring a sense of legitimacy to schools and/or helping indirectly in the recruitment of teachers and staff.

Implementation: Perceptions, Concerns, and Preferences

Like the other mechanisms explored in this book, the implementation of choice policies faced numerous obstacles and concerns at the school level. In contrast to the more positive visions outlined by most system leaders, school-level stakeholders often expressed concerns about enrollment systems and related choice processes or practices. Such concerns were not unique to any one city, type of enrollment system, or type of school. Across all three cities, to varying degrees, respondents at times questioned the efficacy and equity of enrollment processes and related policies.

Mixed Views on Enrollment Systems

In Denver, some school-level educators and parents praised the process of enrollment. "I found the process to be very user friendly. You list your choices and hope that you get one of them," said one parent. However, others in the city complained about the complexity and "stress" involved. According to one traditional public school leader, "The choice process in Denver is literally the most confusing process and parents freak out about it. They have parent forums right before it happens because it's such a painful process. It would be nice to be able to pick kids and bring them here or they have to come to here because that's the neighborhood school. That isn't the case for us, so it is hard. It's horribly confusing."

In New Orleans, some parents also had concerns about their common enrollment system. For example, several respondents critiqued the computer-based system and voiced preferences for paper and pencil forms. One parent characterized the system as "confusing and difficult," adding, "For a parent to have a postsecondary education, it's probably not difficult. When you're talking about parents who have not finished high school, or barely finished high school, or finished high school working two jobs, then no, they're not really tech-savvy because they're not working tech-savvy jobs." Although supportive of the intent, one New Orleans parent noted frustration with the process and the outcome for her child:

> For parents like me, right, who are used to figuring things out and advocating for their kids and what makes the most sense, it can be maddening. It's just clunky. It takes a long time, and you've got to tour all these schools. For equity reasons, I totally support this process. My oldest daughter applied to middle school. . . . We toured, we applied. She listed three schools—she only had one choice, and we said, you have to pick more than one because it's competitive to get in. Everyone said . . . "Oh, everyone gets into [this specific school]." Well, lo and behold, she didn't get her first choice, she didn't get her second choice, she got her third choice, and it was a distant third choice. She cried when she didn't get in. She went. It was a horrible fit.

It is noteworthy that these mixed reviews were coming from Denver and New Orleans, the two cities where the choice systems were highly coordinated. This may point to some of the inherent difficulties of creating choice systems that are simultaneously transparent, simple, efficient, and fair.[14]

The various enrollment systems in Los Angeles encountered a different set of concerns, focused on the ways in which the broader system design allowed for gaming and inhibited access for particular students. The lack of a centralized enrollment process for the various types of schools was one such design element. Several respondents in Los Angeles noted that charter and magnet leaders intentionally set application dates that preceded those of traditional public schools in attempts to "lock in" more desirable students before the traditional schools have the opportunity to enroll them. One central office administrator reported that traditional public schools had complained that "they feel their kids are being taken in October and November. They don't have the chance to compete." Other observers believed that charter school leaders liked to "control their wait lists."

A second design feature pertained to the more centralized enrollment criteria and process for magnet schools. Several Los Angeles educators noted the inequities inherent to the complex magnet school point system. One reform leader explained: "They've been getting so much critique about how wealthy parents game the system of magnets and they recognize that there is an equity issue there, so now they're going to do common enrollment and remove those barriers, but only for district schools, not including the charters." Another city leader pointed to inequities in access to information about the point system and the advantages of more affluent families, recounting that "Westside parents hire coaches to teach them how to 'manipulate' the system. That you apply to a school in elementary school that you do not get into and earn points to use up later. That's a broken system in my mind."

Transportation Concerns

In Denver, school and district leaders cited a lack of district-provided transportation (other than busing for neighborhood schools and enrollment zones) as a challenge in recruiting and retaining students—often bringing this up even when not directly asked about transportation issues. They saw transportation as creating a barrier to parent choice that made it difficult for non-enrollment-zone charters and innovation schools to attract and retain students. For instance, one Denver school leader cited transportation as the primary factor leading students to leave her school: "Typically, the main reason that we lose kids is not because they're unhappy, but because of transportation, which is pretty hard to argue with in terms of, like, if you've got a family and they can't make it here, then yeah, you need to find a school that's closer to you. It's that simple." One administrator in a DPS non-enrollment-zone charter school wanted to join a zone both for the access to transportation and for the perceived boost to enrollment: "They will only give transportation to charter schools if they're part of an enrollment zone. We're not part of an enrollment zone. We want to be part of an enrollment zone, but they won't let us. . . . If you're in an enrollment zone, you could have kids placed with you, which beefs up your enrollment, which allows you to function the way you need to function."

District and school administrators in Denver also indicated that a lack of transportation may inhibit some parents from fully exercising choice options. Some indicated that parents may lose the opportunity to enroll their students in the best school available if they are unable to transport their child to the school. Transportation policies also evoked equity concerns as parents with low socioeconomic status have fewer sources to provide their own transportation.

Much of the concern regarding transportation in Denver centered on the district's approach of providing transportation only to neighborhood and enrollment-zone schools. We heard fewer concerns about transportation in New Orleans and Los Angeles, perhaps because their policies were relatively consistent across schools—New Orleans required all schools to provide transportation, and Los Angeles offered transportation to only a few schools. In comparison, Denver choice schools were often competing with schools where the district provided transportation without charge to the schools.

While transportation did not emerge as a prominent theme in Los Angeles interviews, a few system-level leaders there expressed concern that the lack of transportation and sprawling size of the district presented barriers to parental choice. In the words of an LAUSD district leader, "What makes it a challenge is we're such a large district, geographics alone, and topography to all of that limits the opportunity of choice, and one thing we don't have is busing as part of that formula or even the public transportation system. It's really based on, how much are you willing to walk, or how far is your parent willing to travel to get you to that school?"

In New Orleans, many community advocates and school educators noted that parents did not want their children traveling across the city and preferred having quality options in their neighborhoods. Many educators expressed concerns about the time spent on buses. One school principal said, "We got kids that stay across the street from this school that get picked up by a bus at 5:00 in the morning to go to a school way across town."

"Choice with an Asterisk"

In New Orleans, many stakeholders raised concerns about the authenticity and fairness of the choice system. Some parents complained about the lack of quality schooling options. One principal spoke about it as "choice with an asterisk, because you don't always get your top choice." A parent explained: "I think we have probably three really good schools in the city that give children an opportunity. I mean, there are others, but I'm talking charter. I'm talking that you don't have to pay for and it's difficult to get in. I mean it's very difficult. There's so many children and families that want it and when you go to a lottery, who knows?" Others, too, noted that parents were frustrated when they did not get their preferred choices. A principal stated, "I don't like [the OneApp]. I don't like it. I don't believe that it's fair and equitable as they say it is. Because of the algorithm they actually put together, I've actually seen where kids had a list of, let's say, five schools, and none of those schools they got assigned to." Similarly, a community leader observed: "If you talked to the average New Orleanian, a parent, they'll say, 'I don't really feel like I have choices. There are five schools out of the sixty schools open, or whatever it is now, that I'd like my kids to go to. I couldn't get 'em into any of those.'"

Others expressed concerns about the schools that opted out of centralized enrollment ("the best schools still aren't participating in that kind of stuff") or that used testing requirements. One New Orleans central office administrator said: "You may get a school like this that has a very high [special education] population. Then you may get a school that does not fall under OneApp but can be selective about who they take in the school, so they don't have to deal with some of what we deal with. Then that same school, because they get the best of the best, they look for additional dollars for the gifted kids. We love the gifted kids, but I just feel that money is probably more needed for kids that have special needs."

Failure to Meet Racial Integration Goals

In Denver, several educators and parents in a school belonging to a DPS enrollment zone noted that even with the push to integrate, the schools in their zone remain quite segregated. One Denver teacher explained, "The neighborhood we're in, most of these kids don't come to our school. It's segregation at its best. . . . All of these houses, they don't come to our school. They go to a school down the road. . . . It's just more affluent, I guess, is the way you say that. It's super white. They're choicing out, yep. My understanding is that's been going on for a while; I've only been here for two years. Most of our students are bused." When asked why the neighboring students do not attend this school, another teacher responded: "Parents. They're scared of the diversity."

As noted above, although Los Angeles' choice system was not designed for integration, its magnet schools were. The federal magnet school program, dating back decades, actually requires that these schools seek racial integration. But Los Angeles magnets have struggled to attract the percentages needed to achieve these goals. "There is an ethnic mix; however, it [school enrollment] is still predominately Latino. Is [the magnet schools program] working for integration purposes? Not really," said one magnet school principal. Several parents interviewed were actually unaware that the diversity goals existed.

Trade-Offs Between Providing Choice and Building Communities

A common concern about school choice was that it breaks the bonds of local neighborhoods. Respondents noted that even when families wanted to attend the nearest school, the choice process might not have allowed them. As students went to school farther from home, they were less likely to see their school friends outside of school hours. Similarly, parents of the children in the same schools were less likely to get to know one another. A principal supervisor in New Orleans said: "Because all of the schools transport kids from all over the city, we have kids from the Westbank, almost to Venetian Isles in the East. That's almost with every school, so buses are just going all over the place. We don't have . . . it's not like the community school concept anymore. Maybe that will come back at some point, but right now, everybody is trying to get kids to fill up their school." Similarly, an administrator in the Orleans Parish School Board (OPSB) reported hearing parents ask: "'Why can't I go to this school across the street from my house?' or, 'Why can't I go to the school that I went to and my brothers went to and my parents went to, 'cause it's important to me?' We hear a lot from those parents. There's also some, 'Why do I have to go to a school that's so far away?'"

Denver parents reiterated the concern. A parent at a Denver innovation school reported:

> I grew up my whole childhood down in Colorado Springs. I went to a school down there, and then went to the middle school with all the kids that I knew. I feel kind of sad that my son's probably not going to know, my daughter is not going to necessarily know, the kids that they're going to go to middle school with. The piece that is important to me, wherever they end up at middle school, I want them to be with those kids through high school, too, so that they can establish those relationships.

Another parent from a traditional public school in Denver similarly noted, "I'm kind of torn on choice and charter. Again, I think it's awesome to have options, but it is seeing the neighborhood schools slowly start to disintegrate, which is kind of sad."

It is noteworthy, given how views sometimes differed across cities and educational actors, that this concern about schools and communities was so widely shared. Moreover, fewer comments about this were made in Los Angeles, which maintained the most neighborhood-based system of the three.

CONCLUSION

School choice systems can be designed and implemented in many ways. In all three cities, the choice system design was based on principles similar to those that guided the design of other aspects of the systems, examined in earlier chapters. In New Orleans—consistent with the label of the managed market—essentially all schools were required to participate in the district-managed enrollment system; that is, they were required to compete with other schools. Similarly, they were required to provide transportation to facilitate genuine access. Information was also centralized, albeit provided by nonprofit organizations rather than by the portfolio manager. Equitable access for students and autonomy for schools were prioritized over neighborhood schools and simplicity.

In Denver—the centralized portfolio—the district was more conscious of pursuing citywide goals like integration that were not a natural outgrowth of the market competition. Denver was less aggressive than New Orleans, however, in ensuring that families had access to transportation. The district sought a more equal balance of equity, neighborhood schools, and school autonomy.

In Los Angeles, choice was typified by competing systems—each family could participate in all three kinds of choice systems. Schools that had flexibility in their choice process, according to some respondents, used that to their advantage to lock in the students they wanted through decisions about deadlines. Magnet schools benefited indirectly from the immense complexity of the choice process by drawing in families that could navigate the complex process. The net effect was that neighborhood schools still predominated more than in the other two cities.

System design clearly mattered, and this was shaped by some important elements of the context. In Los Angeles, a climate of mistrust led to continuation of the traditional zone-based approach and the adoption of a more decentralized approach to choice, which many viewed as resulting in gaming and undermining equity. The combination of the large district size and a complex relationship with a strong teachers' association also likely contributed to the lack of trust and the challenges in implementing common policies and practices. District officials were far away from most schools, and the sheer size of the district meant that it would be difficult to manage choice among all schools from one place.

Despite the differences in design, several commonalities in the implementation of choice emerged across the cities. Marketing and recruitment were more common in CMO charter schools. Across sites, stakeholders also expressed common efficacy and equity concerns related to a lack of transportation (mainly in Denver and Los Angeles), to perceived trade-offs with building local communities (in Denver and New Orleans), and to the complexity of enrollment systems and information demands (all three cities).

In the end, there was somewhat limited evidence that the choice mechanisms of each school system operated according to the theory underlying choice. In some cases, schools subverted competition via enrollment practices and gaming strategies. While most schools engaged in recruitment and marketing activities, as one would expect in an environment of competition, schools felt pressure to increase demand even when they already had long waiting lists. Moreover, many parents (particularly in New Orleans) said they did not feel like they had real choices. Schools were choosing as much as parents were.[15] Yet, seemingly contradictory patterns are perhaps not surprising given broader institutional forces at play in all three cities. Schools might be driven to engage in marketing and recruitment activities not as a direct result of market pressure, but rather as a response to a taken-for-granted expectation that schools should recruit students and engage in marketing efforts to sustain their image as high-demand organizations. In this sense, recruitment activities serve to maintain a school's legitimacy in a context of institutionalized choice. Consistent with prior research, providing choice in the unusual market of schooling is more difficult than it appears.[16]

AUTONOMY

Flexibility in Response to Student Needs

with Eupha Jeanne Daramola and Laura Steen Mulfinger

The previous chapter discussed how portfolio systems use school choice as a mechanism to expand educational options for students but face many challenges in implementation. One of the more critical components of implementing school choice is providing schools with the local flexibility needed to design educational programs in response to student needs and to differentiate themselves from other school options. The portfolio model relies on school-based autonomy to achieve this goal of school differentiation.

One of the main assumptions of the portfolio model is that educators who regularly interact with students and parents are better informed and more capable of organizing instruction around student needs in order to improve learning.[1] Accordingly, school leaders and teachers are placed at the center of school governance in portfolio school systems.[2] By providing school leaders and teachers autonomy in areas of school management such as curriculum and instruction, assessment, staffing, scheduling, budgeting, fundraising, discipline, and enrollment, portfolio districts strive to create educational programs that are increasingly responsive to community needs and innovative at improving student outcomes.[3] State policies also play an important role in authorizing greater autonomy for particular school models that operate in portfolio districts, such as charters (in all three cities) and innovation schools (in Denver).

Yet how much autonomy do school actors have in both design and practice across the three cities? In this chapter, we draw on data from school leader and teacher surveys, qualitative school case studies, and system leader interviews to explore this question. Consistent with the intended design of portfolio systems in these cities, the study found that educators in schools formally granted more autonomy from state or district policies and collectively bargained agreements (CBAs) reported more responsibility and influence over school management in practice than their counterparts in school models with less formal autonomy. The overall design of each portfolio system further influenced the level of reported autonomy and the range in reported autonomy observed between school model types. In sum, the implementation of school-level autonomy was quite complex in practice and involved constant trade-offs between competing educational goals.

BACKGROUND ON AUTONOMY IN PORTFOLIO SYSTEMS

In a decentralized environment, one important role of the portfolio manager is to facilitate school autonomy. This facilitation involves implementing state laws, enacting local policies, and negotiating labor agreements that enhance a school's control over its operating conditions. For example, many portfolio districts operate in states with laws that exempt charter schools from district policies and CBAs, or that permit schools to waive out of select policies and CBA provisions.[4] Additionally, some portfolio districts have ratified agreements with teachers' unions to create school models (such as Boston pilot schools) that provide administrators and teachers flexibility in staffing and other critical aspects of school management.[5]

While autonomy is central to the theory of change of portfolio districts, there is considerable debate about when schools should receive autonomy. Certain school districts, in cities such as Chicago and Philadelphia, approach autonomy as something to be earned, with district leaders authorizing it only for school providers with a track record of high performance in education.[6] Conversely, school systems in cities such as New York adhere to the idea of universal autonomy: that all school leaders need to work in autonomous conditions to succeed, especially those in charge of low performing schools.[7] The actual extent and nature of these autonomies also vary:

some schools may be granted limited autonomy around particular functions, such as curriculum, while others are given control of a wider range of functions, including budget and personnel.[8] Additionally, there is evidence to suggest that school autonomy can be misused or underutilized in schools with weak leadership or limited capacity, or in schools faced with perverse policy incentives.[9] In this regard, portfolio managers are seen as responsible for creating a level playing field, shoring up schools with strong leadership, and facilitating school access to support and capacity-building services to ensure that educators can effectively serve students' interests.[10]

DESIGN OF AUTONOMY MECHANISMS

In all of the cities studied, different types of schools and school managers received varying degrees of autonomy from system-level policies and CBAs.

New Orleans' Managed Market

The school system in New Orleans was the simplest in design for providing school autonomy. At the time of this study, the vast majority of schools in the Recovery School District (RSD) and Orleans Parish School Board (OPSB) were charter schools that, as shown in figure 6.1A, had substantial local discretion in setting teacher working conditions (x-axis) and autonomy from state and district policies (y-axis). However, the RSD and OPSB imposed some requirements on charter school operations for student enrollment, discipline, special education, and staff compensation to ensure equitable treatment of students. For example, in response to a lawsuit regarding inadequate special education services and discriminatory practices for student discipline, the RSD and OPSB required charter schools to comply with centralized procedures for special education and student discipline. These schools also participated in a universal school enrollment system, requiring them to enroll students based on a common algorithm for assigning students to schools. Louisiana state law further required charter schools to provide transportation to all students. OPSB charter schools were also required to participate in the school system's teacher retirement plan, limiting control over one aspect of teacher compensation.

There were some exceptions to these rules. For example, a handful of highly selective, "test-in" charter schools in the OPSB exercised their own

FIGURE 6.1A   **Design of school-level autonomy mechanisms in Recovery School District and Orleans Parish School Board**

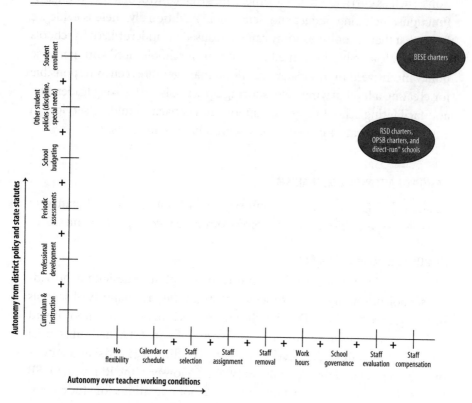

Note: A handful of OPSB direct-run schools that operated with charter-like autonomies have since converted to charter schools.

procedures for student enrollment, based on student test performance. Additionally, some charter schools approved by the Board of Elementary and Secondary Education (BESE) did not have to comply with RSD and OPSB policies for special education and student discipline.

In figures 6.1A–6.1C, autonomies are listed on the y- and x-axes in accordance with how case cities distinguished between schools that were more and less autonomous. School types located farther along the y- and x-axes had more autonomy than school types located closer to the center of both axes.

Denver's Centralized Portfolio

Denver Public Schools (DPS) also supervised school models with varied autonomy from state or district policies and around teacher working conditions. As shown in figure 6.1A, a total of four school models operated in DPS. Traditional public schools were the least autonomous in the system. Charter schools authorized under Colorado's Charter Schools Act (1993/1994) were the most autonomous in design, with freedom from most state and district policies, as well as from personnel management as prescribed in negotiated labor agreements.

Like New Orleans, DPS used a universal school enrollment system that included both charter and district-run schools, requiring those schools to enroll students based on the district's algorithm for assigning students to schools. Charter schools in DPS also had to follow district procedures for special education and for backfilling open enrollment seats (making seats available to new students or those wishing to transfer) to ensure equitable treatment of highly mobile and at-risk student populations and students with disabilities.

Innovation schools were the next most autonomous school model in the district. Under Colorado's Innovation Schools Act (2008), innovation schools could operate with local discretion in educational programming (curriculum and instruction), assessment, teacher professional development, and budgeting, and they could opt out of certain state laws and CBA provisions regarding personnel management, evaluation, compensation, and school calendars and scheduling. Innovation schools could make various choices under school autonomy so long as they were approved by 60 percent or more of the school's staff (hence the dashed box in figure 6.1B to show the range of autonomy afforded by this school model). To make school access to autonomy more equal, DPS also granted all traditional public schools the option to exercise autonomy from district policies regarding curriculum and instruction, assessment, and teacher professional development. DPS also operated magnet schools under the federal government's Magnet School Assistance Program that were similar to traditional public schools in autonomy but could receive federal grants to recruit, enroll, and transport a racially integrated student population.

FIGURE 6.1B   Design of school-level autonomy mechanisms in Denver Public Schools

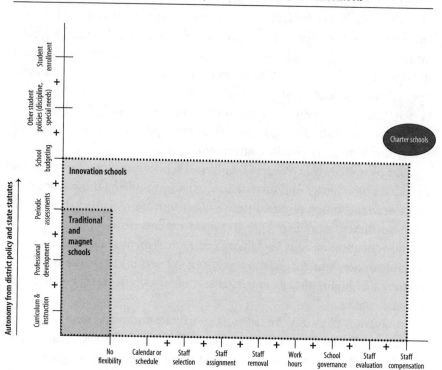

Los Angeles' Competing Systems

As noted, two parallel systems coexisted in Los Angeles: a set of traditional public schools along with six semiautonomous school options overseen by the Los Angeles Unified School District (LAUSD) central office, and a parallel system of independent charter schools authorized primarily by the local school board but with little direct oversight from the central office. These school models operated with varying degrees of autonomy from district policy and/or negotiated labor agreements. As shown in figure 6.1C, the least autonomous of these schools were traditional public schools overseen by the LAUSD elected school board. Accordingly, these schools had to comply with all district policies (y-axis) and negotiated labor agreement terms (x-axis). The most autonomous schools in Los Angeles were inde-

FIGURE 6.1C Design of school-level autonomy mechanisms in Los Angeles Unified School District

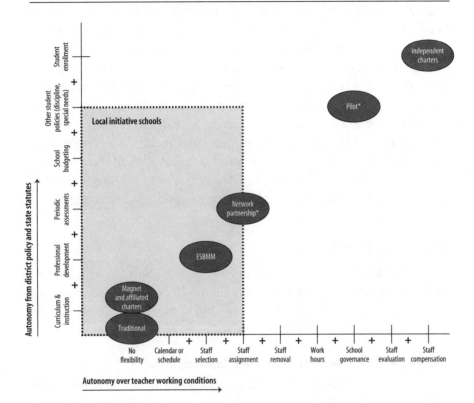

Note: Network partner schools can hire their own principals and implement their own coaching programs to improve school leadership. These schools can develop career ladders for teachers with differentiated compensation. Pilot schools have mutual consent for hiring principals and can hire principals from nontraditional administrator-preparation backgrounds.

pendent charter schools run by organizations with their own self-appointed boards. Under California's Charter Schools Act (1992), independent charter schools were granted autonomy from most state and district regulations regarding curriculum and instruction, assessment, professional development, student discipline, budgeting, and student enrollment. The state law also did not require independent charter schools to hire unionized staff, providing these schools substantial autonomy in personnel management.

Falling between independent charter schools and traditional public schools were a set of semiautonomous school models, including affiliated charter, magnet, Expanded School-Based Management Model (ESBMM), network partnership, pilot, and local initiative schools (LIS), which were internally managed by the district and its elected school board. As shown in figure 6.1C, these semiautonomous schools had autonomy in narrowly defined areas of school management. Because LIS schools could choose to exercise their autonomy in different areas (as approved by a majority staff vote), the dashed box in figure 6.1C demonstrates the range of autonomy that could be realized under this school model. Pilot schools were the most autonomous in this group and could exercise local discretion from most district policies (with the exception of student enrollment). More importantly, pilot schools used an elect-to-work agreement that allowed them to waive provisions in the United Teachers Los Angeles (UTLA) contract for teacher assignment, dismissal, work hours, and school governance structures.

AUTONOMY IN PRACTICE

The *intended* differences between the portfolios in New Orleans, Denver, and Los Angeles are important to keep in mind as we investigate how they play out *in practice*. How are the schools and networks of schools actually using the autonomy available to them?

Alignment Between Intended Autonomy and Autonomy in Practice

Our survey data indicate several important patterns that were consistent with the intended distribution of autonomy in all three school systems. First, school leaders in all three school systems reported more areas of responsibility and influence in school management than they attributed to other education stakeholders (such as the state or district office), which is consistent with the idea of the state and district decentralizing authority over school management and delegating that authority to individual schools.

Second, school leader–perceived influence over school management varied across school types as intended by the formal design of each portfolio. We measured perceived influence as an average of fifteen items, asking how much influence school leaders had across areas of school management such as curriculum and instruction, personnel, budgeting, discipline, and school governance (on a Likert scale of $1 =$ no influence to $4 =$ great influence). We graphed box plots to compare median values of perceived school leader influence by model type (the line dividing the box in two parts) and to examine the distribution of school leader influence within each model category (the 25th and 75th percentiles are illustrated by the shaded area above and below the median line; outliers are illustrated by dots). In all three cities, as shown in figures 6.2A–6.2C, school leaders in stand-alone charter schools reported more influence over school management, while school leaders in traditional public schools in Denver and Los Angeles reported the least influence.

Third, the overall design of the portfolio system informed both the level of reported influence by school leaders and the range in school leader influence between school model types. In Los Angeles, we observed a large difference in school leader–perceived influence between traditional and autonomous schools—those centrally managed by the district central office—and stand-alone and charter schools run by a charter management organization (CMO), which operated independently from the district (see figure 6.2C). Given this disparity between sectors, average reports of school leader influence in Los Angeles (in the system as a whole) were lowest relative to systemwide reports of school leader influence in New Orleans and Denver. In New Orleans, the level of reported school leader influence in stand-alone and CMO charter schools was similar to that observed for schools of

FIGURE 6.2A   **Influence reported by school leaders across school model types in Recovery School District and New Orleans Parish School Board**

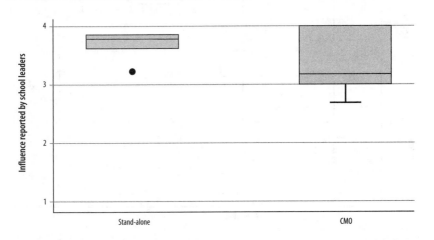

Note: School leader influence was measured on a 4-point Likert scale where 1 = no influence and 4 = a great deal of influence.

FIGURE 6.2B   **Influence reported by school leaders across school model types in Denver Public Schools**

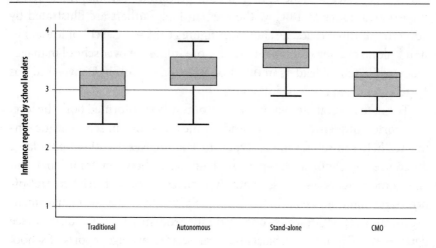

Note: School leader influence was measured on a 4-point Likert scale where 1 = no influence and 4 = a great deal of influence.

FIGURE 6.2C   **Influence reported by school leaders across school model types in Los Angeles Unified School District**

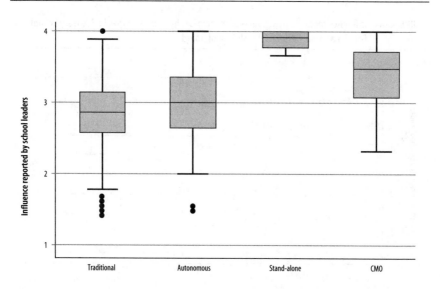

Note: School leader influence measured on a 4-point Likert scale with 1 = no influence to 4 = a great deal of influence.

these same types in Los Angeles (see figure 6.2A). Since the district has no traditional district-run schools, systemwide reports of school leader influence in New Orleans were notably higher than in Los Angeles and Denver, both of which include other school model types with less autonomy.

Denver fell in between Los Angeles and New Orleans in terms of systemwide reports of school leader influence. We also observed smaller differences in school leader influence between traditional, autonomous, and charter school types (see figure 6.2B). This pattern is consistent with a portfolio that institutionalized more autonomy for traditional and innovation schools to make those schools comparable to charters. For example, educators in traditional public schools in Denver reported having flexibility around curriculum, professional development, and assessment in ways that were quite different from the reports from traditional public schools in Los Angeles. In one traditional school in Denver, the school leader noted, "I do think we have discretion with curriculum. . . . Our district gave choices." In contrast, the school leader of traditional public school in Los Angeles noted that the school was required to follow the district-selected curriculum (with limited flexibility to supplement) and added: "[I have to] abide by and respect UTLA: If it's in the contract, I have to abide by it."

Stand-Alone Charters and CMO Charters

In all three school systems, school leaders in stand-alone charter schools reported greater influence over school management than leaders in CMO charter schools. This difference can be explained, in part, by CMO charter schools operating in a nested organizational structure in which they were supervised by and shared authority with a CMO head office. For example, in Los Angeles, school leaders in stand-alone charter schools reported having responsibility in more areas of school management than school leaders in CMO charter schools, who had to share this responsibility with their CMO head office. We observed similar differences between stand-alone and CMO charter schools in Denver and New Orleans.

The difference in enacted autonomy between stand-alone and CMO charter schools was reflected in the case study schools. For instance, a stand-alone charter school leader in Los Angeles boasted about freedoms associated with charter status: "When I hire, I'm not encumbered in any way. That, to me, is the brilliance of charters. Is that you set your vision, you communicate it out to educators, and if they're attracted to it, they're coming to it. Then you can have a culture of shared vision." In contrast, leaders of a case study CMO charter school reported some recentralization occurring within the organization. The principal reported autonomy around staffing but constraints around instructional frameworks and curricula.

Qualitative data from New Orleans also demonstrated clear differences in the reported autonomy between stand-alone and large networked or CMO charter schools. While school leaders in stand-alone charters (and some small CMO charters) boasted about high levels of discretion regarding staffing, budget, curriculum, professional development, and certain aspects of student discipline, their counterparts in large networked organizations often reported limitations in these areas. In one large CMO in New Orleans, an administrator explained, "It's just very standardized." In contrast, leaders in stand-alone charters in New Orleans, particularly those who had converted from prior status as traditional schools, reported high levels of autonomy in all areas. "We're able to get things [done] a whole lot quicker ... than before," said one school leader, "because you ... had to go through so much bureaucracy before you can get something."

Limited Teacher Autonomy

The data suggest that control over school decision-making in the portfolio management model (PMM) is concentrated at the middle-management level of the school principalship rather than distributed across teachers in classrooms. In all three cities, school leaders reported teachers as having responsibility in fewer areas of school management than themselves. That said, in New Orleans and Los Angeles, leaders reported that teachers had more responsibility for school management, and teachers themselves reported more influence over school decision-making in stand-alone charter schools and autonomous schools (Los Angeles only) than teachers in other school types.

For example, teachers in autonomous schools in Los Angeles reported significantly more influence than teachers in traditional public schools. Moreover, teachers in stand-alone charter schools in Los Angeles and New Orleans reported significantly more influence than traditional school teachers and CMO charter schools. These findings are generally consistent with the governance design of autonomous schools in Los Angeles, which include rules and procedures that give teachers greater voice in school decision-making (for example, teachers have to vote to approve the LIS school model), but perhaps surprising for stand-alone charter schools, where there were no formalized provisions on how schools should distribute autonomy between school leaders and teachers.

Case study data suggest similar patterns of teacher influence, although the limited number of schools and teacher interviews within those schools constrains our ability to generalize within a school and school type. In Los Angeles, virtually all of the teachers interviewed in a stand-alone charter reported significant discretion in their classrooms. One said, "In the years I've been teaching, this is probably the most freedom I've had as far as being able to make decisions about how I want to structure my classroom, how I want my day to flow. We have a lot of autonomy." Similarly, teachers in a semiautonomous magnet school reported a high degree of autonomy as well as involvement in budget, school safety, and curricular decisions. "The staff is very active on different committees and local school leadership," said one teacher. "There is some level of autonomy and decision-making there." Teachers in the traditional case study school, however, were more mixed in their reports of autonomy. In New Orleans, teachers in stand-alone charters were similarly more likely to report high degrees of autonomy in the classroom than their counterparts in CMO charters. One stand-alone charter school teacher explained, "I think I'm quite free about what I teach. They trust us."

In contrast, teachers in all Denver schools expressed fairly high levels of autonomy across school model types, again reflecting Denver's characterization as a centralized portfolio system. In fact, reports of autonomy were just as likely to come from teachers in the traditional schools as from teachers in charters and innovation schools.[11] Teachers in one traditional school recognized that DPS was granting more autonomy to all schools; as one noted: "I do think we have discretion with curriculum. I mean, we have curriculums that we chose as a school. Our district gave choices. Our school chose." In innovation schools, teachers also reported having influence over staffing and operational decisions, particularly those serving in leadership roles. "I think our voices are heard," said one such teacher leader. Nevertheless, some teachers in autonomous and charter (particularly CMO) schools in all three cities reported encroachment on their autonomy—a tension examined further in the next section.

Tensions Balancing Autonomy with Competing Goals

In all three cities the implementation of school-level autonomy was not always easy and often involved trade-offs. Unfettered autonomy was not the norm. Instead, there was considerable balancing between competing priorities and goals and some recognition that constraints were needed—either to promote consistent quality, efficiency, equity and fairness, or performance, or to ensure a reasonable burden was laid on educators.

Autonomy and Uniformity

Across cities and school types, educators and leaders reported struggles to balance school- and classroom-level discretion with broader quality and efficiency goals. At a system level, district and CMO leaders noted the difficulties of ensuring quality instruction across multiple schools when there was too much autonomy (and not consistent capacity to lead in each school, which we return to later). As a result, several systems (both district and CMO) had explored adopting common curricula or instructional frameworks. In one Los Angeles CMO, a school leader described the idea of "tight-loose" as the solution to this dilemma: "Some things seem to be really tight across the organization. Everybody has to do such and such the same, everyone must do something or have a plan for experiential learning. Then what's loose looks like, 'Does every school take their kids [on X field trips]?' No. We're the only one. Every school does something within the confines of that."

Similarly, a large CMO in New Orleans began to retract some autonomy around curriculum, justifying this decision by saying, "In the Common Core era, we should not be making up our own curriculum, which is what we used to do." CMO leaders reported efforts to "systematize" more in "areas of risk" to ensure high student performance. They also cited efficiency arguments, acknowledging that although some freedoms were removed, standardizing across the network ensured "that teachers can collaborate on a high level" because they are using the same curricular materials. A CMO leader in Denver made a similar argument, defending a greater level of re-centralization "to improve collaboration and improve results."

These tensions around autonomy were particularly acute in larger CMO networks, whose leaders often attributed their decision to recentralize to their size. One leader in a New Orleans RSD CMO explained: "For the first time in our history as an organization, we have common curriculum so that what children are learning at [this school], they're also learning at [school A], [school B], and [school C]. Teachers are trained in the same fashion. Now, you will have to tweak that and make adaptations at each school site, but I thought that was important as we grow as an organization, as we seek to brand, as we seek to attract teachers, and as we seek to attract children." Some leaders in New Orleans and beyond, in fact, began to question whether autonomy was the most important lever of change. A leader in one New Orleans CMO observed: "I think most CMOs are already starting to go, there's less and less autonomy. I feel like where we started as a city . . . [was] from this premise that autonomy is the most important thing. I feel like where big CMOs are coming to—and big—big in New Orleans is not that big but maybe eight schools or four schools . . . or even three schools—is that in order to actually get the gains that we need to get as a city, we have to stop reinventing the wheel."

Similarly, a Denver CMO leader even questioned whether "uniform autonomies are going to be the best solutions for kids." It is possible these concerns about consistency and the growing doubt about the value of autonomy could explain the lower levels of reported autonomy in CMOs that surfaced in the survey data presented above.

Yet these tensions were not unique to CMOs and systems. Leaders in individual schools often struggled to provide teachers with some discretion while also ensuring a consistent educational experience for all students. We uncovered efforts to tighten up curriculum, instruction, and assessments in several schools in Los Angeles, including a pilot and magnet school. "We have a lot of freedom here to do what we want," explained one magnet school teacher, "and [the school leader], I think, is adding some structure to that and trying to make our classrooms a little more uniform but still allowing us to be who we are."

Of course, not all educators in these schools and systems were happy with the balance being struck between autonomy and uniformity. One school leader in New Orleans, for example, expressed frustration with changes being considered by OPSB (at the time of data collection) to align school calendars across all schools (a move intended to advance efficiency and assist families with children in multiple schools). This leader feared the move would remove important freedom around scheduling of school trips and niche programs. Similarly, teachers in a Los Angeles pilot school resisted the effort to create schoolwide assessments and bring more consistency across classrooms. CMO leaders were not blind to these concerns and often acknowledged that their efforts to balance autonomy and uniformity remained a work in progress. A CMO leader in New Orleans explained:

> I think what all of us would say is, we, as a network, are still figuring out that balance, and that we started off way to one side where we were all doing our own thing, and loved it to a degree. Also, we're not reaping the benefits of the collaboration. I think we've pushed maybe past the middle point. Maybe we're a little bit more lockstep than we would want to be and are seeking to reclaim some of our own identity in certain places. That I think what most people would say is that it's a balance. It's an ebb and flow. We may not have exactly found the happy medium yet.

Autonomy and Equity

Broader system goals of student equity, access, and fairness came to be in tension with the promise of freedom underlying the portfolio model—often leading to recentralization. For example, as the result of increases in expulsions in the early years of the post-Katrina reforms, and subsequent public and legal outcry, New Orleans administrators in the RSD and the OPSB created a centralized expulsion process, a unified enrollment system, and uniform procedures for special education to ensure that all students received fair treatment.[12] Similarly, in Los Angeles, the district recentralized procedures for student suspensions for willful defiance (nonviolent student behaviors that can be perceived as disruptive to the classroom) for all district-run schools. This followed pressure from the Office of Civil Rights in the US Department of Education over disproportionately high suspension rates for black students, and it resulted in dramatic declines in student suspension rates.[13] Some CMOs went further, centralizing particular practices in these areas as well—such as mandating common special education processes across network schools—to further ensure compliance and protect students.

Portfolio managers frequently wrestled with a desire to grant school educators flexibility while also protecting students. "A school leader should have the ability to create the climate and culture that they want in their own school," an OPSB administrator noted. "I'm not in the best position to tell every school here in the city when they should suspend a child and when they shouldn't. And I should be humble about that, but I worry about it."

An RSD administrator expressed a similar struggle: "We have . . . debated it internally, but have always come down on the side of . . . this is part of what autonomy is, because . . . Let's say if we come up with a solution, do we mandate that they follow XYZ? If we do, then we're sort of infringing on the autonomy that we gave them in the first place."

District leaders in Denver reported learning from the New Orleans experience to deter "cream-skimming" by creating a unified enrollment system and common policies, such as requiring all schools to take late arrivals. "If you're only charter schools and no charter school took late arrivals, that's not going to work very well. Right?" said one DPS leader, "This has to be philosophically coherent where you can't opt into the goods and opt out of the bads." DPS charter schools had access to district services and resources such as transportation and facilities that in some sense helped compensate for the reduced autonomy that came with some of the centralized policies to which they had to adhere.

These system-level tensions were clearly felt at the school level. Some educators who were interviewed appreciated the constraints, recognizing that they helped protect students and prevented schools from encountering legal difficulties that might have otherwise developed. "Discipline and special education are probably the most heavily restricted areas," said one New Orleans charter school leader, who went on to explain: "The district does tend to have lots of 'You must do's' in place in those areas. Honestly, I don't mind those very much because I would prefer to have a laundry list of things that I must do to make sure that I maintain compliance, rather than just giving me carte blanche access to how we sculpt those policies, and we miss something that's important." Yet others were not as accepting. Interviewees in another New Orleans charter, for example, decried the common enrollment system because it facilitated enrollment of families without a deep understanding of and commitment to that particular school's mission. One parent explained, "We're different, and I feel already right now some parents don't understand. . . . Oh, they hear that [school A is] a great school, but they don't understand what [specialized educational approach] means, and they don't do the background [research]. . . . They just are enrolling their child . . . without knowing what we're all about and then it's not for their child."

In Los Angeles, while charter schools were not required to adhere to the same centralized suspensions and enrollment processes, there were mandates in the area of student safety that met resistance. For example, several charter school leaders decried district requirements around the use of metal detectors. One CMO leader viewed it as an affront to their freedom and to their educational approach:

> We ... tried to push back on one policy in particular. ... This policy essentially required us—for any schools that are on district campuses, we had to implement a what they called "random," in quotes, daily metal detector wanding, whether they're ten years old, they're in a wheelchair, or they're eighteen years old. We were forced to implement that, even though it flies completely against everything we try to do, philosophically, in our buildings. The relationships that we try to build with students—we're able to have a student-to-adult ratio that far surpasses anything you'll see in a secondary school in the district and yet, that wasn't taken into consideration.

Importantly, several observers expressed deep concerns about too much autonomy in Los Angeles and the threat this posed to student equity. Without centralized management of enrollment, some argued, individual charter schools were able to create an uneven playing field. Others extended this concern to the enrollment processes for within-district magnet schools, which gave families with greater social capital and understanding of the complex application process advantages that enabled them to "game the system" and enroll in the more competitive schools. (For further discussion of these enrollment issues see chapter 5.) "This autonomous schools concept, to me, in some ways it borders the concept of states' rights," said a UTLA representative. "At the end of the day, poor people suffer when there are not centralized—when there's not centralized accountability and standards. I think that's a real problem."

Autonomy and Performance

The PMM concept rests on the idea that autonomy is an important mechanism that facilitates improvement. Yet in the course of the research, several system leaders across cities asserted that autonomy should instead be a reward for improvement, and that until a high level of performance was demonstrated, one could not risk granting autonomy to schools ill-equipped to handle it. In fact, some of the CMO leaders in Los Angeles who reported tightened controls over curriculum and instruction were considering a shift to allowing schools to "earn more autonomy" once they've demonstrated some "success." An administrator of a CMO in Los Angeles, having observed uneven performance across its network, reported trying such an approach: "If your school has implemented the instructional framework with a degree of success, then we will give you more autonomy to try on something, to pilot some things to see if they will further inform the quality of instruction at the site."

In other places, the relationship between performance and autonomy was less explicit but was clearly acknowledged. Some school leaders interviewed in New Orleans believed they had received greater freedoms than other schools in the CMO network: "Autonomy is given realistically to who is viewed as deserving autonomy at this point. If you have a proven track record of success, or you're moving in that direction of success, you're allowed more autonomy." Similarly, a leader of a small CMO in Denver reported considerable freedom from district central office intervention or oversight: "With a proven track record of the results which we have had, I suspect there is a lot less district-to-[school] engagement from what you might see at other schools where there [are] interventions because of the chronic underperformance." A Denver innovation school teacher believed "what buys [the school's] freedom" had less to do with their "innovation status" and more to do with their "high test scores." Overall, the varied use of earned autonomy could help explain the variations in reporting among autonomous, traditional, and CMO charter educators, as reflected in the survey data.

Autonomy and Burden

Across all three cities, study participants commented on the unintended consequences of autonomy, including added burden and burnout. For some educators, the added burden was worth the trade-off for greater freedom and the ability to innovate. Others, however, believed that some autonomies were either inefficient or overly labor intensive. This was particularly true in the area of curriculum and instruction. A Los Angeles pilot school leader who led teachers in developing their own assessments confessed, "It was daunting because teachers thought it was going to be a simple process, but it's a lot of work. That's why they pay people to actually write assessments."

Several CMO leaders who had chosen to recentralize cited burden as their rationale. One national CMO leader explained, "Because what we have learned over time is that we were burning out our teachers because everyone had so much autonomy they could do whatever they wanted. They were spending hours upon hours creating lessons and making plans and creating their own tests. We didn't have consistent data sources and we didn't—our teachers were just tired. We did take away some of those choices." Similarly, a small CMO leader in Denver reported intentionally taking control of school finance tied to purchasing, food services, and transportation, so that school leaders could devote their limited time and attention to "learning and extended relationships."

At times educators, particular newer educators, were grateful to forgo freedom in the classroom in exchange for less work. A relatively new teacher in a Denver charter school greatly appreciated the detailed instructional materials on "day-to-day instruction," including units, assessments, and activities, which made her work easier. In a nearby school, another new teacher was relieved to receive premade materials, citing a lessened psychological burden: "It honestly takes a little bit of pressure off. Like, what if I choose to teach the wrong thing? That's not really my call." Even school leaders at times expressed relief at not having to handle operational or budget issues, noting a preference to focus elsewhere. "I'm grateful that I don't have to figure out money," confessed one CMO charter school leader in Denver. Other educators simply used their autonomy selectively, opting not to unnecessarily invest time to reinvent the wheel when good tools or policies already existed. This was particularly true in Denver, where schools were given many opportunities to opt-in to district policies. A charter leader explained, "There's a lot of things that we don't opt out of. The discipline ladder, we follow that. I mean, we follow [the district's] at the core. Then there are things that surround that that, of course, we have our own systems of how we deal with kiddos around discipline."

In summary, systems and schools faced important trade-offs when granting autonomy. The desire for uniformity, efficiency, quality, equity, and ease of burden created pervasive tensions that at times led to recentralization and limitations on autonomy.

Conditions Shaping Autonomy

In addition to these tensions, even when school-level autonomy was offered, it was not always enacted. For example, figures 6.2A–6.2C show variation in

enacted autonomy within school model categories, with substantial variation in school leader influence among traditional and autonomous schools
and, to a lesser degree, for school leaders in CMO charter schools in Los
Angeles and stand-alone charter schools in Denver. This variation suggests
that there could be system and school conditions that afford school leaders
in these school model categories more influence than leaders in other categories. Across the three cities, three interrelated conditions—leadership,
capacity, and central office commitment and creep—appeared to help or
hinder autonomy in practice.

Leadership

In many case study schools, the nature of leadership played an important
role in facilitating or hindering the realization of school-level autonomy.
In fact, many observers across the three cities believed that school leaders,
more than formal governance arrangements or school models, determined
autonomy. "A lot of it comes down to the individual school leaders," said
one LAUSD administrator. "Our really dynamic school leaders, I don't
think [it] matters what model they're using. They figure out a way to get
it done." In Denver, a charter school leader who had previously taught in
a traditional setting described himself as a "renegade" in his prior school,
carving out autonomy by simply pushing back on district mandates.

School leadership was particularly important for the level of autonomy
teachers felt in their classrooms. For example, several educators in a traditional school in Denver reported high levels of autonomy and attributed
it in part to the school leader who felt empowered to take control and advance autonomy just as a charter school might do. Even leaders in school
models granting significant autonomy played a part in the extent to which
they embraced those freedoms and extended them to teachers. A charter
school leader in Los Angeles admitted that she needed to "loosen up a little
bit" and adjust her leadership approach to give teachers more leeway and
accept that all classrooms do not need to "look the same." Repeatedly, we
found that leaders' ability to build trust with teachers allowed teachers to
lead in their classrooms.

A lack of school-level leadership may also explain why some schools
did not enact the autonomy spelled out in their charters, plans, or memo-
randums of understanding (MOUs). In several cases, the founding leaders

of a school had left, and the current leadership (school leader or site coun-cil) was not familiar with the autonomies spelled out in the plan. In other cases, school leaders did not display strong buy-in for a plan because they were not involved in its development. Two individuals interviewed in Denver, for example, noted that some innovation plans in the early years were "cut-and-paste" documents created by district leaders, and the school leaders did not necessarily develop the plans nor commit to enact-ing them.

Intermediate-level leaders also played critical roles in enabling the en-actment of autonomies granted to schools. In Los Angeles, a pilot school leader identified her supervisor as critical to enabling or constraining au-tonomy in practice. While some supervisors served to "protect" the free-doms intended for pilot schools (and magnets), she noted that at other times turnover led to individuals who either did not understand or were not willing to advocate for the autonomy afforded by the model. This was particularly true when central office leaders assigned personnel to the school in ways that violated the pilot MOU (see more on this below). Simi-larly, a leader of an innovation schools network in Denver believed her role was "to protect and advocate for the autonomy and flexibility of [the net-work's] schools ... acting as the intermediary between them and the school district, ensuring that they have a high level of autonomy."

Individual Capacity

Closely tied to leadership is the capacity of individuals to make use of granted autonomies. Portfolio managers and CMO leaders in all three cit-ies commented that not everyone knew how to take advantage of discre-tion afforded to them—and these managers and leaders often used such explanations to justify recentralization. An administrator in OPSB in New Orleans noted that even under the prior system, leaders had autonomy but "did not really know it or use it," particularly in the area of budgeting. "I used to always tell them, 'Okay, you have these funds, why don't you all make decisions about how you want to use it? If you don't want a coun-selor, then you can take the amount of money you pay a counselor and you maybe can get two other people who can do the function better, but think out of the box.' We had one or two [school] principals to do that, and we had others who just were not able to."

In Denver, a CMO leader expressed similar concerns about the lack of capacity to utilize freedoms, particularly in the areas of finance and management:

> Simply giving school autonomy for folks who maybe have not had direct training or support on building capacity for somebody in finance or human capital, or marketing and branding or—how do you take data and transform it into a new system and how do you engage in change in order to do that when buy-in is strong? So, there is a lot of layers there, right? So, when you give those levels autonomy and you have not done the prep work to get people ready for it, what, does it actually lead to a change in outcome in performance or is the autonomy leveraged to make change?

In Los Angeles, a community leader questioned the assumption that after a school has been granted pilot status, "suddenly, they're going to know how to act differently, how to make decisions together, how to share authority."

These concerns around capacity also extended to midlevel managers, who may have also lacked the capacity and shared understanding to support school leaders in exercising their autonomy. In a Denver small CMO, school leaders noted that they had multiple "partners" to contact at the district regarding special education, enrollment, facilities, transportation, and other issues, and that often they received mixed messages related to "what do we have autonomy over versus when do we have to include DPS." Several LAUSD administrators reported that school leader supervisors were unfamiliar with the details of the MOUs for semiautonomous schools or how to support school leaders to use them—indicating again how the sheer size of Los Angeles presented challenges for developing shared understandings of the various school models. "There's local autonomies and you have directors who are going to have different levels of understanding around how to support a school leader," said one administrator. Another central office leader characterized the problem as a combination of will and capacity, noting that not all directors were "open to schools being creative." As an example, he attributed the failure of many schools to enact granted scheduling autonomy to this lack of openness. Even though they could have moved to different configurations, many pilot, ESBMM, or LIS schools were operating with a traditional schedule due in part to directors encouraging conformity.

In fact, portfolio managers in Los Angeles and Denver reported not doing enough to build the capacity of school actors to use their autonomy. Referring to innovation schools, a Denver central office administrator explained: "They're really leveraging HR and scheduling flexibilities and autonomies, and less so education program autonomies. . . . If you think about the role of school-based flexibilities and curriculum assessment and professional learning, we had opt-in rates. Schools are using the district options at about . . . an average of around 80 percent. Like, I think there's several reasons for that. I think partially we haven't set school leaders out to be successful in using their own options. Right? We haven't trained them." Similarly, an LAUSD board member admitted, "We haven't done a really good job of explaining it [autonomy] and of training them [school leaders and teachers]. . . . I think that the real promise there has not been fulfilled, because people don't understand their true autonomies, and don't know how to push back on the system, right?" Other LAUSD leaders similarly acknowledged their failure to disseminate clear information and training around "what does it look like or what does it mean for [them] to implement this autonomy?" Some of these leaders proudly reported new efforts to create better materials (such as a pilot school manual) and assistance with the transition to becoming a semiautonomous school, "so that they don't feel like, if I want autonomy, I have to make such a huge leap, and you might not be ready to really take on what is expected of you when you become that school model."

Portfolio Managers' Commitment and Creep

In some interviews, individuals felt confident in portfolio managers' commitment to advancing autonomy. In New Orleans, for example, interviewees believed the new OPSB superintendent had demonstrated his commitment by giving all school leaders greater discretion. "He wants [school leaders] to have more say-so," said a traditional school leader. "Now I could say, 'I don't want a teacher. I want two para[professionals].' I think I should have that." Nevertheless, interviewees in all three cities voiced concerns about portfolio managers' true investment in autonomy and the ability of the system as a whole to embrace change. This was particularly true in Los Angeles, where individuals questioned not only LAUSD leadership but also the overall bureaucracy itself. Some study participants said that school leaders and teachers had been placed at pilot schools and other semiautonomous schools in violation of the schools' staffing autonomy. Justified by LAUSD leaders as necessary due to "budgetary issues," one such "forced" placement resulted in a teacher at a case study pilot school who simply did not want to be at the school and was not committed to its vision. In another example, schools were given autonomy around assessments, but were then required to deliver the data to the district in a format compatible with the central office's data system—a requirement generating considerable cost and burden.

In the charter sector, several Los Angeles interviewees reported increased bureaucratic requirements placed on charters (like the metal detector wanding example mentioned earlier). One stand-alone charter leader saw such requirements as a reflection of a general bureaucratic view of government that "they can't trust anyone to act well, [so] they have to literally spell out everything." Even some district leaders acknowledged their inability to truly support autonomy. An LAUSD board member said,

> This district loves to talk out of both sides of its mouth. . . . We believe in local control and autonomy, but we're going to pass a budget that says . . . we're going to give you all each a new counselor for—you can't do both, right? Either you're decentralizing and you let people decide what they're going to do, or you're going to be a centralized system and say we're going to tell you exactly how many teachers, and when we have a new initiative on getting more counselors in school, we're going to tell you how many you're going to get based on your normal day enrollment. You can't do it both.

Although Denver interviewees were more optimistic about the district's willingness to advance autonomy, citing that all traditional schools had gained more freedoms, there were also reports of "district reach and creep," as one foundation leader explained. Some reported that the district had started to "take back" some of the autonomies initially granted to innovation schools. One cited example was a requirement that all schools housed in district buildings, including innovation and charter schools, had to adopt a district-approved literacy program tied to new funding from a local mill levy—even if they already had their own approach to literacy. Reflecting on these moves and the district's perceived inability to "keep themselves from trying to erode the very autonomies that make charters," one foundation leader recalled the parable of the frog and the scorpion who both want to cross a raging river.

> [The scorpion] says, "Will you give me a ride?" The frog says, "Well, you'll sting me. You'll kill me." The scorpion's like, "No, I just want to get across the river." He says, "All right, hop on." They swim across the river. About halfway on the scorpion stings the frog. The frog said, "I thought you said you wouldn't do that." The scorpion's like, "It's my nature . . ." That's a district. I mean, it's not bad intent or anything. It's just their nature to try to directly manage schools.

CONCLUSION

In summary, the experiences in the three educational systems studied indicate that autonomy can be implemented as designed. In broad strokes, consistent with the portfolio design in all three school systems, school leaders in autonomous, stand-alone, and CMO charter schools demonstrated significantly higher levels of influence than school leaders in traditional public schools. School leaders in New Orleans, followed by Denver, also reported higher levels of autonomy than their counterparts in Los Angeles—another pattern consistent with the overall design of the three portfolio models. We also found considerable differences between the reports of leaders in stand-alone charter schools and reports of those in CMO charter schools, consistent with the idea that CMO central offices claim some authority for schooling at the expense of school leaders. And while teachers generally had less influence than school leaders, in New Orleans and Los Angeles teachers reported more influence in schools that included governance conditions for redistributing autonomy (the stand-alone charter and autonomous schools) than teachers in traditional and CMO charters said they had. In Denver, teachers reported more consistent levels of influence across school model types, reflecting Denver's design as a centralized portfolio system.

At the same time, data showed that implementing autonomy can be complex in practice. In particular, the survey data showed substantial variation in school leader influence within school model categories, suggesting that there could be conditions aside from school governance model that enable and/or constrain how principals exercise authority over schooling. At a more fine-grained level, leaders and educators in all three cases struggled with a set of common tensions in efforts to balance autonomy with competing goals related to uniformity, equity, efficiency, quality, and ease of burden. In all three cities, even when autonomies were granted, they were not always used.[14] This variation in implementation often related to leadership at multiple levels, the capacity of individuals, and broader forces resisting change within school systems.

In the end, the observed trends raise questions about the underlying assumptions of the portfolio model. In many ways, the pattern of recentralization occurring across the three cities, particularly among CMOs, and the direct challenges articulated by portfolio managers and CMO leaders about the merits of decentralization as a strategy for improvement, suggest that autonomy is a complicated tool for aligning the goals of system leaders and schools (see chapter 2). Efforts to create more uniform policies indicate that portfolio managers and CMO leaders believed constraints on autonomy may be needed to advance system goals, such as protecting student rights, providing equitable access to high-quality education, promoting quality instruction and performance across schools and classrooms, and running efficient systems where school educators can collaborate across sites and focus limited resources where they are needed most. In the end, unfettered autonomy may threaten these higher-level goals and the responsibilities of portfolio managers.

Efforts to recentralize, and the common practices and tensions observed across school systems and sites, might also suggest that there are broader institutional forces pushing against efforts to use autonomy as a lever of change. Scholars have long argued that to maintain legitimacy, over time organizations must adhere to common, taken-for-granted practices and norms. The study's finding that CMOs, particularly larger ones, may be limiting autonomy and adopting centralized practices similar to those in traditional school districts is consistent with these ideas and arguments made by other scholars.[15] Concerns expressed in Los Angeles and Denver about school district "creep" and an inability to be "open" and embrace change further support these arguments. Ultimately, more than a conscious effort to advance other system goals, the recentralization and limits on autonomy may reflect broader field-level expectations and norms favoring centralized models of schooling.

Finally, for leaders committed to autonomy, there may be opportunities for improvement and ways to create more fertile ground for its enactment.

Notably, leadership and capacity appear to be central. Without greater attention to building the knowledge, skills, and dispositions allowing for individuals at all levels to support and use various flexibilities, the promise of improvement via local discretion may not be realized. Chapter 8 develops these issues further when reviewing school support systems, and chapter 10 provides more specific implications for policy makers and leaders.

Of course, autonomy is just one of the many mechanisms of change embedded in the portfolio model. In theory, greater discretion will not bring about the improvement on its own, but instead will work in concert with rigorous planning and oversight, enhanced student choice, flexible human capital, and school supports. In fact, it is quite possible that it is the intersection of these multiple mechanisms that helps us understand the particular practices observed herein. For example, is the press to recentralize driven in part or exacerbated by new accountability demands that put even greater weight on the competing goals of equity and quality? Is the idea of earned autonomy due to planning and oversight mechanisms emphasizing student performance? Cross-cutting findings are revealed in chapter 10.

HUMAN
CAPITAL MANAGEMENT

A Pipeline of Diverse, Qualified Educators

with A. Chris Torres

Human capital management in school systems encompasses policies and practices pertaining to the recruitment, hiring, development, retention, and dismissal of educators. Managing schools' and districts' educator workforces—in particular, teachers and school leaders—is critically important for school and district success. It is well known that teachers and school leaders are the most significant in-school factors that contribute to student achievement growth, and that finding the right fit between teacher and organization is beneficial both for the teacher's persistence in the position and for their performance.[1] Therefore, the ways in which teachers and leaders are recruited, developed, and retained are crucial to the success of any school improvement reform.

In traditional public school districts, human capital management is often centralized at the district level. Critics of the traditional system argue that district policies and collective bargaining agreements (CBAs) can prevent school leaders from staffing their schools with teachers who are the right fit for their schools—for example, by assigning teachers with tenure and seniority to schools rather than assigning teachers based on school-teacher match.[2] By contrast, systems that embrace the portfolio management model theoretically create policies and procedures that enable educators and schools to have different kinds of flexibility and autonomy when it comes to human capital management, bringing the core tenet of *autonomy* (discussed in chapter 6) into this crucial function. Some argue that this allows portfolio managers, recognizing that different types of schools have different needs and preferences, to actively support heterogeneity in school staffing via a flexible "talent-seeking strategy."[3] This strategy involves granting schools autonomy from state and district policies and CBAs in areas such as educator hiring, assignment, evaluation, and dismissal, while other schools work within a traditional framework.

Under this system, the intent is for portfolio managers to work to build a pipeline of diverse and qualified educators by recruiting new educators, connecting school leaders to traditional and alternative supplies of teachers and leaders, helping generate systems and processes to evaluate and develop the professional practice of in-service teachers and leaders, and helping to create processes to retain effective educators. These measures, alongside school-based autonomy, are intended to increase teacher and school leader supply and fit for varied schools, with the goals of greater mission and pedagogical alignment, higher job satisfaction, increased retention, and better student outcomes.

This chapter provides examples of how each city implemented human capital management policies as aligned (or not) with the general portfolio model. The chapter argues that each city approached human capital management in ways generally consistent with its PMM characterization. Denver was the only portfolio manager that attempted to navigate the balance between building capacity across the system and allowing all schools flexibility to choose human capital supports, while the charter sectors in New Orleans and Los Angeles largely took on the work of human capital management on their own. By contrast, Los Angeles' district-operated schools (including traditional and autonomous) had more traditional restrictions based on the district's financial constraints and the strength of unions and CBAs. Despite these differences, all three portfolio managers struggled to resolve issues of educator supply, turnover, and compensation. The data also point to the varied roles of organized labor in shaping human capital policies in portfolio systems, and suggest that many of the differences across the case cities could be a function of the individual school model types that operate in the cities' respective school systems.

BACKGROUND

Historically, educational governance systems have grappled with the tension between centralization and the idea of providing substantial flexibility and autonomy to individual schools.[4] Attempts to decentralize decision making and empower schools and communities have been consistent features of governance reform for decades. For example, "site-based management" proliferated in the 1980s and 1990s, with an estimated one-third of districts embracing some form of this reform approach.[5] Site-based management is based on the concept that schools are better able to improve processes and outcomes without a reliance on assistance and intervention from a centralized local education agency or district office, and thus many decision-making processes should be undertaken at the school level by committees of community members and school-level actors.[6]

In recent years, the push for increased school-based autonomy has stemmed in part from the belief that schools need more flexibility to hire, develop, and retain educators. Attempts to remove or diminish the power of local and state policies have been at the heart of legislative and judicial actions in almost every state in the country and even in the US Supreme Court.[7] In response to high-stakes accountability policies, tightening fiscal constraints, and competition from charter schools, many states and districts across the country have pushed for school leaders in public schools to have enhanced autonomy in school management, especially with regard to management of teaching staff.[8] This push comes in response to critiques of CBAs negotiated between teachers' unions and district administrators and of state policies that are seen as impediments preventing teachers and school leaders from making decisions that fit their specific school and student contexts.[9] Critics believe that state policies requiring local education agencies to hire certain kinds of educators and provide job protections to teachers both early in their careers (via tenure) and later in their trajectories (via retirement benefits and layoff and dismissal policies) constrain administrators from staffing their schools with the personnel they want or need to improve schools.[10]

PMMs are a new chapter in the decentralization movement and offer some interesting examples of how school districts balance centralization with school-based autonomy in the management of human capital. For example, charter schools in all three case cities have substantial flexibility relative to CBAs and other district policies, but in Denver and New Orleans they can work in coordination with the portfolio manager and other external providers to address issues of teacher and school leader supply, retention, evaluation, and development. Innovation schools in Denver are another example of this hybrid, as they are district operated but can apply for waivers to be autonomous from specific policies. For example, many have the same flexibility as charter schools to hire and fire teachers using school-specific procedures that do not adhere to CBA regulations. At the same time, innovation schools can work with the district and other providers to support them with human capital–related functions such as teacher evaluation. While not identical in construct or (especially) in practice, pilot schools in Los Angeles represent a similar hybrid option for autonomy. Pilot schools operate under a "thin" union contract that allows them to set work hours and select and dismiss teaching staff outside of standard CBA provisions, while still participating in centralized district procedures for teacher hiring, compensation, and evaluation.

While PMM is gaining prominence as a reform strategy for decentralizing school management and optimizing human capital for schools, little is known about how portfolio managers are undertaking this important work in different contexts. Specifically, we need to know more about whether portfolio managers are designing their school systems to make human capital resources broadly accessible to schools, and if so, how; how portfolio managers, leaders, and teachers perceive and navigate flexibility and centralization; why schools in a portfolio system implement certain human capital policies or practices; the perceived efficacy of choices by educators in portfolio schools; and what other contextual factors might be shaping the enactment of various human capital mechanisms by portfolio managers and schools.

DESIGN OF HUMAN CAPITAL MANAGEMENT SYSTEMS

The three cities had common but also distinct approaches to educator preparation, recruitment, placement, evaluation, retention, and dismissal. For example, the cities shared common strategies for educator preparation that emphasized diverse pathways to the classroom: from district or charter network "grow your own" programs, to alternate routes, to purposefully crafted district-university partnerships.

The majority of human capital management strategies, however, varied by city in ways consistent with this study's characterizations of each city: as a centralized portfolio, managed market, or pair of competing systems. Rather than report data from each human capital mechanism (evaluation, retention, dismissal, and the like), we chose a small number of human capital management strategies that help to illuminate the overall approach found in each system. For example, in Denver's centralized portfolio, all schools were afforded some autonomies and flexibilities, but the central office also took a more active oversight and coordination role across school types. Evidence of this dynamic appeared in how the district both facilitated and designed efforts to recruit educators for all schools in the system. By contrast, the managed market of New Orleans, which consists almost entirely of charter schools, exhibited little central coordination and was associated with more variation across schools in their human capital management strategies. Since New Orleans is composed of local and national charter networks alongside stand-alone charter schools, the Recovery School District (RSD) as portfolio manager demonstrated a hands-off approach to human capital management, allowing charter schools to instead design their own strategies and systems. Filling this gap in support were external providers such as nonprofit organizations, for-profit entities, and universities that offered relevant services to schools wishing to use or purchase them. Despite a network of external providers, many noted significant issues with teacher supply and turnover in New Orleans and felt unclear about who would take primary responsibility for addressing this capacity issue at the system level. This points to a limitation of relying on school-based autonomy at the expense of more centralized coordination.

In Los Angeles the role of the district central office as portfolio manager was clearly split with regard to human capital management. As a system of competing sectors, it included traditional public and autonomous schools operating in a highly centralized structure where the district central office determined most (if not all) human capital procedures, allowing for little to no flexibility for schools. Accordingly, little variation in human capital management was evident across district-run school types in Los Angeles, with school leaders and teachers (particularly in autonomous schools) voicing frustration with their inability to staff schools with well-matched and high-quality staff. In contrast, charter schools in Los Angeles operated with minimal interaction or support from the district central office, much like charter schools in New Orleans.

Denver

In Denver, the centralized portfolio approach was visible in the ways that Denver Public Schools (DPS) strategically coordinated autonomies and partnerships while continuing to offer centralized supports across the system. DPS was balancing the coordination and creation of human capital procedures in school leader and teacher recruitment, such as undertaking initiatives to increase the diversity of the teaching force and using an evaluation system called Leading Effective Academic Practice (LEAP). As part of these efforts, schools were allowed to flexibly participate in procedures based on what suited their local context. This balance of support and flexibility for all schools likely contributed to there being fewer differences in human capital management practices between charter and noncharter schools than were evident in New Orleans and Los Angeles, as well as contributing to their high ratings of satisfaction with human capital management across school types.

For instance, Denver's centralized approach was reflected in its management of teacher supply and, in particular, its efforts to increase teacher diversification. DPS worked to increase the supply of teachers and leaders, but it did not place principals and teachers in schools. Rather, this pipeline was available to school leaders, who could work with the central office to determine an appropriate match for schools in the system that opted in. As a result, many DPS-run schools across model types availed themselves of this pipeline, whereas CMOs for the most part did not. As a human resources director explained: "We don't have CMO participation [in hiring systems] . . . We do have high-level participation in innovation schools." CMO leaders explained that they worked to develop their own pipelines, and they had significant autonomy to do so.

In a similar vein, a DPS central office employee explained how the district implemented "grow your own" (GYO) initiatives to prepare educators for working in the specific context of their school, to support them in their work, and to help school leaders and teachers of color work in whatever school model they might choose as the best fit for them:

> We have some initiatives targeted at increasing the size of the pipeline, the number of diverse teachers in the pipeline. We have some efforts about ensuring early hiring of teachers of color. . . . We're starting a new Black educator superintendent's team. We have mentoring opportunities, educators

of color mentoring other educators of color. We do a lot of growing of our own talent. The majority of our principals that are hired, we grew. We have an opportunity to ensure the diversity of our—who we're growing into principalship.

DPS also stood out from both the New Orleans system and the Los Angeles Unified School District (LAUSD) for its coordinated attention to both creating its own programs and collaborating with CMOs and external providers around other programs. For instance, DPS worked with Relay Graduate School of Education to develop educators and increase the supply of teachers and leaders for all schools in the system, whether charter, innovation, or traditional. A Relay representative applauded this intentional coordination with DPS: "In our launch year, we had meetings with [a DPS director]. I have to say, we are thrilled to be working with [them]."

The centralized portfolio in Denver was also visible in the choices leaders and teachers made (and could make) about whether to opt in to district-designed systems such as the LEAP evaluation system. As with their GYO program, Denver provided this evaluation and support system for all of its schools (charter, innovation, and traditional), but also allowed for charter and autonomous schools to opt in to the LEAP system, waive it, or adapt it to fit their own needs. In the traditional public and innovation schools in the study, DPS allowed teachers flexibility to decide *who* would conduct their formal evaluation—namely, a teacher leader or peer observer—highlighting the level of choice and teacher autonomy at the school level even for district-run schools. Innovation and charter schools had the freedom to adopt LEAP wholesale, adapt it to their own contexts, or opt out entirely, and some did just that. However, not all schools that could have adapted or opted out of LEAP did so. One DPS employee noted that while innovation schools *could* create their own teacher evaluation system or adapt LEAP to suit their context, they often did not. She said: "The feedback we get about our tools is not perfect, but it's really strong. Since it was built by our teachers and leaders, there's a strong degree of belief that it captures a lot of really important things." Since the system was "built" by teachers and leaders, the perception was that there was stronger buy-in and motivation for these school-based actors to meet the goals set by the portfolio managers for educator performance. Even some charter schools ended up adopting the LEAP system.

Accordingly, interviews with teachers and school leaders in DPS suggested general satisfaction across school models with evaluation systems, whether LEAP or self-designed. Schools that designed their own evaluation systems enjoyed the autonomy of being able to match their evaluation process to the instructional system, while those who opted for LEAP were most satisfied with the ability to "localize" and fit the system to their context. Similarly, teachers appreciated having the autonomy to choose the type of evaluator at the school level. These dynamics illustrate how centralization and autonomy in Denver's centralized portfolio can complement one another when it comes to schools' choices around teacher evaluation.

New Orleans

Just as Denver's centralized approach to management was evident in its human capital strategies, New Orleans' managed market orientation extended to human capital management. As a whole, the system evinced much less coordination and substantially more variation than DPS. The vacuum left by having no centralized "manager" enabled a market of individual schools, charter school networks, and external providers working in tandem to address human capital needs. Accordingly, wide variation in human capital practices was evident across schools, largely arising from which entities provided human capital services and the processes used by those entities. However, school leaders across the board reported facing persistent issues with teacher supply and high rates of teacher turnover that detracted from their ability to effectively staff schools.

One way this became evident throughout interviews and case studies with teachers, leaders, and central office staff was in a recurring questioning of ownership of human capital initiatives. For example, an RSD representative spoke about tracking teacher supply and retention data, highlighting the "red flag challenge in [the] ecosystem": "We need to make sure we are working with partners to figure it out, so working with NSNO [New Schools for New Orleans], working with others to say hey, who's doing—who's taking the lead on this? We need to know who's taking the lead on this because this is an issue for our schools." Although the problem was clearly recognized, this question of "who's taking the lead" remained and, in contrast with Denver, illustrated uncertainty about the role of the RSD. In this and in other instances, external actors provided their own solutions to support schools in New Orleans. For example, a leader of a prominent nonprofit outlined how his organization was working to address issues related to teacher preparation and supply in New Orleans, laying out strategies that went beyond simply relying on alternate routes like Teach for America to expand the teacher pipeline, such as working with local universities to create residency programs that would help attract and retain teachers. In this sense, outside providers acting within the market environment of New Orleans were tackling pressing human capital problems, though not necessarily in coordination with RSD or the Orleans Parish School Board (OPSB).

Examples of schools experiencing New Orleans' decentralized managed market abound in the case study data. Recruitment and retention practices, for example, were often highly informal or varied school by school. Leaders across five out of seven case study schools discussed recruitment as a major challenge for them, often due to the market approach that persisted in New Orleans not just for students but also for educators. Exemplifying a consistent refrain, one principal at a larger CMO noted that schools competed intensely for high-quality teachers. As a result, he reported having to "speed up the process" and use an informal, relaxed interview style to attract teachers. Since there were few central mechanisms to support recruitment efforts, principals often found themselves using word of mouth and their own and their teachers' social networks and personal connections to attract educators to their schools. For instance, at a small, RSD-authorized CMO, the majority of teachers and school leaders with whom we spoke (five out of seven) reported that the most effective avenues for recruitment were word of mouth and TeachNOLA, a New Orleans–based alternative certification program run by the New Teacher Project (now known as TNTP). Similarly, at a stand-alone charter school, several interviewed teachers noted that they had previously worked with the current principal at a previous school. Survey data echoed these findings, as 71 percent of teacher respondents in New Orleans stand-alone charters and 57 percent of teachers in CMOs reported that they applied for a position in their school because they had "heard good things about the school." In contrast, a lower share of teacher respondents across school model types reported the same decision-making process in Los Angeles (between 20 percent and 31 percent) and Denver (between 45 percent and 68 percent).

At times, this informal recruitment strategy enabled school leaders to recruit and select teachers who they believed would fit well with their schools and students. For instance, one principal at a small CMO noted a preference for veteran teachers who know or have lived in the community. Her own background as a community member and former principal helped her attract many teachers and minimized challenges with recruitment. As she explained: "I basically know everybody down here. It's just being vested back into where I was born and raised in." Even a principal at a large CMO reported using informal strategies to recruit well-matched teachers because of the "teacher shortage" of highly qualified candidates. This, despite having a centralized structure to help with recruitment. He explained: "I think our best teachers are word of mouth from our best teachers who have like-minded people that they refer to us."

Closely tied to this issue, most of the same schools experiencing issues with recruitment also noted issues with high turnover. Here again, the autonomy that enabled school leaders to implement highly localized approaches to recruitment allowed them to use targeted and flexible retention strategies. Many teachers in case sites noted that school leaders were making proactive and varied efforts to retain teachers. In this instance, the lack of managed structure and the ability for teachers to move with relative ease to other schools resulted in giving principals more incentive and flexibility to sit down with teachers to understand what would make them want to stay. Thus, the market approach appeared to result in teachers having more voice. For instance, one teacher at a small RSD CMO explained: "If they think you might even want to leave, they will meet with you, and many times they ask you what you want. I know for next year, I wanted to do a little bit more coaching, and my principal's like, 'Okay, let's figure this out.'" Another teacher at a small OPSB CMO similarly noted that the principal had an "open door" policy to talk about issues related to retention. One principal at a large CMO noted that he used mechanisms to give teachers more voice as a strategy to retain teachers, specifically a "staff council." He explained: "I give them a comfortable space where they can talk and then they can have that one person relay that information to me. If it's things that I can reasonably fix and address I will. The teachers love and appreciate that." Similar evidence appeared in the area of teacher compensation. School leaders, unconstrained by a single salary schedule or a negotiated pay structure, were also able to use varied forms of compensation to retain teachers. For instance, teachers at the small RSD CMO referred to above noted that the school provided them with salary raises after two years, which they felt helped with retention.

Los Angeles

As described in chapter 3, Los Angeles' portfolio management approach included two separate but competing systems. LAUSD's central office managed and coordinated all traditional public schools and autonomous schools, but there was also a set of charter schools, many of which were technically overseen by LAUSD but in practice received little support or services from the district for human capital management.

This difference in central office oversight across sectors manifested in substantial differences in human capital management strategies between district-run and charter schools. In particular, both system-level interviews and survey data suggested that traditional and autonomous schools were sometimes hindered in their ability to hire well-matched and high-quality teachers (particularly in the autonomous, district-managed schools), due to regulations, policies, and politics surrounding teacher hiring, placement, and dismissal. Much of the perceived constraint emanated from the district's strong CBA with the teachers' union, United Teachers Los Angeles (UTLA).

In interviews with traditional public school leaders in Los Angeles, they described working within LAUSD's teacher placement and dismissal process, which was largely prescribed in the district's CBA. One traditional public school leader noted: "So the district has a pool of applicants, and out of this pool, she can interview and select the one that she decides fits better for [the] school." A different magnet school leader explained why she found this problematic, particularly the timing of the process: "To be honest with you, by the time you get to July, who's left on the list to be hired is usually, not always, but usually not your premier candidates. I was texting people . . . I was like, 'I don't know anybody in middle school. I need a middle school English language arts teacher.' It's the end of July. Recruitment, they send us a list. We interview people. We picked the best candidate that we could find at that moment in time."

While traditional public schools in Los Angeles were clearly bound by the CBA, many of the autonomous schools had explicitly written agreements that removed them from some of the most restrictive staffing provisions within the CBA. In practice, however, the district's CBA superseded the agreements the schools had with LAUSD, lessening their ability to manage their own labor force in ways they perceived as best for their schools. For instance, numerous interviewees from the central office and the LAUSD board said that the provision of autonomy in hiring staff in the district's theoretically autonomous pilot schools had not always been implemented as was intended. A prime example of this lack of autonomy in practice was found in the requirement that pilot schools accept "must place" teachers and administrators, even when they had agreements with LAUSD that suggested they would not have to. A central office representative explained: "[The superintendent] didn't want teachers or administrators out there without an assignment, but they have contracts with the district so still have to be paid. You're essentially paying somebody without them doing any work. He needed to make sure those people were placed first before— so a lot of schools, I would say there were four, at least three or four pilot schools that had principals placed without them having any input into who would be the next principal if they had a vacancy." Similarly, an administrator in a district network partnership school said that they faced pressure from these "must place" placements and had to work multiple angles to avoid hiring teachers they believed were not good fits for their schools. He said: "In many cases, if we're looking for a solution to forced placements, we're doing it with the office of general counsel, with the local superintendent, with district personnel at every single level."

Leaders from the charter case study sites in Los Angeles reported having significant autonomy around human capital management strategies. One CMO school leader, in describing the autonomy to coordinate and manage the hiring process, explained: "Right now, I'm working really closely with our recruitment specialist to hire new teachers. They do the initial phone screen for us. By the time we're speaking with them, they've already filtered through some of the people for us."

Tight district regulation did not always put traditional and autonomous schools at a disadvantage, however. During the time period under study, LAUSD was itself focusing on implementing human capital management strategies that would enable them to support and retrain a strong teacher labor force. One major initiative was the district's multimeasure teacher evaluation and support system, labeled Educator Development and Support for Teachers (EDST), and a parallel system for school leaders (EDSSL).

As was the case in Denver, the process of working with school-based staff to develop an evaluation system they would eventually use bolstered satisfaction and motivation to work toward the goals of the portfolio manager. Interviews confirmed this belief, with district-level respondents noting that training around the mandated system was strong: "We have teachers who really appreciate the developmental aspect of the teacher evaluation system, but also the fact that their principals have been given so much support in that. We put a lot of energy and time into making sure our principals [were trained]." Results from surveys also support this assertion. For instance, with regard to the EDSSL system, the vast majority of school leader respondents at traditional and autonomous schools (82 percent or higher) agreed that the school leader evaluation process was fair and that they used feedback from the evaluation process to improve their practice. These results reinforce the idea that there is a greater incentive for school-based staff to work toward the goals of the portfolio manager when the manager strives to incorporate teachers' and leaders' input thoughtfully.

Despite the popularity of EDST and EDSSL and the immense resources required to develop these evaluation systems, LAUSD did not make these systems available to charter schools, which instead developed their own evaluation systems (if any) with different data components. For instance, survey data show that principal respondents from CMO and stand-alone charter schools were more likely to report using value-added measures of effectiveness in their teacher and school leader evaluation systems, whereas value-added measures were not included in EDST or EDSSL. Even though LAUSD charters were not able to choose the district's evaluation system and often created their own systems, the vast majority of surveyed school leaders in stand-alone and CMO charter schools expressed satisfaction with their evaluation system in terms of perceived fairness and using evaluation feedback to improve their practice (upward of 91 percent of school leaders in stand-alone charter schools and 74 percent of school leaders in CMO charter schools).

DIFFERENT PORTFOLIO MANAGERS, SIMILAR PROBLEMS: EDUCATOR SUPPLY AND TURNOVER

Turnover

Although each city's human capital management strategies largely reflected its specific approach to portfolio management, the three were clearly facing similar challenges related to their educator labor force (both teachers and leaders). In all three cities, the most prominent human capital issues facing each system involved educator retention and, particularly when it came to charter schools in each city, educator supply.

In terms of supply, charters in Denver and LAUSD seemed to be experiencing teacher recruitment struggles similar to those described above in New Orleans. In Denver, this issue seemed most pronounced in stand-alone schools rather than CMOs, as one charter advocacy group representative reported: "I think [CMOs are] thinking a lot about retention through teacher leadership and master teacher career ladders. I think all the CMOs have developed those in recent years. I think our 'mom and pops' are taking largely whoever walks in the door. I mean, that sounds awful, but when you talk to them, they're like, 'Well, we had openings until June.' I think for them, they're not—they're trying to be strategic. I just don't think they have the resources to compete." In Los Angeles, both CMO and stand-alone leaders cited issues with filling positions with teachers who were, as one CMO principal put it, the "right fit." However, the issue was not just about fit, as the same principal explained: "Filling our positions this year has been really difficult. We have a couple of long-term subs in positions, one who's been here almost the whole year."

Representatives from each system also uniformly noted that it was difficult to retain both teachers and leaders. This challenge was more pronounced in Denver and New Orleans than in Los Angeles. For instance, when asked to report the number of teachers who left their school in the past three years for reasons unrelated to performance, school leader respondents in New Orleans and Denver reported an average turnover rate of 10 and 6 teachers per school, respectively, while school leader respondents in Los Angeles reported a significantly lower average turnover rate of 3 teachers per school, even as average school enrollment in Los Angeles was larger (632 students) than in Denver (432 students) and New Orleans (608 students). While we observed higher rates of turnover in stand-alone (5) and CMO charter schools (5) in Los Angeles than in traditional public schools (2), the turnover rates for Los Angeles charter schools were still notably lower than those reported in Denver (6 for stand-alones and 9 for CMO charters) and New Orleans (14 for stand-alones and 9 for CMO charters). The relatively high rate of turnover in New Orleans and Denver also tracks with the average experience level of teachers in each city.

LAUSD educators were, on average, more experienced than educators in the two other systems, and there was a far greater proportion of novice teachers and school leaders in New Orleans schools than in either Denver or Los Angeles. These trends suggest that the higher rates of turnover in New Orleans and Denver could have been influenced by the less experienced teacher workforce in these cities.

Regardless of these differences in context, similar frustrations with teacher and school leader mobility appeared in interviews with respondents across all three cities. In Los Angeles, average teacher experience was greatest and reliance on novice teachers was lowest. However, educators in charter schools tended to express more difficulty with turnover. One CMO teacher who used to work for traditional public schools in Los Angeles explained that the workload was more difficult in the charter context: "Our school does have the stereotypical high turnover rate. Considering I'm the only teacher here that's been here all five years. It's only been five years . . . Even the office staff, that's high turnover as well. There's nobody here that's been here longer than two years. Not just here, but across all schools [in the CMO]. It's that way because it's so demanding."

This same issue was salient in Denver as well. One employee at the DPS central office worried: "I would also say that our turnover rate among principals is far too high to have an effective organization. . . . We're talking upwards of a third of our principals at times not being in the same role the following year." Similarly, in New Orleans, an RSD employee explained: "We see that we have this looming gap in the number of—number of teachers that are being hired every year is increasing, but the supply of teachers is not. We know that teacher turnover here is not really higher than in other urban districts, but it's relatively high, and a lot of the schools that have higher turnover are the ones that are—schools and CMOs are the ones that are expanding."

Recruitment and Retention

Several human capital policies and strategies were used by portfolio managers and others in each system to address problems of educator recruitment and retention.

Teacher Supply: Alternative Educator Pipelines

One way that systems tried to fill teacher and leader vacancies was through exploring alternative educator pipelines. A sizable share of teacher survey respondents from Los Angeles (19 percent), Denver (25 percent), and New Orleans (39 percent) indicated completing an alternative teacher preparation program prior to entering the teaching profession. While this strategy brought with it some benefits—for example, filling vacancies with motivated, young teachers—some felt that this strategy exacerbated the problem. Leaders in New Orleans and Los Angeles described tension between addressing the supply of teachers through alternative pipeline programs and addressing later retention concerns, as teachers recruited from these avenues had higher rates of turnover, thus leaving districts and schools with more vacancies to fill. A leader of a nonprofit in New Orleans emphasized the need to develop new strategies to recruit educators because of this tension: "Some of the talent pipelines that we have—Teach for America, teachNOLA, et cetera—may not have the same sort of longevity in the classroom. We're working with Xavier University right now on a pilot program, partnership between charter organizations and a university preparation program to try to build residencies for undergraduates that can then get master's degrees and go into teaching." System leaders in LAUSD and Denver also described trying to create stronger university partnerships in an effort to expand the pool of teachers and increase their longevity. It has yet to be seen if any of these partnerships improve retention issues.

Teacher Supply: Teacher Compensation

Across cities, numerous participants argued that teacher compensation exacerbated or caused teacher staffing problems. Respondents in all three cities suggested that low pay was a significant barrier to growing and retaining an effective educator labor force. Only 31 percent of respondent teachers in Denver agreed or strongly agreed that they were compensated fairly. While higher rates of satisfaction were observed among teacher respondents in Los Angeles (51 percent) and New Orleans (49 percent), there were just as many teachers in these cities who were dissatisfied with compensation (50 percent in Los Angeles and 51 percent in New Orleans). Echoing these concerns, a state-level leader in Louisiana noted: "We're working on both of those fronts [to improve preparation/recruitment], I think, as aggressively as any state, but let's be real. Pay is gonna have to change."

This focus on teacher compensation and the belief that the current level of compensation was insufficient to reward teachers for their efforts was consistent across cities in case data and interviews. Indeed, in both Los

Angeles and Denver, the teachers' unions coordinated strikes in the years since this study's data collection in response to lagging teachers' salaries. For instance, a DPS employee explained:

> I think that Denver has become—became an attractive and has become an attractive place to teach, but the turnover is still super high. One in four teachers they're turning over still. . . . Even with all the hype around ProComp, we pretty much have a traditional compensation thing. Denver has become a crane-filled, hip city with real estate prices jumping by 30 percent in the last year. A living wage is now $70 grand, which is at the high end of the teacher pay scale. That's going to be a real problem, actually, for everyone, charter or district schools.

Denver's Compensation System

Although compensation was an issue across cities, the data from Denver revealed perceived compensation inequities between different school models that may have been related to ProComp, Denver's incentive-based teacher compensation system. Denver implemented ProComp as its compensation system of record in 2005, funded by a local annual tax approved by Denver voters. While ProComp was intended to attract and retain teachers for DPS's highest need schools and to reward the highest performing teachers, this compensation system, and the extra funding that went along with it, only applied to teachers in traditional public and innovation schools, not to those in charter schools. Importantly, ProComp generated differences in pay even within the traditional sector; the compensation structure provided financial incentives for performance and for teachers who worked in "hard to serve" and "priority" schools. This differentiation fueled feelings of inequitable treatment among charter schools, particularly since DPS, as a portfolio manager, had largely implemented centralized policies for the opposite purpose—to provide equal opportunities to educators across school types. Moreover, as noted earlier, issues of compensation and teacher recruitment were seen as the most critical barriers to achieving optimal staffing in DPS schools.

One CMO leader discussed some of the disparities brought about by ProComp: "ProComp's a big challenge within the portfolio, because part of the portfolio gets it and part doesn't." Another CMO leader explained how they needed to adjust their compensation system because of Pro-Comp: "We very purposely start middle range, so we're not the most competitive offer you're going to get. We offer base-pay salaries based on merit that are significantly higher than what you'd get anywhere else." Yet this same leader felt that they could not compete with some of those incentives offered through ProComp, that it was a huge "equity issue," and that they often lost teachers to DPS. He added: "We cannot offer $10,000 bonuses for teaching in a hard to fill school or an at-risk school. We can't tell you that if your school hits distinguished, you're going to get x, y, and z. Teachers come to us with $14,000 to $18,000 of bonuses included in their paycheck. We have zero capacity to be able to do that. That's fully paid for out of the levy that explicitly says only DCTA teachers have access to that money." As mentioned above, the levy funding ProComp was only for traditional public and innovation school teachers who belonged to the Denver Classroom Teachers Association (DCTA), which put the portfolio manager in a difficult position by restricting who had access to this pool of money and for what purpose.

These disparities surrounding compensation are reflected in the survey data as well. Whereas 59 percent of traditional school leaders and 51 percent of autonomous school leaders reported using monetary rewards to retain effective teachers (relative to no school leaders in traditional or autonomous schools in Los Angeles), only 16 percent of stand-alone charter school leaders in Denver were able to use monetary rewards in this way. Notably, as the CMO leader who discussed offering starting salaries at the "middle range" explained, 87 percent of CMO leaders reported using compensation as a retention strategy. As the charter advocacy leader quoted earlier suggested, it could be that stand-alone charter schools in Denver did not have adequate funding or the resources to use differentiated teacher compensation as a strategy for recruiting effective teachers.

On the flip side, the presence of differentiated teacher compensation for teachers in traditional public schools in Denver raised questions about fairness. As reported above, a lower proportion of teachers agreed or strongly agreed that they were compensated fairly in Denver than in Los Angeles and New Orleans. Moreover, within Denver, a significantly lower proportion of teachers in traditional public schools (25 percent) reported that they were compensated fairly than teachers in innovation (33 percent), stand-alone (46 percent), and CMO charter schools (37 percent). In contrast, no significant differences were observed in teacher reports of compensation fairness between school model types in Los Angeles or in New Orleans.

Teachers' Unions

While the main human capital challenges facing each system were the same—teacher and leader supply and retention—the state policy and local labor market contexts concerning the educator labor force in each city were markedly different. The strength of teachers' unions varied across the cities, with organized labor heavily influencing human capital practices in Los Angeles, but much less so in Denver and New Orleans. The UTLA was described in the data and media coverage as a very strong and active union with a restrictive CBA that regulated the great majority of teachers' work in schools governed by LAUSD (traditional and autonomous schools).[11] For instance, the CBA in LAUSD dictated how any teacher employee of the district could be voluntarily or involuntarily placed within or removed from schools. Consistent with this highly regulated context, approximately 86 percent of school leader respondents in traditional public schools and 82 percent of school leader respondents in autonomous schools in Los Angeles reported that UTLA posed a barrier to the dismissal of ineffective teachers from their schools, whereas only 21 percent and 17 percent of school leader respondents in stand-alone and CMO charter schools (respectively) reported the same. In interviews, LAUSD teachers expressed their view that the union was a strong force and expressed appreciation for it. One teacher explained in response to questions about the role of the union: "I think teachers are really vocal. They really stick up for each other and they really go to battle for each other and I'm just going to leave it at that. . . . You really see it. It's like, 'Whoa, that is a real sense of community.'" Consistent with Los Angeles' competing systems characterization, case study participants in charter schools described the union as not playing much of a role in their schools, with the exception of one CMO where the union bargained regarding pay scale and teacher evaluations. However, even in that context the principal noted that the union did not play a role with regard to autonomy with staffing.

By contrast, Denver's teachers' association (the DCTA) was seen as a far less involved teachers' union, with a more collaborative relationship with district leadership. Accordingly, a lower share of principals across school types reported the teachers' union as a barrier to the dismissal of ineffective teachers (62 percent of school leaders in autonomous schools, 74 percent in traditional public schools, and 0 percent in stand-alone and CMO charter schools). The middling level of union influence in Denver was reflected in case interviews. School leaders and teachers alike almost uniformly described the union as having little influence, and they expressed little knowledge of the DCTA beyond the option to pay dues and the existing teacher contract. However, the teachers' union was raising important concerns to the central office, especially pertaining to compensation. As one teacher at a traditional public school explained: "I just don't have—it's just my first year out of college and I just don't have $70 a month [to pay dues]. I can't fit that into my budget. I know that pay is one of their big stances right now, is getting everyone a $40,000 salary, which is nice."

At the other end of the spectrum, there was no uniform teachers' union representing New Orleans schools, although a small handful of charter schools had unionized at the time of data collection. The decentralized nature of the New Orleans system, and the fact that the majority of schools were charter schools (therefore not necessarily unionized), were key drivers of the relatively low level of union constraint felt by school leaders. New Orleans case study participants noted that unionization efforts in the city happened on a school-by-school basis and were contentious and taxing. Survey data suggest that these school-by-school unionization efforts were perhaps more concentrated among stand-alone charter schools than among CMO charters. As one stand-alone charter teacher explained: "I know individual charter schools are having to unionize, which sounds—I know teachers who have gone through that process and lost their jobs or decided to leave because it is so much work to start a brand new union at a charter school."

IMPLICATIONS FOR HUMAN CAPITAL MANAGEMENT IN A PMM

The study's PMM case sites all demonstrate the importance of human capital management in motivating and enabling school-based agents to meet principal goals in the PMM. In one case, schools exercised autonomy to recruit and retain well-matched and high-quality teachers with little oversight from a portfolio manager (New Orleans), and in a contrasting case, the portfolio manager provided centralized and coordinated support to supply schools with effective educators regardless of school model

(Denver). In the third case, Los Angeles, the portfolio manager interfaced with schools differently across sectors, providing extensive support and regulation to district-operated schools and little to no oversight and support to charter schools.

As these cases suggest, human capital management is a critical mechanism in fueling school success. Specifically, the satisfaction of school-based agents with human capital management depended on whether or how the portfolio manager, as principal, managed processes and expectations that would allow for greater choice and capacity to meet goals. Indeed, the data elucidate several challenges and benefits to a portfolio system having a more hands-off approach and granting substantial flexibility versus one that is more coordinated and centralized in its approach. The decentralized approach in New Orleans meant that efforts to recruit diverse teachers into the school system were coordinated mainly by outside providers, and New Orleans school leaders reported substantial competition for teachers. This caused school leaders in New Orleans to resort to informal and ad hoc recruitment and retention practices. While this created challenges for the schools, the end result was that charter leaders developed various ways to listen to teachers' concerns and ideas in an effort to retain them. While the absence of centralized recruitment efforts could be seen as problematic because the portfolio manager was doing little to solve the systemic problem of teacher supply and retention, the informal processes that were observed could at the same time be seen as encouraging more responsive or innovative retention strategies from school leaders.

There were also advantages to the portfolio manager taking a more proactive role to coordinate human capital support for schools. For instance, Denver partnered with outside providers such as Relay while still developing their own recruitment, retention, evaluation, development, and preparation policies and initiatives (ProComp, the Teacher Leader initiative, LEAP, and diversification pipelines, among others) and allowing schools substantial flexibility to select policies and providers that fit their context. Survey observations and interview data indicated that this combination of coordinated support and flexibility resulted in fewer perceived differences between school models in Denver, and that it potentially aided in overall recruitment and retention efforts across the system.

However, ProComp is an important counterpoint to this dynamic. ProComp as a centralized DPS initiative offered substantially greater support to a subset of traditional public schools but not to other schools in the system. This support was particularly important because it addressed recruitment and retention, which stakeholders described as the most pressing problem facing schools in the system. This led to feelings of inequitable treatment, as school-based agents felt that the portfolio manager (as principal) was offering advantages for a certain kind of school to the detriment of their own capacities to meet academic goals. Indeed, ProComp and compensation more generally were driving factors behind the teacher strike that occurred in DPS in 2018, after this study's data collection ended.[12]

In Los Angeles, schools struggled with a lack of autonomy around human capital management that was influenced by district policies, with the portfolio manager regulating district-operated schools in ways that were both helpful and detrimental to flexible staffing and, on the flip side, providing little to no support to charter schools. Although CBAs were responsible for restricting staffing autonomy in LAUSD, more research is needed to discern whether union strength leads to lower turnover and higher levels of teacher experience, and if so, what the benefits, challenges, and tradeoffs are in terms of achieving various outcomes. For example, some pilot schools, though theoretically they had hiring autonomy, were required to hire from the district's pool of teachers because of financial constraints in the system. At the same time, LAUSD developed a robust teacher and school leader evaluation system for its schools that was largely perceived as helpful to schools and was not accessible to charter schools. Previous work that studied the development and implementation of these support and evaluation systems in LAUSD (EDST and EDSSL) showcases how the district negotiated with its bargaining partners to develop and adapt the system in ways that served the needs of both the educators and schools.[13]

This coordination by the portfolio manager is particularly important when individual schools do not have the capacity to exercise autonomy in a particular area (for example, in creating an evaluation system) or to solve system-level problems such as a low supply of teachers who are willing and able to work within the system. By contrast, autonomy can be an important incentive in cases where school leaders have the capacity to use their autonomy to fit their context. Finally, the case of DPS shows that these ideas need not be mutually exclusive. Centralized supports and ideas can be shared across school types, but teachers and school leaders can still have autonomy to decide *what* to adopt and *how*. When done thoughtfully, this balance between autonomy and centralized support has the potential to increase agents' motivation and capacity to meet principals' goals.

Finally, reflecting on the role of flexibility and centralization as it relates to human capital management, some of the examples discussed, especially those pertaining to charter schools, may be less attributable to the portfolio structure and more characteristic of the autonomies that are associated with individual school models. The charter sectors in all three cities had substantial autonomy in human capital management—for example, autonomy from general state and district policies and from the teachers' and administrators' union CBAs. Therefore, charter schools have far greater ability to implement policies that impact educators than do schools overseen by district policies and CBAs (both autonomous and traditional public schools) or by just CBAs (traditional public schools). This raises a tension inherent in the PMM approach: How many of the "innovations" theorized to stem from portfolio districts in the area of human capital are actually a result of centralized management, and how many are a result of individual autonomies associated with discrete school governance structures?

The study's findings appear to be driven by the combined influence of portfolio governance and school-based autonomy. The study found that certain human capital management strategies are more dictated by school governance type—teacher placement, dismissal, and compensation in charter schools, for example—but that there are key human capital management strategies for which a portfolio manager can provide important resources and supports regardless of school governance model. Denver represents an interesting hybrid case, with different policies for charter and noncharter schools, but with DPS still maintaining some active coordination and management across school models, including in the charter school sector. In sum, understanding the enactment of human capital management strategies may require us to consider the interaction of state policy, system design, school-based governance, and the role of outside organizations.

SCHOOL SUPPORTS

Administration, Instruction, Compliance

with Jane Arnold Lincove

Public education systems are expected not only to perform but also to constantly adapt and improve in response to changing conditions, such as increasing enrollment, emergence of new student populations, changing student needs and community conditions, or the fluctuating needs of labor markets. In a traditional, centralized school district, the central office is largely responsible for the holistic growth and adaptation of the system. Districts facilitate improvement through both broad efforts and targeted interventions for schools or populations. What happens, then, when the traditional central office is partly or completely removed from those responsibilities in a decentralized portfolio management model?

In shifting responsibility for school management to school sites, decentralization changes the mechanism through which districts build support capacity to serve students. Portfolio managers give school operators an incentive to improve by giving them the autonomy they need in order to adapt to student needs as they believe appropriate, respond to family preferences as a result of competition, and meet external expectations through performance-based oversight, but it is unclear how the work needed to maintain and build capacity is conducted in these settings.

While the central function of most public schools is classroom instruction, myriad activities, services, and supports must be provided to make effective instruction possible. These include supports directly related to instruction and the expertise of educators, such as assessment, curriculum development, and teacher development; they also include an expanded list of peripheral but necessary supports that require a broad range of complementary expertise, such as transportation, facilities management, employee benefits, and nutrition programs. Decentralization of decision-making to the school level is meant to take full advantage of the expertise and local knowledge of school leaders, teachers, and parents to create a better suited environment and curriculum for students. But a potential downside of decentralization is the loss of centralized support for tasks that fall outside the expertise of teachers and principals. If the needed expertise for tasks such as employee payroll, optimal school bus routing, or plumbing repairs is not provided by someone external to the school, who on campus provides it?

This chapter describes how support services are currently provided in the three case districts and identifies some of the key challenges for designing school supports in portfolio systems. The chapter identifies current capacity-building activities and examines how district supports are similar or different across school types, school needs, and student population; it also considers how potentially unequal distributions of resources could impact the adequacy of education provided to all students. Finally, the chapter considers the larger question of whether and how capacity building occurs when it is not provided by a central school district, including the role of charter management organizations (CMOs) and the emerging nonprofit support sectors in portfolio-managed schools.

Drawing on a broad range of data, the analysis examines how stakeholders at the system and school levels described the nature and sources of administrative (human resources and building maintenance), instructional (professional learning and coaching), and compliance (special education and legal services) supports available to and utilized by schools, as well as the ways in which schools accessed available supports (whether by choice or by mandate). The study found that the design of each unique system substantially shaped approaches to support, resulting in very different conditions for schools both across and within the three systems. The analysis revealed emerging systems that are still working through the innate conflicts and compromises of decentralized governance. Central to these conflicts is the concern, raised repeatedly, that having a portfolio manager support schools directly would almost inevitably reduce school autonomy.

DECENTRALIZATION AND SCHOOL SUPPORTS

Decentralization carries both risks and potential benefits for schools and school systems. A substantial downside is the loss of economies of scale, where a centralized school district can provide supports to many campuses at a lower cost than the campuses can support themselves.[1] One example of economies of scale is the money-saving strategy of bulk purchases of supplies, such as textbooks and furniture, and services, such as IT support and transportation. The concentration of expertise to solve problems that occur frequently across a district but rarely on an individual campus is another common benefit of the traditional district model. Traditional school districts aggregate expertise to support schools in many ways—such as designing services for students with rare disabilities, correcting building code violations, or supporting families in crisis.

While little is known about how decentralized schools receive supports, some prior research in New Orleans indicates a loss of economies of scale. In the years following decentralization, administrative and transportation costs increased in New Orleans, while expensive but optional services like preK were diminished.[2] This evidence suggests that market-based reforms, intended to improve efficiency, might sometimes have the opposite effect, by increasing costs or diluting expertise.

A second concern with decentralization focuses on the equity effects of removing centralized support. School districts are meant to look out for the well-being of all students and take steps to ensure that input, access, quality, and outcomes are equitable across schools. Often, districts are expected to ensure that all students receive a minimum, adequate level of educational quality—for example, by ensuring that all buildings meet standards for safety and security, that classroom sizes are not too large, and that resources like librarians, nurses, and enrichment programs are available for all students. With limited resources, school districts act as arbiters of what is fair and just across campuses, programs, students, and employees. Often this means allocating extra supports based on specific campus needs, such as facilities investments for older buildings and intervention programs for academic improvement.

Accountability systems typically focus on outcomes by holding schools to transparent minimum standards of student performance, but often, funding and other resource allocations are not adjusted based on individual school needs.[3] It is unclear whether decentralized systems address the idea of adequacy when schools begin on unequal starting points; and if they are addressing it, then how? Many systems use some form of compensatory funding to enhance equity of inputs based on concentrations of student poverty or special needs.[4] Equity of inputs is complicated by decentralization. Should a school that is struggling academically in a decentralized system receive extra support to access experts and interventions? Should a school with an older building receive extra funds for maintenance? Should a school located far from accessible public transit receive extra transportation funds? Who should step in if a charter school cannot make payroll? These are all questions that must be eventually addressed in the design of portfolio management.

THREE TYPES OF SUPPORTS

To structure the analysis, the study examines how and why schools are supported in portfolio management systems—both for implementation of supports and for research—and potential implications around variations in the general purpose of supports. The chapter focuses on three areas of support typically present in centralized school districts, each addressing unique challenges in a decentralized setting. The first area is instructional program support, such as curricular materials, assessment, and teacher professional development. This type of support directly addresses the core educational mission of a school system, but also typically replicates or reinforces the expertise of teachers and administrators. Schools with autonomy over instruction and curriculum may or may not value centralized support for these activities, and portfolio managers need to consider whether they can support differentiated programs across schools.

The second type is administrative support, such as maintenance, human resource management, and transportation. These activities are necessary to the daily operation of a well-functioning system but often fall outside the expertise of professional educators. School leaders trained as educators may lack expertise in these areas, and administrative functions performed by educators might subtract from instructional inputs for students. It is often challenging for charter school leaders and teachers to adopt new administrative skills that are not part of typical educator training. However, it is unclear in what contexts autonomous school leaders welcome administrative support from districts rather than rejecting it as a threat to autonomy.

The third area of support is compliance-related, such as special education services and standardized testing. Compliance is often part of the core educational mission, but can also require more specialized expertise in laws and regulations. In addition, compliance is time-consuming and often considered a drain on educator time and resources. Finally, compliance activities are unique in that failure to comply at the school level often has consequences at the district level. Thus, in the area of compliance, districts might feel the need to maintain a greater level of control over schools.

THE ROLE OF CENTRAL DISTRICTS

The three systems we studied had very different designs for support, both in overall orientation and in the specific ways each balances the idealized hands-off approach with the goals and responsibilities (such as equity and legal compliance) that can be in conflict with such an approach. Reflecting this, the data suggest that supports vary dramatically across portfolio districts.

Figures 8.1A–E illustrate, by city and school type, how the surveyed school leaders perceived district supports in five specific areas: student assessment (instructional); building maintenance, transportation, and human resources (administrative); and special education (compliance). The figures show how infrequently New Orleans schools received supports from their portfolio managers, with virtually no support in any area except the federally mandated areas of assessment and services for special-needs students. By comparison, Denver Public Schools (DPS) provides supports for most schools of all types in areas such as transportation, building maintenance, and special-needs services, as well as support for human resource management for both traditional and semiautonomous district-governed schools. The Los Angeles Unified School District (LAUSD) provides supports in all five areas for most district-governed schools, both traditional and autonomous, but provides virtually no support for charter schools. Thus, we observed three distinctly different profiles of supports: New Orleans with minimal supports, Denver with

FIGURE 8.1 **The role of portfolio managers in school supports**

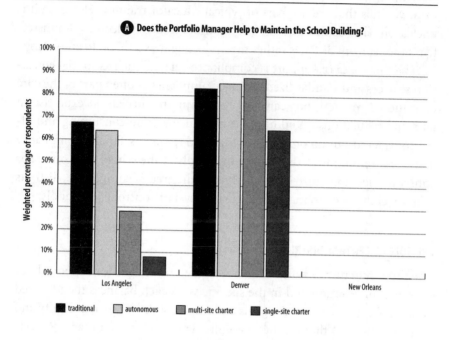

A Does the Portfolio Manager Help to Maintain the School Building?

(y-axis: Weighted percentage of respondents)

Legend: traditional · autonomous · multi-site charter · single-site charter

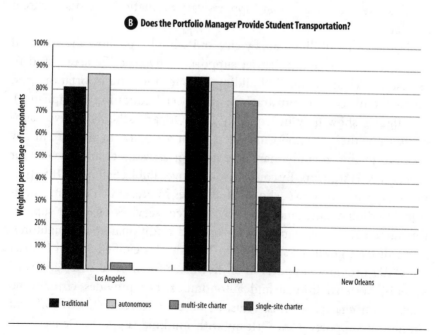

B Does the Portfolio Manager Provide Student Transportation?

(y-axis: Weighted percentage of respondents)

Legend: traditional · autonomous · multi-site charter · single-site charter

FIGURE 8.1   The role of portfolio managers in school supports, *continued*

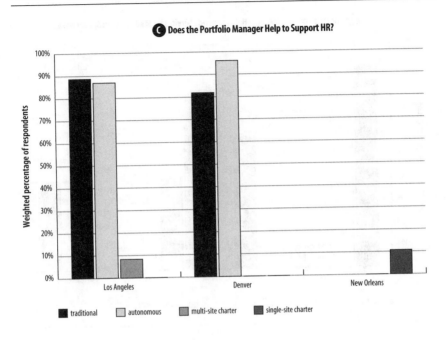

C Does the Portfolio Manager Help to Support HR?

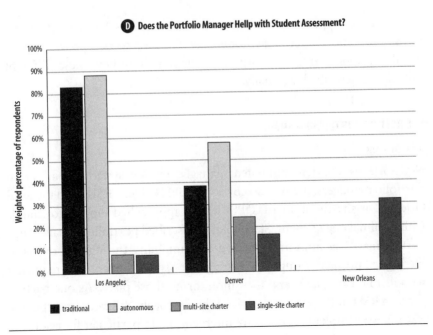

D Does the Portfolio Manager Hellp with Student Assessment?

FIGURE 8.1   The role of portfolio managers in school supports, *continued*

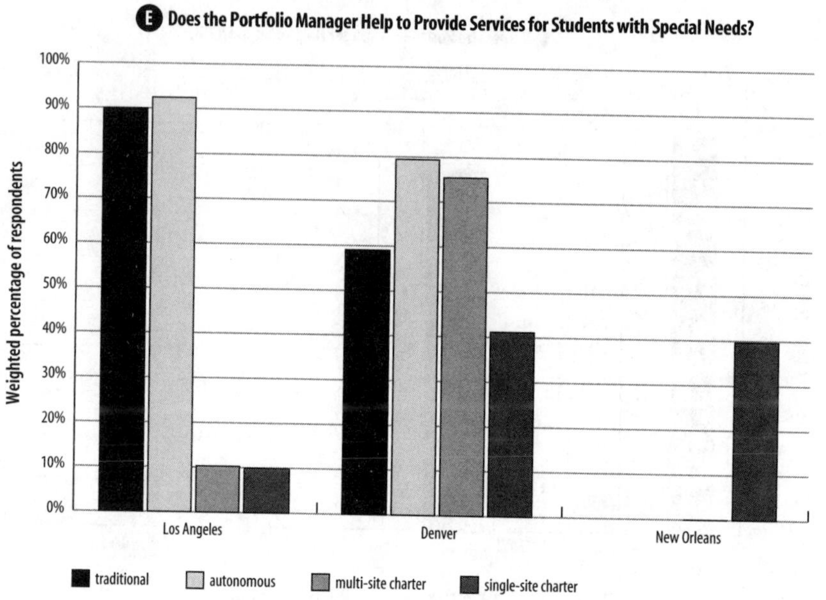

E Does the Portfolio Manager Help to Provide Services for Students with Special Needs?

support for all types of schools in some areas, and Los Angeles with selective support for district-run schools only. The next section provides more detailed evidence from case studies to demonstrate how these different models are described internally.

THE ROLE OF PORTFOLIO MANAGERS

New Orleans

New Orleans' charter-dominated managed market system includes two portfolio managers, the state Recovery School District (RSD) and the local Orleans Parish School Board (OPSB). Both approached support to schools with minimal engagement. Stakeholders described portfolio manager support primarily as authorization and accountability through a process of identifying problem campuses, placing schools in interventions, requiring schools to create plans, and then monitoring those plans. As one participant, an RSD staff member, described the approach, "It's not support in the way that you think of . . . intensive intervention. In particular for academic concerns, we're not sending in the curriculum team to go help them fix their third-grade math curriculum." Instead, participants described port-folio managers helping schools self-identify areas of improvement and connect with other organizations that could provide support through holding up a metaphorical mirror to schools in order to "give them an objective view on things."

Even the small number of traditional district-run schools in New Or-leans noted a shift to a minimal district role. District staff described how instructional supports that were broadly provided by the district in the past were now only offered on an as-needed basis. One OPSB staff per-son suggested that "Our relationship with [traditional public schools] is different . . . because they are not charter schools, but there, too, we want to empower those educators and hold them accountable. We do have more obligations to provide support but want to do that in a way that's empowering, as opposed to an intervention process." OPSB maintained some involvement around issues of compliance for both direct-run and charter schools, particularly in the areas of special education and student expulsion. While this could be seen as infringing on school autonomy, one charter school principal viewed this involvement more positively: "I would prefer to have a laundry list of things that I must do to make sure that I maintain compliance, rather than just giving me carte blanche access to how we sculpt those policies, and we miss something that's important." This orientation may make particular sense for compliance supports, where the tensions between autonomy and support may be minimized, since the focus is on meeting federal legal requirements with consequences of non-compliance for both the school and the portfolio manager.

The RSD had even less internal capacity to directly support schools under its authority. Recovery district staff described a deliberate strategy of minimal supports to the charter schools it authorized, as most support was viewed as being in conflict with school-based autonomy. For example, one RSD staff person commented: "Let's say we did [identify] this set of issues that were there. Now do we mandate that they do XYZ? Let's say if we come up with a solution, do we mandate that they follow XYZ? If we do, then we're sort of infringing on the autonomy that we gave them in the first place."

Overall, the role of portfolio managers in New Orleans is narrower than the role of portfolio managers in the other cities we studied, and is focused primarily on helping schools identify needs, access external sources of support, and address critical compliance issues. This is explicitly related to a systemwide commitment to autonomy over top-down interventions and mandated strategies.

Los Angeles

In Los Angeles, the central school district is responsible for district schools, while charter schools are typically authorized by the state. Thus, as has been mentioned, the systems are in competition with one another. In terms of school supports, this plays out through starkly different levels of supports provided by the local school district. The district's traditional and semi-autonomous school models received substantial support from the district, while charter schools received virtually no support. Interviews suggested that even among district-run schools, the district grappled with the best ways to deliver support to schools with varied levels of autonomy.

Since the LAUSD is a large district covering a vast geographic area, its central office faced the challenge of delivering supports to hundreds of diverse campuses across a large geographic area. The district allocated support services through subunit offices located across the city. Not long before data collection, the LAUSD had reorganized local offices from a structure based on both geography and school type to one based entirely on geography. In the prior organization, one subunit had housed an Intensive Support and Innovation Center that provided tailored supports for schools with similar governance structures. This allowed semi-autonomous schools, such as pilot schools, to receive supports in a way that acknowledged the challenges of balancing supports with autonomy. The new structure has the advantage of moving supports geographically closer to schools, but there is no longer a subunit with specific expertise in supporting more autonomous school models. As one central office staff member noted: "Most of the directors we work with at pilot schools when we had [the Intensive Support and Innovation Center] were either former pilot school principals themselves or directors who had worked with pilot schools before. They understood what it meant or what it would look like. When we reorganized last year and we were moved into this local district . . . that wealth of knowledge and experience waned." Despite this, principals at pilot and magnet schools reported getting good support from their directors. At the pilot school, the principal said: "I think my needs are very different than traditional needs. I may not need support every day. I may not need feedback every day. I know from my leadership that I can call my director. If he doesn't have the answer, he would seek out the assistance and support. That way I think it's beneficial."

Respondents in Los Angeles also reported that the availability of district resources was inconsistent across schools. Some respondents lauded the availability of professional development opportunities and school-based instructional coaches. Others, such as this administrator at a traditional public school, noted that the district experts are hard to access: "We don't see [those experts] in the school. If you want them in the school, you really have to call and make an appointment at the beginning [of the school year]. It's very hard. It's very hard. It's not something that the district regularly does with the schools."

The portfolio manager's approach to compliance-related supports was similar for traditional and semiautonomous district schools, but there was substantial variation in how different semiautonomous school models received other types of support. For example, network partnership schools that, by design, operated in collaboration with a nonprofit partner received support from both the partner and the school district. One such partner, the nonprofit Partnership for Los Angeles Schools, takes on many typical support activities for a cluster of semiautonomous schools. This model allows for more differentiated supports across schools.

Other semiautonomous models were supported only by the district directly. In this case, accessing district support often came into tension with semiautonomous schools' missions to provide unique programs and innovations. District-provided supports and expertise were limited to selected programs (curriculum, assessments, or professional development), and comparable support was not necessarily available if schools wanted to opt for alternative programs. Thus, the benefits of economies of scale might pivot semiautonomous schools toward programs selected by the central office when extra support was needed. For example, one pilot school decided not to use the district's assessments but, as a result, did not get any district support for professional development around the form of assessment that the school did choose. One teacher said, "We [in the school] miss out on the additional resources that other schools receive when they adopt whatever curriculum the district is adopting. We don't get professional development money that goes along with that."

This institutionalized support system for district schools was contrasted with minimal supports around the instructional and administrative work of charter schools. The district operated a substantial charter school office that primarily focused on compliance, both with charter contracts and federal and state regulations (see chapter 4). The leader at one stand-alone charter found this type of oversight helpful, commenting, "What I appreciate about [the district] is that they do remind—it's like good reminders: 'Oh, did we send that letter out, did we do that?' It's compliance." Those working in charter schools found this approach appropriate, as they saw it as allowing them to largely maintain their autonomy.

Denver

Compared to the other portfolio management systems, Denver's centralized portfolio strategy was designed to provide broad support to both charter and district schools, with specific types of support differentiated based on school needs as well as school type. A consistent message from those working with DPS was that decisions were tied back to thinking around the "three equities" central to the district's vision: the "equity of opportunity," "equity of responsibility and access," and "equity of accountability."[5] Denver stakeholders acknowledged the possibility of a transition to portfolio management creating more unequal and less adequate levels of school supports. Centrally provided support was considered important to counteract potential limitations of market approaches. One high-level DPS staff person said: "[In this district, we ask,] How do you create systems and structures in a multiple provider environment that drive greater equity rather than decrease equity? Because part of the experience in many marketplaces, and marketplaces are not equity-driven, and we certainly see that in many places with charters across the country that I think that charters in many ways have not been forces for equity."

In Denver, achieving equity of opportunity was described as requiring resource support for all school types and structures that balanced supports with accountability and responsibility. In practice, this included providing charter schools and semiautonomous innovation schools with supports in specific areas such as transportation, facilities, and special education, with the expectation that schools would work toward shared district goals. For example, charter schools could receive support for transportation and facilities only if they adopted certain enrollment practices that help the system as a whole, such as accepting new students after application deadlines and/or during the school year. Thus, Denver's autonomous schools often chose to implement district preferences in return for extra support and resources.

An illustrative example of deeper integration of district supports into charter schools is the district's practice of requiring some charter schools housed in district buildings to operate specialized centers for students with particular disabilities. Because of the central role of these centers in delivery of special-needs services in the system, housing a center transformed the relationship between the charter school and the district to increase both district oversight and district support. According on one foundation representative, "Now that we have so many charters that run center-based programs, they really rely on the district for support and help there."

While the equity-of-opportunity focus meant an emphasis on sharing resources across school types, there were important differences in supports offered to district-run schools and charter schools. This approach was designed to minimize the potential for support to restrict innovation. Supports for charter schools tended to focus on building internal capacity to improve through principal support and intervention, while supports for district schools could include more direct intervention by the district. For example, while the district might intervene directly with professional development for school teachers in a struggling traditional school, such an effort at a charter school might include central office staff advising school leaders, who would then enact their own interventions for teachers. The DPS website described these supports as "building the capacity of [the charter school's] leaders and school boards to improve a school's program in alignment with its mission." This focus on working with leaders reflected one way to try to balance autonomy with support.

While Denver's central office did not prescribe specific strategies for charter schools, it did offer opportunities for charter educators to participate in district-provided trainings. Supports were also available for newly opened charter schools, including leadership coaching and strategies for serving English language learners. Finally, one notable overall aspect of support for Denver charter schools was how district staff sought to intertwine oversight and support by focusing specifically on leaders and charter boards. One former district staff person described the approach in this way:

> There's a couple things that are nonnegotiable. We come in and walk your building in year one and give you our best analysis of what's happening, because, in our experience, if you're still struggling by year three, your chances of getting it right for year four when you're up statutorily for renewal are pretty minimal. Lots of schools can turn from year one to year two . . . be able to really engage in deep continuous improvement, so it's the early gift of reflective feedback that I think is really important. We sit in on board meetings—that's not a standard part of all authorizing practices— because we understand that the board is the lever for change in support of the CMO's CEO or the single-site principal, and so we want to make sure we understand if there's high governance capacity.

While Denver stakeholders sought to treat all schools as part of the same system, the district also tried to differentiate supports based both on school autonomy and school needs. In this system, both the level and type of supports experienced by individual schools varied substantially.

THE ROLE OF CHARTER MANAGEMENT ORGANIZATIONS

The varied approaches to school support in the three case cities affect how CMOs offer and provide support to the schools they operate. A school operating with oversight from both a CMO and a portfolio manager may experience conflicting pressures. Figure 8.2 reports survey data from school leaders demonstrating the important but also varied supports provided by CMOs in all three cities. The data indicate some areas of consistency across the cities in the role of CMOs, as well as some ways in which the local role of districts shaped the practices of CMOs.

In the New Orleans and Los Angeles charter sectors, principals reported that portfolio managers were mostly not engaged in the basic operation of charter schools (for example, building maintenance). For these two cities, CMOs supported at least some schools in all the categories shown in figure 8.2. Some CMOs in New Orleans and Los Angeles (and, to a lesser extent, in Denver) operated similarly to small district offices, providing

FIGURE 8.2   **The role of CMOs in school supports**

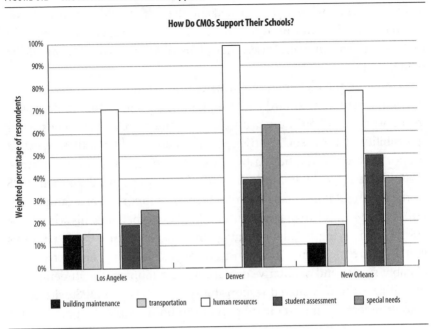

administrative supports as well as largely directing the educational program. This combination of supports and control had emerged over time in response to challenges that a given CMO's schools had faced. As a staff member from New Orleans CMO described, issues around compliance and special education led the CMO to be more prescriptive:

> We've definitely seen the bad side of—I don't know that I'd call it autonomy—but mistakes made with special ed or that kind of thing. . . . We just had an audit from our authorizer, who was like, "Your folders in special education are a mess" . . . We went to [the school] and said, "Look, this will never happen again. Here's a list of things that need to happen. We're going to review every single folder that we have. We are going to send network people to support you, and we want a list that all these things are correct."

In another example from Los Angeles, one staff person described how, if a school was struggling, CMO staff would first meet internally and then meet with the leader. In the latter meeting, CMO staff and the leader would "reflect on what had happened and the areas that they had successes and the areas that they need to grow in. Then we would create a plan for that to happen." In some cases, that plan could lead to the firing of the school leader.

In Denver, the higher level of district involvement created a somewhat different orientation toward CMO support. CMOs were still very engaged in the work of schools, but with clearly defined areas that were the responsibility of DPS (such as transportation and facilities), these types of supports were not duplicated by CMOs (see figure 8.2). In other areas, CMOs were responsible for both support and oversight. Even then, DPS worked with CMOs to create comprehensive supports. For example, the leader of one CMO-managed charter school described how his school had "really been trying to take advantage of [its] partnership with DPS this year in more individual departments like [its] learning support teams." Notably, survey and qualitative data found that supports for students with special needs were a shared responsibility of CMOs and DPS, with some schools reporting important supports from both. While the potential for conflicting demands from CMOs and district personnel was present, regular conversations helped to mitigate this potential through a clear shared understanding of the support responsibilities of each.

THE ROLE OF OUTSIDE ORGANIZATIONS

A diminished role for the school district creates the opportunity for other private sector organizations (both nonprofit and for-profit) to emerge. While potentially important for all schools in a more decentralized system, this might be particularly important when district supports are minimal and for stand-alone charter schools that operate without a CMO. All three systems, as described in examples below, included large nonprofit organizations that took on multiple direct support activity with groups of autonomous schools, often operating in a district-like capacity. This was complemented by smaller, more specialized organizations that expanded or enhanced services in areas such as the arts, family supports, and even school culture, instruction, and curriculum. Finally, the systems differed as to how the full system supported schools, whether outsourcing school activities to external providers or developing leadership within schools to build internal capacity.

As illustrated in figures 8.3A–E, Denver school leaders reported very few outside supports in a system where the district continued to provide many supports for all types of schools. By comparison, outside organizations often provided support for charter schools in Los Angeles and New Orleans. Stand-alone charter schools, which lack the support of a CMO, more frequently reported support from outside organizations in most areas. These findings suggest that to understand portfolio management, we must also examine the broader ecosystem of organizations that contribute to school capacity.

Nonprofits in New Orleans

New Orleans is notable for the expansive ecosystem of nonprofit organizations that are actively involved in public schools of all types. The post-Katrina school reform movement included a planned effort to develop

FIGURE 8.3   **The role of outside organizations in school supports**

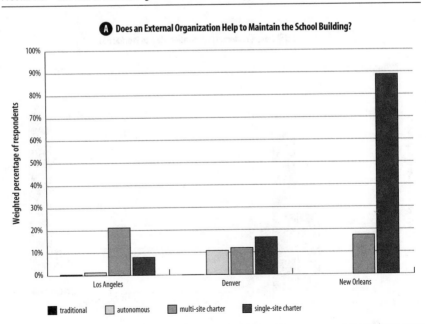

A Does an External Organization Help to Maintain the School Building?

FIGURE 8.3   **The role of outside organizations in school supports, *continued***

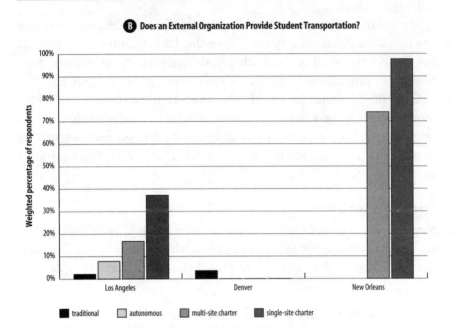

B Does an External Organization Provide Student Transportation?

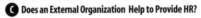

C Does an External Organization Help to Provide HR?

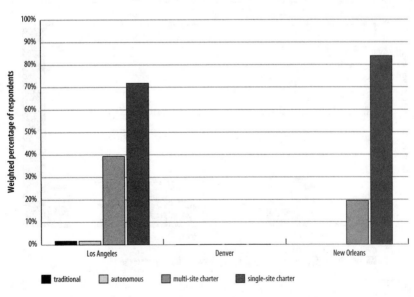

FIGURE 8.3   **The role of outside organizations in school supports, *continued***

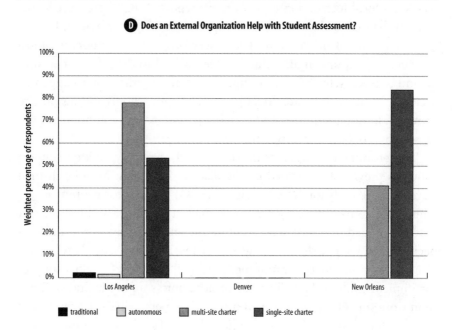

D **Does an External Organization Help with Student Assessment?**

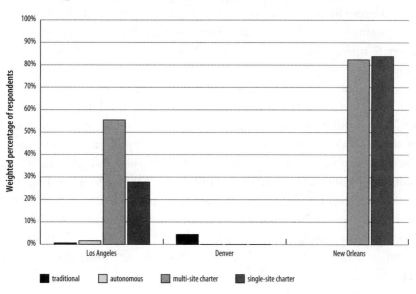

E **Does an External Organization Help to Provide Services for Students with Special Needs?**

nonprofit capacity to support schools in the absence of a powerful central district. A local foundation representative reported that there were, at the time of data collection, over 440 nonprofits serving children and youth in the city (about one nonprofit for every one hundred students), most of which were founded after Katrina. He pointed to the intentional work behind this ecosystem: "This [nonprofit sector growth] didn't happen by accident, some of them are directly in response to schools and needing to provide additional supports and gaps in the system that were not being addressed by a decentralized system."

Two prominent nonprofits in New Orleans explicitly took on support activities previously provided by the district—although in quite distinct ways. New Schools for New Orleans (NSNO) is the most prominent example of a nonprofit taking on typical district support activities in a way that is intended to honor school autonomy and build internal school capacity. NSNO supports a large group of local charter schools with curriculum, instruction, programming, coaching, and even financial support for implementation. Specific areas of academic support included Common Core transition, data-driven instruction, personalized learning, and special education. NSNO also conducted school reviews of some charter schools, in partnership with the RSD, that were intended to shine a light on challenges schools were facing and potential areas for improvement. NSNO brought substantial new resources to the city through active fundraising from private donors and foundations. Filling a traditional school district's role, NSNO also served as the lead agency for large federal education grants to the city.

Importantly, NSNO is associated with a specific set of instructional practices, including the use of data and teacher coaching to foster instructional improvement. While supports are provided at the discretion of school leaders, schools that receive NSNO supports are signing on to the organization's preferred strategies. The reach and influence of NSNO is quite substantial. One participant estimated that NSNO is involved in at least half the schools in the city. While the supports have been instrumental in both basic school operations and improvement processes, NSNO's broad reach raises the possibility that the preferred curriculum and instructional approaches of its donors and staff have replaced the democratic representation of the school district.

A second organization providing support to a large number of schools—in a very different way—is the East Bank Collaborative (EBC). EBC emerged to provide district-like supports for single-site charter schools that lacked the economies of scale of CMOs or districts. EBC's mission is to support diverse and independent charter schools without imposing preferred models or strategies. The supports provided by EBC were considered important to the goal of maintaining a diverse selection of charter schools in the city and preventing the consolidation of schools under a small number of large CMOs. Contrasted with NSNO's more comprehensive education support strategy, EBC is described as providing mostly administrative services, such as human resources management and legal services, that fall outside the expertise of educators and do not impose any particular educational or instructional preferences. Similarly, the state-level Louisiana Association of Public Charter Schools provides support for charter boards, governance, and operations without dictating preferred education models.

Among the hundreds of nonprofits in the city, national organizations provided a broad range of typical district supports. For instance, Teach for America, Relay Graduate School, the Teacher Advancement Program, and others provide professional development and training for a large number of New Orleans teachers and support the teacher pipeline. The Achievement Network also has a substantial presence in the areas of student assessment and data analysis techniques.

Many peripheral education programs are outsourced to local nonprofits in New Orleans. This was facilitated to some extent by local nonprofit incubators, such as the Propeller Incubator, which provided seed grants to start-ups in education and other areas, and 4.0 Schools, which supports the development and scale-up of educational innovations. School services that were outsourced to local nonprofits included arts education, physical education, mentoring, tutoring, family support, and school social workers. These partnerships gave nonprofits the opportunity to influence the core values of charter schools.

Overall, practices in New Orleans suggest that a broader portfolio system can include numerous external organizations that fill gaps caused by diminished district support. These included both capacity-building supports such as principal and teacher development and ongoing outsourcing of both instructional and noninstructional activities. Whether these supports are available consistently across schools, however, is unclear, and the distribution of support is an important potential distinction between supports from a traditional central office and those obtained from a nonprofit ecosystem.

Nonprofits in Los Angeles

The intentional development of a system of school support organizations was not as visible in Los Angeles as in New Orleans, but schools did tap into a broad network of education-related organizations and interested funders in the city. Survey results suggest that charter schools were more likely to receive support from external organizations than district-run schools. Single-site charter schools were most likely to report external support in areas such as human resources management and building maintenance, while CMO schools were most likely to receive support for instructional services.

Los Angeles offers another interesting example of school supports being intentionally shifted from the district to an independent nonprofit. The nonprofit Partnership for Los Angeles Schools (PLAS) was created to support schools in the network partnership model, specifically taking on some district support activities for these schools. The partnership school model was designed to provide opportunities for district-run schools to gain both autonomy and more focused support from a nonprofit organization, thus providing a distinct response to the tension between autonomy and support. However, in a centralized hierarchy, this arrangement of dual support from the district and the nonprofit created new challenges.

On the one hand, partnership schools that were consistently low performing had access to additional financial resources through PLAS, as well as assistance from PLAS with fundraising and instructional expertise. On the other hand, participants identified challenges in balancing the dual expectations of the district and the nonprofit. A union representative who had worked with personnel in multiple partnership schools said: "[Principals] are taking direction from the local district and from the outside partner. It is really making the life of the principal next to impossible . . . because the pattern has been what's important to the local district is not necessarily important to the partnership. . . . Sometimes it's like, 'Oh my God.' You're being pulled in two different—because you're still a district school."

In addition, teachers expressed that promised resources, such as technology, playground equipment, and facilities improvements, were sometimes not delivered due to breakdowns in the communications among school, district, and nonprofit. This reveals problems that can emerge when multiple organizations provide oversight and support for a single school. Fewer problems emerged when those school leaders had autonomy that allowed them to choose supports. For examples, one school leader said that both the district and PLAS provided data and analysis, but that the school worked more closely with PLAS in this area and found their support more helpful.

Other supports reported in Los Angeles came from community-oriented nonprofits that partnered with schools outside of the district structure; such relationships are not necessarily particular to a portfolio management context or to charter schools. For example, school leaders across school types cited organizations such as museums and universities providing enrichment programs for students. In addition, many charters, including some managed by CMOs, also contracted for administrative and compliance support from organizations that had specifically emerged to serve the growing charter movement. One such organization, ExED, describes itself as "a mission-driven nonprofit" that is "advancing public education in Southern California by providing quality charter schools with sound business solutions."[6] Overall, both the survey data and case studies point to important involvement by nonprofits in Los Angeles, but not to the extent found in New Orleans. However, there are indications that some instructional and administrative supports that continue to be provided by the district for its direct-run schools are now being provided to charter schools by an emerging nonprofit sector.

Nonprofits in Denver

Denver also has an ecosystem of nonprofit school support organizations—both newly emerged and long-standing—but survey evidence suggests a smaller presence than in Los Angeles or New Orleans. In line with the DPS focus on supporting school leaders as a primary way to enhance school improvement efforts, both district staff and outside organizations provided leader-focused capacity-building services to district-run and charter school leaders. For example, Relay Graduate School of Education initially supported local charter leaders and then was brought in to provide professional learning opportunities for some leaders in DPS-run schools as well.

The provision of services to both district-run and charter schools by outside organizations reinforced the idea of the centralized portfolio, with

support organizations working across school types. There are indications that the use of outside organizations offers greater flexibility than
district-driven support. For example, one traditional school principal
cited a nonprofit organization, Achievement Network, as providing school
improvement services in place of direct district intervention: "When we
first started doing Guided Reading Plus, that was all district support for
that. . . . That was a mandate back then, but next year we have autonomy
for who we work with for our assessments, and we've chosen ANet again.
It's started as working with them, but it's something we see [as] valuable."

Other organizations, however, focused exclusively on the charter sector.
For example, the Colorado League of Charter Schools offers its services
to any charter school in the state, including networking, board training,
and administrative support for purchasing and facilities. One study participant indicated that stand-alone charter schools are particularly likely
to use these services. "We act as that district for charter schools," said one
League staff member, "so they can access group purchasing power with
our umbrella. That's a great advantage to them." As in other cities, this
is another mechanism to address the loss of economies of scale faced by
stand-alone charters.

Finally, the Luminary Learning Network (LLN) was a distinct type of
support organization that worked with four innovation schools in Denver
at the time of the study. The LLN provided or facilitated some supports to
schools and also negotiated for additional autonomy and budget control
with the DPS central office. This idea of a third party negotiating school
autonomies with a district is unlikely to be seen outside of a portfolio management context. While the LLN had some similarities with a CMO, it explicitly had less authority over schools, and schools could choose whether
to be a part of the network. An educational advocate who had supported
the emergence of the LLN as the first "innovation zone" of schools said
that the organization was intended to "allow schools to empower and lead
on their own." He added, "I think the people involved in the zone believe
that the schools are the unit of change, and that it's identifying leaders with
the capacity to run a truly autonomous model, and that the LLN serves
as the accountability system to ensure that's being done accurately and to
be some sort of facilitator on best practice sharing and distribution of resources, but not a management organization."

Overall, outside organizations were cited less often in Denver than in other cities and often in conjunction with district school improvement programs. The smaller role of outside organizations in DPS aligned with the larger role the portfolio manager plays in all types of schools.

ISSUES AND TENSIONS IN SUPPORT SYSTEM DESIGN

While the study cannot point to an ideal model for portfolio management, evidence from New Orleans, Los Angeles, and Denver points to several tensions, particularly related to the multiple PMM mechanisms, that are likely to be found in any PMM system. While decentralization is meant to improve upon the limited capacity of district central offices to effectively support all schools and all students, it introduces risks and uncertainty. Achieving balance between centralized support, fair and effective oversight, adequate access to needed supports, and school manager discretion will require responsiveness to these tensions.

Support Versus Oversight

The first tension relates to whether the school district, as the principal in the district-school contract, can simultaneously be a support agency for school managers. Does the new district role of overseeing contracts and accountability with consequences conflict with the traditional district role of helping schools to identify needs and work toward improvement?

Of the three case study cites, Denver is the one where the PMM design institutionalized the district as central to both accountability and school support and improvement. Participants saw this as potential conflict of interest: one respondent told us that Denver has "blurred the line" between accountability and support. In this context, one board member expressed concerns that involvement in school supports made high-stakes accountability decisions more challenging: "I think there's an inherent conflict of interest in the system, the way we do it now. . . . If you've got people who are on the same team in schools all day long trying to help those district-run schools do a better job, and those same people then are deciding . . . how schools are evaluated, what schools need to be closed. I think you're going to have just a human-built bias to bend over backwards to help the schools that they're managing on a day-to-day basis."

While DPS has taken on this expanded role in school improvement with potentially problematic consequences for accountability and resources, the portfolio managers' roles in New Orleans are more minimal, and CMOs or outside organizations are more commonly providing school support. The consequence of this arrangement in New Orleans, however, was a lack of consistently available supports for improvement, which may be tied to more school closures. One representative of an advocacy organization, who was generally supportive of the reforms, described it this way: "We've kinda said, 'Here's your operating agreement. We'll see you in four years.' All of a sudden, it's like, 'Oh, you've done terrible. You're done. We're moving on.'"

This debate also played out in efforts in Los Angeles to create a variety of models of semiautonomous district schools. For example, network partnership schools were jointly supported by nonprofit partners and the district. School leaders sometimes felt pulled in multiple directions; for example, they might have to attend redundant meetings and give redundant assessments. One principal commented,

> I've worked under two local districts, and within each local district, there seems to be different priorities, and there's different management systems. Even within the partnership, because they're a whole different entity that has their own management. Working here at the partnership school, I have to be tactful in the ways that—how I utilize my time, and how I interact with both entities, because I have an LAUSD boss. I have a partnership boss.

Thus, greater autonomy and enhanced support were accompanied by more complex oversight.

Support Versus Autonomy

A closely related tension that emerges in any decentralization process is the degree to which support systems conflict with the benefits of autonomy. In portfolio systems, this tension suggests that reliance on external support can diminish a school's independence. This was a topic of ongoing debate in all three case study sites and was managed differently in each. For example, a staff person in New Orleans' RSD described explicit and ongoing debate about when the district should intervene in struggling schools:

As we've debated it, not just us as an organization, but us as an ecosystem, there is a divide amongst the reformers about this very issue. I squarely fall on the side of we should intervene, because we are government and ... we're the backstop and we are responsible. If a school isn't doing what they're supposed to do, then we should intervene, and if intervening means scaling back some ... or infringing on their autonomy at some point, then it kind of is what it is. That's the exchange, because we are ultimately responsible.

While supports from organizations that have oversight responsibilities, especially portfolio managers, can diminish autonomy, in some schools supports were intentionally optional, such as when charter schools in Denver had access to district-offered professional development. However, rendering supports optional does not completely eliminate the tension between autonomy and support. For example, while semiautonomous schools in Los Angeles did not have to use district-provided systems, the lack of available resources for alternative systems sometimes left them with the choice of either using district systems or trying to identify additional resources to pay for other systems or developing systems within the school. This may leave schools that have fewer resources in a position where it does not make fiscal sense to move away from district-driven options even if such moves may be more consistent with the school's mission.

Looking across the systems, we see that portfolio systems must determine areas in which schools can exercise discretion and areas in which portfolio managers' direct involvement and support are necessary to meet system goals. New Orleans' design intentionally seeks to maximize school discretion in most areas, and both portfolio managers saw this as necessitating minimal support. However, these authorizers also removed school discretion and mandated centralized supports in areas where equity problems emerged in the system, such as enrollment and student expulsion. The district office in Denver also maintains control of enrollment and other areas. Other supports are typically optional, giving schools some control over the degree of district involvement in the schools. The LAUSD offers broad autonomy to charter schools through minimal, compliance-based involvement, but struggles to provide meaningful autonomy for its district-run autonomous school models. To prevent this tension between autonomy and support from being a problem, districts need to find the appropriate balance between portfolio manager involvement and school autonomy.

Inequality of Support in Decentralized Systems

A third core tension is whether increased local control creates problematic inequalities due to differences in school capacity. In portfolio management systems, schools will vary in the capacity and expertise of school managers and staff, as well as in financial resources, social networks, and student and neighborhood context. Absent potentially equalizing efforts by a central district, this can create inequalities that impact students. The three case studies showed that these types of inequalities are real and important in portfolio systems, and that there are no easy solutions.

LAUSD sought to balance these issues by providing district-run schools with intensive district supports while prioritizing autonomy over support for charter schools, which relied largely on CMOs or other organizations. District schools were receiving more support directly through central or regional offices than charter schools, and so charter schools needed to seek supports elsewhere. Charter schools unable to build a support system through fundraising or partnerships were less able to access potentially valuable opportunities.

This was also the situation for most schools in New Orleans. While OPSB provided some additional supports to its direct-run schools, support available to charter schools varied depending on school resources, networks, and context. Some schools were supported by large, well-funded CMOs, while others operated independently. Some principals participated in school leader support groups, while others were more isolated. Some schools received services from nonprofit partners, while others did not. Some paid fees out of school budgets for supports, while others were able to access supports for free from nonprofits with external funding. This created inequalities between schools, with some struggling to obtain needed supports.

Denver provides an example of a middle ground, where the district committed to provide support, if needed, to try to tackle some inequities in school resources. DPS specifically targeted supports in areas tied to potential inequities—such as student transportation—so that students could access more school options. We see above that this creates an uncomfortable role conflict for the district.

Support from Private Organizations Versus Democratic Control

In addition to the issue of inequality in access to external support, diminished central office capacity opens the education system to broader participation of, and therefore greater influence from, external organizations. This creates a tension between democratic control, as enacted through elected school boards, and the power of private organizations. A familiar concern about privatization of school management is the threat that large, well-funded organizations will come to dominate local education decision-making—for example, through the role of national CMOs such as KIPP, Achievement First, and Success Academies. Because these CMOs are governed by private, nonelected boards, there are concerns that their involvement in public schools may undermine local democracy and stakeholder participation. Similar concerns exist about stand-alone charter schools, whose board members may also represent private or corporate interests, as well as about the role of large, private organizations in school support and improvement processes and the role of major foundations that support nonprofits and charter schools.

These concerns are playing out in the expanded ecosystem of school support organizations, particularly in New Orleans, but also in Los Angeles and Denver. Granting school managers discretion to choose new sources of support does not guarantee that they have access to a broad range of choices that reflect local preferences. In all three systems, large national organizations played a substantial role in teacher and leader development and student assessment, suggesting that the preferred instructional, classroom management, and assessment strategies of these organizations may be privileged.

While New Orleans had a significant locally grown ecosystem of supportive nonprofits, NSNO in particular provided so many low-cost resources to charter schools that the preferred instructional approaches of their board members (and presumably their donors) appeared to be given greater validation in the city—again, without the approval of a democratically elected school board. This creates an additional tension between autonomy and support, because not only CMOs but also other supportive organizations are indirectly making education policy by serving as the only and/or the most affordable provider of necessary services.

Portfolio Management and the Internal Capacity of Schools

A final tension implicit in both the design of PMMs and the fundamental issues of school autonomy is the opportunity for school supports to be delivered in the form of outsourced services rather than in the form of internal capacity building. In short, should PMMs be designed such that school leaders have access to ongoing assistance, or should supports be designed for the short term, with a long-term goal of school-based self-sufficiency? We observed distinctly different approaches toward capacity building across the cities and also within cities across school types. Overall, districts that provided supports tended to provide direct assistance to traditional schools and leadership development to more autonomous school models. Leadership supports are, in theory, a strategy to provide support while honoring the leaders' autonomy and their consequent right to make decisions about school programs. Supports that were provided by CMOs included a mix of direct assistance and leadership development, with direct assistance often focused on operational tasks such as human resources and accounting.

At the school level, outside organizations provided both fully outsourced services and support for internal development. Outsourcing primarily included areas outside of the typical expertise of educators, such as school bus services and building maintenance. Many schools also outsourced direct education services such as physical education and art classes, student assessment, and student support services such as social workers, mentoring, and tutoring. Other schools used outside providers to help build internal capacity. For example, rather than outsourcing art instruction, some programs trained teachers to integrate art into all classrooms.

The conditions under which schools can exploit economies of scale through outsourcing, and whether the financial gains are offset by losses in educational quality, are open questions. When a portfolio system is looked at overall, outsourcing of central educational services raises the question of whether expanding the ecosystem of involved organizations enhances or impedes the system's capacity to improve. In practice, autonomy and capacity are intrinsically linked such that a school leader with low school capacity who must rely on external support is not as free to execute autonomous decision making. Thus, a system focused on school innovation and improvement may want to consider investing in capacity-building activities for all types of schools around the instructional program, school culture, and so on. However, in areas outside the expertise of educators, outsourcing to specialized providers (food services, transportation, legal experts, and the like) might free up space for school leaders to focus on instructional improvements rather than day-to-day operations. Outsourcing may also have benefits in schools with high staff turnover (see chapter 7), as building the capacity of educators could be less useful or efficient in the long run.

The portfolio management systems in New Orleans, Los Angeles, and Denver all have the potential to benefit from the specialization and innovation that can result from decentralization. However, these benefits potentially come at the cost of lost economies of scale and more varied access to resources across school sites. In our analysis, we found that portfolio management systems struggled to identify and implement a level of support for schools that both offered expertise and resources and worked in tandem with efforts to grant schools broad discretion. For example, in both Los Angeles and New Orleans, there was often an implicit assumption that schools either have support from the PM alongside limited autonomy, or limited support alongside substantial autonomy. In Denver, on the other hand, the district office sought to identify ways in which the system could be designed such that schools could receive enhanced autonomy (although less than the most autonomous schools in the other cities) while also benefiting from portfolio management supports in an effort to promote systemwide equity.

LESSONS FROM EXISTING PORTFOLIO SYSTEM DESIGNS

In theory, the decentralization found in PMMs enables schools to tap into an array of support resources to better address the needs identified within a building. Overall, some similarities in approaches to support appear across the systems, but critical differences reflected the distinct orientation of leaders and portfolio managers in each city, and there were also critical differences in context. For example, all portfolio managers provided at least some level of support around issues of compliance, while instructional and administrative supports varied across settings. Schools were most likely to rely on internal capacity for instructional program supports, while some CMOs and districts also provided substantial supports in this realm if they were focused on a clearly defined instructional program implemented across schools. Administrative supports were often provided by districts and CMOs or contracted out to other organizations.

New Orleans offers evidence that a vibrant private sector can replace a bureaucracy as the primary support system for public schools. However, this required a planned and well-funded effort to create a system of supportive organizations. In a few areas—including enrollment and expulsion—severe inequity for students led to the recentralization and expansion of the central district role.

In Los Angeles, the district maintained expertise and capacity to provide a broad range of supports to district-run schools, but limited its involvement in supporting charters, as was consistent with a focus on charter autonomy. This system led to common conflicts regarding support and discretion alongside different ways of viewing the allocation of public resources to schools by type (with resources largely devolved to charter schools but held more centrally for district-run schools).

In Denver, the portfolio manager explicitly took responsibility for the successes and failures of schools across the system, taking a larger role in support for all types of schools (especially when they were struggling). However, this expanded role often complicated the tensions between support and oversight, as the district played an active role in both promoting success and taking responsibility for sanctioning failures.

The study's findings suggest that there may be important trade-offs in PMMs between schools receiving adequate supports and portfolio managers' efforts to provide both discretion to and oversight of those schools. With portfolio managers historically serving as the primary source of school supports, the study's findings raise questions about the conditions under which other organizations can fill those gaps and the new sets of skills needed by school leaders, especially, in terms of determining what supports are needed and who can best provide them.

Additionally, the idealized PMM includes an ever-evolving ecosystem of supports and support organizations that adapts and changes in response to school needs. However, as seen in the example of New Schools for New Orleans, as particular organizations gain power and become institutionalized within those ecosystems, the organizations themselves may begin to drive what supports and approaches are deemed legitimate, re-creating the structures of the centralized traditional school district that the PMM was designed to replace.

In conclusion, PMM systems can create new ecosystems for school supports that question traditional assumptions about what supports are needed, how supports should be allocated, and who should deliver supports. However, the specific design and delivery of support may be fundamental to school improvement, but it can, at the same time, be in conflict with other values of the portfolio management model, including the fundamental values of granting schools broad discretion and the role of the central district as authorizer and enforcer of accountability rules. This balancing work will, no doubt, continue as PMM systems evolve and continue to struggle with these persistent challenges for educational governance.

SECTION 3

CHANGING SYSTEMS, COMMON STRUGGLES

DOES PMM ALIGNMENT TRANSLATE TO HIGHER SCHOOL QUALITY?

with Tasminda K. Dhaliwal

The PMM theory of action suggests that enacting the mechanisms studied in the previous chapters will result in school improvement. The preceding chapters explored each of the five core mechanisms of the PMM and how they were enacted, and offered insights into how these mechanisms separately translated into school practices.[1] Here, we step back and look at the systems and sectors overall, focusing on three key questions. First, how closely does each city approximate the ideal PMM model in its enactment of the five mechanisms? Second, do differences in the degree of alignment with the PMM model seem likely to yield differences in intermediate outcomes associated with school quality and student achievement, either within or across cities? And finally, what does this analysis of the connection between alignment and intermediate outcomes tell us about the promise of PMMs? With only three cities and largely cross-sectional analysis, we obviously cannot make causal claims, but the analysis does allow an examination as to whether the patterns in the data are broadly consistent with the theory as reflected in figure 9.1.

Overall, while we find some consistency with the theory of action, the inconsistencies are notable and point to two puzzling findings. First, analysis of the systems and sectors showed relatively high alignment between the PMM theory of action and the systems/sectors in Denver and New Orleans.

FIGURE 9.1   Understanding the Portfolio Management Model

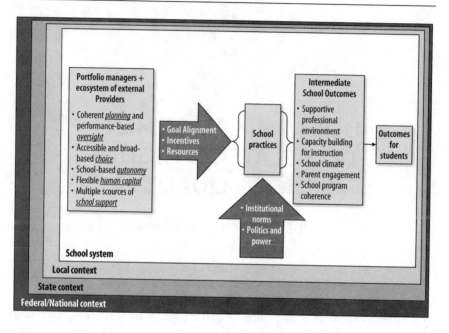

According to the theory of action, then, PMM implementation should lead to greater improvements in intermediate outcomes in those systems relative to Los Angeles. While the analysis of intermediate outcomes found that teachers and leaders in New Orleans consistently assigned more positive attributes to their schools than teachers and leaders in the other cities, outcomes in Denver were more similar to those in Los Angeles than to those in New Orleans. Second, in the Los Angeles context of parallel systems, we anticipated the charter sector would have more positive intermediate outcomes than the district-run system because the charter sector is more closely aligned with the PMM theory of action. However, we saw more similarities than differences in survey responses from teachers and leaders in the two sectors. Below, we share our analysis; in the following chapter, we explore some of the possible explanations for these puzzling findings.

HOW SYSTEMS WERE (AND WERE NOT) ALIGNED WITH THE IDEALIZED PMM

Throughout this book, we have sought to show the subtlety and complexity of how the five mechanisms have been designed and enacted in New

Orleans, Denver, and Los Angeles. An analysis of how strongly each city and sector demonstrates alignment with the PMM mechanisms, however, requires stepping back from that complexity to assess how closely the use of these mechanisms aligns with the PMM theory of action. Based on the analysis presented in the previous chapters, table 9.1 compares the five PMM mechanisms under study in the book across school governance models within each of the three systems. Larger checkmarks indicate closer alignment with the PMM theory of action. In the case of Los Angeles, we indicate the two parallel systems of district-run and charter schools by separating them with a dotted line.

New Orleans: The Managed Market in Practice

In many ways, the provision of publicly funded education in New Orleans aligned particularly well with the PMM ideal. Reviewing the chapters on the core mechanisms, it is clear that *oversight* incorporated explicit performance expectations and high-stakes consequences for not meeting those expectations. In response, as described in chapter 4, schools emphasized improving test scores. Portfolio managers, in conjunction with New Schools for New Orleans, clearly worked hard to be proactive in terms of *planning* who would operate schools in what locations; however, these efforts were sometimes criticized, particularly around the limited engagement with communities.

Parental *choice* in New Orleans' charter schools was broad-based and cohesive, with accessibility facilitated by the required provision of transportation and centralized information and enrollment processes. However, school-level actors did express mixed views about the efficacy of the enrollment system, and actors in multiple roles raised concerns about the lack of quality school options. As with other aspects of the system, nonprofit organizations were engaged in choice work, and efforts were made to enhance equity. The small number of remaining district-governed schools varied in their engagement with choice processes, with some declining to participate in the common enrollment system (hence the smaller checkmark for those schools).

The design of the system, with charter schools as the presumptive school structure, enabled substantial school-based *autonomy*. Although we saw substantial autonomy even in the district-run school that we visited, district-run schools still were not granted the same autonomy as

TABLE 9.1 Alignment of mechanism design and enactment to PMM theory of action

	NEW ORLEANS			DENVER				LOS ANGELES			
	Autonomous District-Run Schools	*CMO Charter Schools*	*Stand-alone Charter Schools*	*Traditional Public Schools*	*Autonomous District-Run Schools*	*CMO Charter Schools*	*Stand-alone Charter Schools*	*Traditional Public Schools*	*Autonomous District-Run Schools*	*CMO Charter Schools*	*Stand-alone Charter Schools*
Coherent *Planning and Performance-Based Oversight*	✓	✓	✓	✓	✓	✓	✓	✓	✓	✓	✓
Accessible and Broad-Based Choice	✓	✓	✓	✓	✓	✓	✓	✓	✓	✓	✓
School-Based Autonomy for School Leaders	✓	✓	✓	✓	✓	✓	✓	✓	✓	✓	✓
Human Capital Flexibility with Multiple Providers	✓	✓	✓	✓	✓	✓	✓	✓	✓	✓	✓
School Support from Multiple External Sources	✓	✓	✓	✓	✓	✓	✓	✓	✓	✓	✓

Note: Larger checkmarks indicate closer alignment with the PMM theory of action.

stand-alone charters. However, CMO charters experienced lower levels of school leader autonomy and teacher influence on school decision-making relative to autonomous stand-alone charter schools. Autonomy around issues of *human capital*, such as flexibility in hiring, compensation, and retention, was generally high. The teacher labor market in New Orleans was shaped by substantial school-level flexibility around compensation, little formal job security (through tenure), and high turnover. This distinct labor market created different dynamics around recruitment, retention, and competition for teachers, including teachers who felt that they had more ability and space to assert their voices than did those interviewed in other cities.

The availability of multiple sources of *support*—not limited to the portfolio manager—is central to the idealized PMM. For example, nonprofits can be an important alternative to a traditional central office as a source of resources and services to schools, giving school leaders the opportunity to select those organizations that best serve the needs of their particular schools. In New Orleans, the broad and deep ecosystem of nonprofit organizations seemed representative of this vision. This included alternative educator preparation organizations, and the unusual teacher labor market noted above included a substantial number of educators who had completed such programs. In addition, while the portfolio managers offered some supports to schools, most of the systemwide capacity building was left to nonprofit organizations. Indeed, one organization—New Schools for New Orleans—played such a large role that it raised concern about the organization's limited public accountability.

Denver: The Centralized Portfolio in Practice

While both cities are sometimes held up as positive examples of the PMM idea, the design and enactment of Denver's centralized portfolio was quite similar to that of New Orleans in some areas but distinct in others. Notably, more centralized approaches, which placed some boundaries around school-based autonomy in different areas, were linked to the stated commitment by Denver Public Schools (DPS) to provide "equity of opportunity" to both schools and students. For schools, this included access to central office resources for all school sectors.

As in New Orleans, performance-based *oversight* was central to the Denver system and included a focus on high-stakes consequences. Interestingly, leaders in Denver schools run directly by the district (both traditional and autonomous innovation schools) reported more concerns about closure than did their charter school colleagues. *Planning* which schools would operate and where was largely centralized to the portfolio manager, with access to district facilities serving as an important incentive for potential operators to respond to the portfolio manager's priorities. Distinct from the other two cities, Denver's planning processes were also used to target specific system priorities around serving students with special needs.

The centralized enrollment system and processes for providing information about school options facilitated parental *choice*, as did district transportation available for some schools. Consistent with a strong equity orientation, the portfolio manager used resources such as access to transportation and district facilities in an effort to address concerns, including concerns about school segregation. However, the lack of required transportation, along with the ability of schools to define geographic boundaries such that few seats were actually available in the choice system, limited student access in important ways.

One of the most striking aspects of Denver's centralized portfolio can be seen in the availability of substantial *autonomy* across the full range of school sectors, including traditional, autonomous, and charter schools. While formal autonomy for school leaders was varied in the system design, leaders' perceived influence on school management did not differ greatly between sectors (as it did in Los Angeles). Teachers in all sectors reported relatively high levels of influence on school decisions. As shown in chapter 6, leaders in the innovation schools actually reported slightly more influence than did those in CMO charters. Denver's centralized portfolio also had implications for *human capital* issues, with forms of collaboration and integration not seen in the other systems. For example, the portfolio manager actively sought to increase the supply of both teachers and leaders for all sectors through collaborating with alternative preparation programs. In addition, DPS offered charter schools access to relevant district systems required of traditional and innovation schools, including those for human resources and teacher evaluation. While system leaders did appear to build a more collaborative environment, there remained considerable challenges around human capital. These included high leader turnover and teacher dissatisfaction with compensation. The compensation issue, in particular, was complicated by the availability of dedicated incentive funds via DPS's

ProComp program for teachers in district-run schools—funds unavailable to charters.

Finally, Denver's approach included more broadly available school *supports* provided by the portfolio manager. Centrally provided supports, many of which were oriented toward school leaders, such as opportunities for coaching, were considered important to counteract the potential limitations of a market-oriented system, especially limitations tied to issues of equity for students. While the specifics of the supports available to (and required of) schools varied by sector, their availability was generally valued, even though it required some reductions in school autonomy. An ecosystem of external organizations, including the alternative preparation programs referenced above, also supported schools; however, this ecosystem did not have the breadth, depth, or resources of that seen in New Orleans.

Los Angeles: Parallel Systems in Practice

Los Angeles, distinct from Denver or New Orleans, functioned as two different but parallel systems both in design and in how the mechanisms were enacted. As shown in table 9.1, both of the other cities had mechanisms that were enacted consistently across all sectors. In Los Angeles, however, there were no mechanisms enacted systemwide, and thus district-run schools and charter schools are separated with a dotted line.

While planning and oversight were not as closely aligned to the PMM ideal in any of the sectors in Los Angeles, there were some common elements. For issues of *oversight*, educators in both sectors reported multiple and sometimes shifting accountability frameworks, more emphasis on non-test-score data such as graduation and dropout rates, less concern about high-stakes consequences tied to accountability, and a portfolio manager grappling with developing and maintaining the capacity to oversee a sprawling and complex landscape. In terms of *planning*, small pockets were found in specific district-run sectors, but little coordinated planning at the system level was evident. These patterns are reflected in table 9.1 by the small size of the checkmarks in the planning and oversight row for all sectors in Los Angeles.

Similarly, parental *choice* operated in a complex environment with a wide range of largely uncoordinated rules and practices around enrollment and information. In the district-run system, there were some "zones of choice" at the high school level that sought to bring more coordination, as well as magnet schools that were centrally run and offered choice. However, there were also concerns that access to some particularly desirable autonomous options could be "gamed" by more savvy and advantaged parents. Choice processes were also not coordinated either between the charter and district systems or within the charter system. Instead, within the state requirement around lotteries, charters used their own individual enrollment processes and timelines; these timelines, which sometimes happened prior to district processes, were seen as exacerbating competition between the sectors.

The *autonomy* available to different school sectors differed dramatically in Los Angeles, with school leaders in the traditional public school sector reporting the least influence on management of any sector across the three cities, and stand-alone charter leaders reporting the most. For teachers, both autonomous school models and stand-alone charters offered the greatest opportunities to influence school decisions.

Issues of *human capital* in district-run schools were shaped more by the engagement of unions and central office processes than in the other two cities, and leaders reported challenges in staffing their schools with well-matched and high-quality teachers. This was true even within less restricted autonomous schools, as the collective bargaining agreement carried considerable weight. At the same time, educators in district-run schools benefited from aspects of the portfolio manager's approach that focused on supporting and retaining a strong teacher labor force, including a collaboratively developed evaluation system with a strong developmental emphasis. In addition, the district-run sector boasted the lowest turnover rates and most experienced educators in the systems we studied. Consistent with the hands-off approach taken by the portfolio manager, charter schools in Los Angeles had significant autonomy around human capital. While turnover was higher than in district-run schools, and CMO teachers described heavy workloads, charter school leaders reported lower rates of teacher turnover than charter school leaders in the other two cities in our survey.

Finally, consistent with the idea of parallel systems, school *supports* in Los Angeles were bifurcated. Specifically, the portfolio manager offered substantial (although sometimes inconsistently available) supports to district-run schools while staying largely uninvolved in supporting charter schools. Outside organizations, in addition to CMO central offices, did provide supports to charter schools. However, the depth, breadth, and resources of such organizations, especially considering the vast scale of the system, did not appear to match the resources seen in the much smaller New Orleans system.

BRINGING IT ALL TOGETHER: ASSESSING INTERMEDIATE OUTCOMES BY PMM ALIGNMENT

Comparing the Three Systems

Taken as a whole, our analysis of alignment leads us to several specific expectations about the likelihood of the PMM model in the different cities and sectors yielding positive outcomes for students. At its core, the PMM idea is about changing educational *systems*, rather than sectors within those systems. This section considers how the systems compare to one another. Based on the study's findings around system design and enactment, the educational systems in Denver and New Orleans aligned most closely with the idealized PMM, while neither of the two systems in Los Angeles was as closely aligned. This leads us to predict that, as systems, New Orleans would have slightly more positive outcomes than in Denver, and both New Orleans and Denver would have better outcomes than Los Angeles.

We examined a wide range of school-level practices, relationships, and culture that are important for creating and sustaining high achieving schools, and are more proximately related to the practices of the portfolio manager. This approach allows a closer examination of the theory of action inherent in the portfolio management model by allowing us to see if portfolio managers are indeed able to facilitate high-quality school conditions through their governance of diverse school types.

The intermediate outcomes found in the case cities are tied to broader constructs that are central to the study's theory of change, shown in figure 9.1. Most of the intermediate outcome measures come from prior studies and are positively correlated with student outcomes.[2] The constructs and scales, as well as the survey participants for which they were measured, are as follows:

- Supportive professional environment
- Teacher collaboration and trust (leader survey)
- Teacher-teacher trust (teacher survey)
- Teacher-principal trust (teacher)
- Capacity building for instruction

- Principal instructional leadership (leader, teacher)
- Quality professional development (teacher)
- Data use (teacher)
- School climate (leader, teacher)
- Parent engagement (leader, teacher)
- School program coherence (leader, teacher)

While it is inherently difficult to establish causal relations among these factors, they are consistently correlated with student achievement.[3]

New Orleans: More Positive

Overall, responses from educators in the New Orleans surveys—both teachers and leaders—show more positive intermediate outcomes than in the other two cities (appendix B provides more detail about the intermediate outcomes across systems and sectors). This pattern carried across almost every city-to-city comparison, as is shown in figure 9.2. The differences are

FIGURE 9.2   **School leader responses on intermediate outcomes across cities**

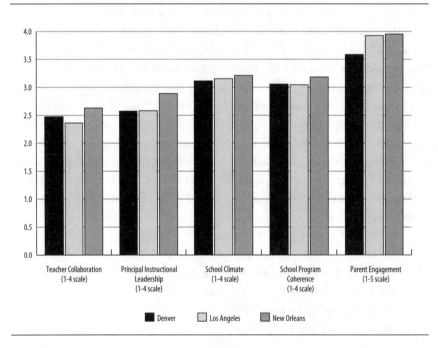

clearest (and statistically significant) with both teacher and leader reports of principal instructional leadership. The principal instructional leadership scale drew from items about the amount of time principals spend in developing professional development, observing classrooms, providing feedback on instruction and curriculum, and analyzing student assessment data (measured on a Likert scale from 1 = not at all to 4 = almost daily). The same pattern appeared in teacher survey reports of professional development and data use for instruction. These differences were statistically different from Los Angeles and Denver for both teacher and leader reports of principal instructional leadership.

Denver and Los Angeles: More Similar Than Different

While we found strong support for the hypothesis that, at the system level, New Orleans would have the most positive intermediate outcomes, the comparison of intermediate outcomes in Denver and Los Angeles did not match with the study's prediction. Instead, the findings were mixed. Overall, the intermediate outcomes in the two systems were more comparable than different from one another. In fact, we find few instances where Los Angeles and Denver differed significantly from one another in terms of school leaders' (as illustrated in figure 9.2) and/or teachers' reports of intermediate outcomes, and these differences did not consistently show Denver outperforming Los Angeles (in parent engagement, teacher data use, and teacher-principal trust). There were also outcomes for which we did not observe consistent evidence of differences between the two cities in our school leader and teacher survey data (principal instructional leadership, school climate, and school program coherence). This analysis of the links between system alignment and intermediate outcomes points to our first puzzling finding—that, despite their similar system designs, leaders and teachers in New Orleans reported notably more positive intermediate outcomes than in Denver, while educators in Denver and Los Angeles had more similar responses despite Denver being much more aligned with the PMM theory of action.[4]

Comparing Sectors

Within the three systems, our analysis also pointed to variations in the level of PMM alignment across school sectors, with stand-alone charters the most aligned and traditional public schools the least.

New Orleans and Denver: Little Variation

The structure of the PMM in both New Orleans and Denver suggest that we would see relatively little in the way of differences in intermediate outcomes between sectors within each city, and our analysis supported that expectation. In New Orleans, our data allowed us to compare intermediate outcomes for the two main school sectors (CMO and stand-alone charter schools). To the extent that school-based autonomy would be the priority, consistent with the origins of the PMM idea, we anticipated that more autonomous stand-alone charter schools would see modestly better outcomes. In fact, we saw few differences in the reports of school leaders and teachers between the CMO and stand-alone charter sectors. We only observed one statistically significant difference between CMO and stand-alone charter schools, and it involved more positive responses for the CMOs rather than the stand-alone charters—CMO school leaders reported higher ratings of principal instructional leadership than did their stand-alone charter counterparts. This finding was accompanied by two other outcome measures with ties to teacher instruction in which CMOs again outperformed stand-alones: teacher reports around the quality of their professional development and use of data. Taken together, this provides hints that CMOs in New Orleans were perhaps better at supporting instructional practice. However, considering the larger set of outcomes we analyzed, we saw more similarities between CMO and stand-alone schools than differences.

One of the priorities expressed by system leaders in Denver was the creation of a cohesive system of schools. The study's findings suggest that this was achieved across a number of mechanisms. Given this approach and how it was put into place, we anticipated that there would be less variation in intermediate outcomes across the different school sectors than we would see in a more varied system such as Los Angeles. Overall, the study's results provide some support for this expectation and suggest that the intermediate outcomes emerging from different school types in Denver were more similar than those in the other cities (at least with respect to school leader and teacher responses). Moreover, in instances where we do observe differences, we do not see consistent patterns for any school model type and observe very few statistically significant differences.

Los Angeles: Competing Systems, Similar Intermediate Outcomes

Los Angeles' competing systems—district-run and charter—differed substantially in how they measured up to the PMM ideal. While neither of the two systems lined up as closely to the ideal as in the other two cities, the charter system was more closely aligned in terms of choice, autonomy, and flexibility around human capital. In this context, the PMM theory of action would lead one to expect more positive intermediate outcomes in the two sectors that comprise the charter system than in the two sectors that make up the district-run system.

The analysis lends some very modest support for the expectation that charter schools would have better outcomes than district-run schools. The intermediate outcomes in schools within each system in Los Angeles were substantially similar, with the one exception being stand-alone charter schools. On a majority of the full set of intermediate outcomes, and three of the intermediate outcomes highlighted in figure 9.3, school leaders and teachers (not shown) in stand-alone charters provided more positive

FIGURE 9.3   **Los Angeles school leader responses on intermediate outcomes by sector**

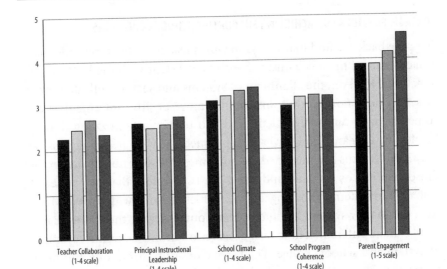

responses than educators in any of the other school sectors. However, other than for stand-alone charter schools, we did not observe consistent patterns of differences between the remaining school types in Los Angeles. School leader and teacher reports from CMO charter schools, autonomous schools, and traditional public schools included some outcomes on which leaders and teachers in each type of school offered the most positive reports. For example, educators in autonomous schools reported higher levels of parent engagement than in traditional public schools, but lower levels of principal instructional leadership. There are also outcomes such as teacher collaboration and trust, school climate, and school program coherence for which we did not observe any consistent differences between these school sectors in our school leader and teacher survey datasets.

While our analysis of sectors within cities met some of the expectations we identified based on the alignment between sectors and the PMM idea, it also pointed to our second puzzle: if the charter sector in Los Angeles was so much more closely aligned to the PMM theory of action than was the district-run sector, then why were there only negligible differences in outcomes between these sectors?

NO MAGIC FORMULA FOR ACHIEVING SUPPORTIVE SCHOOL CONDITIONS

Stepping back, we find many ways in which leaders in the three cities have, in fact, enacted the mechanisms in ways consistent with the PMM theory of action. However, the alignment of systems and sectors with that theory of action does not clearly translate into more positive intermediate outcomes. In fact, our analysis led us to two particularly puzzling findings. While New Orleans and Denver both pursued PMM strategies aggressively, only New Orleans had intermediate outcomes that were notably better than those seen in Los Angeles, and while the two sectors that comprised the district-run system in Los Angeles were far less aligned with the PMM ideal than the charter system, the intermediate outcomes for the two were more similar than different. These results serve to remind us of the complexity of system and school change. The three cities differ from one another on many dimensions, not all of which can be identified and observed. Indeed, in chapter 3, we describe some of the important contextual differences between these three cities, including differences in size, resources (such as the above average relative funding for students in New Orleans), leadership stability (great stability in Denver and considerable instability in Los Angeles), and teachers' union presence (nonexistent in New Orleans, weak in Denver, and strong in Los Angeles). All of these broader conditions may also influence school functioning and therefore intermediate outcomes.

Those who are or are not in favor of PMMs might point to these contextual differences between cities to explain our results. Opponents of PMMs, for instance, might point to the NOLA/Denver puzzle and say it is just a matter of money. Proponents of PMMs, on the other hand, could point to the political challenges and contextual factors that make it difficult for LA to provide the level and kinds of supports needed for their charter sector to really excel. In the final chapter, we look at these intermediate outcome findings as illustrative of the complexity of enacting an idealized PMM model in real-world settings. Specifically, we examine the ways in which mechanisms come into tension with one another and institutional, contextual, and political conditions push against the intentions of the PMM system. If those broader conditions in cities outweigh the potential benefits of the PMM idea, then our findings raise serious questions about the PMM approach—and the system and community disruptions that accompany it—as a means for system and school improvement.

NOTES ON METHODS

Finally, a few notes on our methods. The study is not intended to be broadly generalizable; it involved only three cities and is largely exploratory in its approach. There are many contextual factors that might have affected the implementation of PMMs and/or how PMMs impacted intermediate and student outcomes, including those discussed in chapter 3, that—given the focus of our study—we did not capture. For instance, in theory, it could be that New Orleans has somewhat better outcomes because teachers and school leaders work in smaller schools, with different student populations, and/or with more alternatively certified teachers/leaders. One alternative hypothesis to explain the consistency in leader-reported intermediate outcomes across school models in DPS might be that the characteristics of the schools are more similar in Denver than they are in the other cities, although analyses of administrative data in Denver suggest that this is not the case. Examination of school and teacher characteristics in DPS schools revealed differences across school models in terms of size, underrepresented minority (URM) students, years of experience, and alternative teacher certification.[5] Moreover, if stand-alone charter schools in Los Angeles were smaller or had fewer URM students, less experienced teachers and leaders, and/or more alternatively certified teachers and leaders, this might potentially lead them to report higher intermediate outcomes than are reported in Los Angeles traditional schools.[6]

It is important to note that even if it were possible to establish causal relationships between mechanism enactment and intermediate outcomes, this analysis does not attempt to connect them to the ultimate objective of student outcomes. Rather, the study has tried to lay out a clear set of predictions based on alignment with the PMM idea and to examine what teacher and leader responses tied to meaningful intermediate outcomes tell us about how well the theory seems to hold up. More definitive tests will have to wait for future studies, which we hope will build on the present one.

10

TENSIONS, TRADE-OFFS, AND LIMITATIONS IN THE PORTFOLIO MANAGEMENT MODEL

Changing systems is complicated, messy, and influenced by a broad array of factors. Our purpose in this volume is not to evaluate the idealized portfolio management model (PMM) so as to tell leaders, "Yes, this works" or "No, this doesn't work." Rather, it is to shed light on the complex work of altering deeply institutionalized school systems and to examine what changes have emerged in these three very different systems, what has influenced those changes, and how leaders across these systems have struggled with the tensions within the model itself and negotiated trade-offs between prior practices and new directions.

As described in chapter 2, the idea that altering structures and governance—especially at the level of school systems—will lead to improvement has a long history in educational reform.[1] So, too, do ideas around shifting incentives in order to create better alignment within organizations.[2] In this chapter, we highlight a number of trade-offs and tensions involved in the enactment of PMM that those in policy and practice may wish to consider. We focus on the idealized PMM as a system of educational governance in which a series of interlocking policy mechanisms are expected to bring about improved educational quality, including centralized *planning* and performance-based *oversight*, parental *choice*, school-based *autonomy*, flexible *human capital*, and school *supports* from multiple sources. These mechanisms are expected to reinforce one another by bringing the goals of those working at the school level into alignment with those of system leaders, while also enabling those school-level actors to better work toward shared goals.[3] Central to this approach is a strong focus on developing systems of continuous improvement in which, as Paul Hill put it, "leaders add more of what's working, assess, and repeat."[4]

In this chapter, we first revisit our findings through the lens of the designers and supporters of the PMM idea, considering the extent to which the system and school practices we observed in New Orleans, Denver, and Los Angeles lend support for the PMM theory and the ways in which the mechanisms were at times in tension with one another. We then examine a number of areas in which our findings suggest that conditions beyond structure and system design have shaped these systems and schools.

The three education systems varied in the design and enactment of the five policy mechanisms in important ways:

- New Orleans was a managed market, in which many of the conventional responsibilities of district central office—including managing budgets, hiring staff, and determining educational programs—shifted to schools and nonprofit organizations. In turn, portfolio managers assumed responsibility for a defined and narrow set of tasks, including fostering accessible information and the enrollment processes for families; determining what existing schools will continue to operate and, when schools are closed or taken over, what operators will replace them; and overseeing issues of students' rights, including disciplinary processes and special education.
- Denver was a centralized portfolio, in which the portfolio manager retained many of the functions of a traditional central office, such as providing professional development and overseeing special education programs, but shifted substantial decision-making about how to utilize resources to school leaders. In addition, the portfolio manager added structures and systems to facilitate student access to choice, including deciding which schools opened and in what locations, and making centralized policies on enrollment, information, and transportation.

- Los Angeles was a pair of competing parallel systems, in which the portfolio manager directly operated schools in its district-run system (with some variations around autonomy) while schools in the competing charter system had substantial autonomy but limited access to portfolio manager expertise and resources. School choice and oversight processes varied in this expansive district, and there was little centralized planning.

In chapter 9, we looked across the mechanisms and considered the overall alignment between the PMM theory of action and the systems and sectors that we studied. Our analysis of intermediate outcomes identified two puzzling findings that we did not expect: First, while both Denver and New Orleans were, overall, well-aligned with the PMM idea, school leaders and teachers in Denver did not report as positive intermediate outcomes as did educators in New Orleans. Second, though the Los Angeles district-run schools were far less aligned with the PMM idea than the parallel charter system, the two systems had similar intermediate outcomes. These puzzles show that the PMM theory of action, as we have described it, does not always unfold in anticipated ways. Throughout this chapter, we reflect on how we might better understand these unforeseen findings, in light of the tensions in the model as well as the broader institutional, contextual, and political conditions.

In the introduction to this volume, we asked how our research in these three cities can inform a broader understanding of how American public education systems may be changing and whether changes in systems are leading to school-level changes in practice. We conclude by returning to those questions, highlighting both the potential and limitations of the PMM idea specifically and, more broadly, of reform efforts that center changes in structure, governance, and incentives to enhance organizational alignment (as opposed to other kinds of reforms, such as those emphasizing changes closer to the core technology of teaching and learning). In doing so, we consider implications for system change and school practice.

INTERSECTING MECHANISMS IN THE PMM

The PMM idea includes, at the system level, *oversight* involving the setting of clear performance expectations for schools and high-stakes consequences tied to the achievement of those expectations, thus creating more powerful incentives for those in schools to meet system goals. Oversight is coupled with centralized *planning* processes for adding additional schools or installing new operators in existing schools. Through the inclusion of student *choice* and common enrollment systems, market-based accountability is expected to motivate schools to improve, while the ability to choose from among different school options is expected to help parents better meet the needs of individual students. In theory, schools will be able to respond to the particular needs of their students as a result of substantial *autonomy*, including in the educational program and in *human capital*. Finally, the availability of varied school *support* is expected to assist schools in their ability to respond to local needs. Ideally, a varied set of educational preparation organizations offer the needed human capital, and schools have the opportunity to select school supports from the portfolio manager and others that meet their particular local needs.

The PMM idea is a rejection of the "one size fits all" approach to schooling. Even the PMMs themselves can differ across places. Advocates expect that each system that incorporates the mechanisms we study will look different, and that the specific set of schools within each system will also look different as the portfolio is adapted to best meet the needs and desires of their particular contexts and students. Therefore, we would not expect to see that the schools and systems look the same, but we would expect the results to look better as the PMM is adopted with greater fidelity, and as these mechanisms link up to improve intermediate and individual outcomes for students and educators.

In chapters 4 through 8, we delved deeply into each of the five individual mechanisms, finding ways in which the systems varied in both design and enactment. In doing so, we consistently found an internal tension in one of the central intersections of mechanisms in a PMM: site-based autonomy, school-driven selection of supports from multiple providers, and high-stakes oversight by the portfolio manager. Ideally, by providing schools with autonomy and access to a range of support providers, portfolio managers enable schools to adapt their practices to meet the needs of local stakeholders and the high expectations of school quality and student performance set by portfolio managers. In New Orleans, we saw this most closely enacted. Specifically, schools had high levels of autonomy and used that autonomy to access supports from a substantial ecosystem of nonprofit organizations. The supports that they used, such as those provided by New Schools for New Orleans (NSNO), were often targeted specifically at helping schools to meet performance expectations.

This triad of mechanisms becomes a source of tension because the responsibility of the portfolio manager to evaluate and make high-stakes decisions about school openings and closures, and to ensure that laws and regulations are being followed, is at odds with its simultaneous role to provide or facilitate school support. On the one hand, portfolio managers may want to maintain distance between these roles to avoid infringing on school-based autonomy and to ensure that oversight is applied fairly and consistently (and not muddied by overinvestment in the success of a particular school). However, in order for this distance to be maintained, portfolio managers—who may have the most expertise around support in the system, and who are primarily responsible to the community for the quality and availability of schools—can also feel pressured to remain uninvolved when schools are floundering, and to not require struggling schools to use supports such as centralized systems or offices, selection of particular curriculum, or participation in specific professional development. This tension between autonomy, oversight, and support emerged in all three cities and in both of Los Angeles' parallel systems.

The case systems resolved this tension in distinct ways, often by trading off some mechanisms over others. In Los Angeles, the portfolio manager resolved these tensions quite differently for each system. For charters, the central office weighted autonomy over support and oversight. Charter leaders reported feeling that encroachment around compliance tied to oversight challenged their autonomy (such as the example in chapter 6 in which district requirements for metal detector searches to advance safety districtwide conflicted with the perceived autonomy of a charter school to approach discipline/safety with less punitive and more restorative practices), while, as described in chapter 8, they had little access to district supports. For district-run schools, support was clearly the priority, with a distinct but limited range of autonomy for different school models, and oversight that highlighted additional support rather than high-stakes consequences.

The two portfolio managers in New Orleans emphasized oversight and autonomy, although keeping a distance from supporting schools sometimes created discomfort for portfolio manager staff when they saw schools struggling. The availability of and coordination with nonprofit organizations that provided supports to school leaders and others, especially NSNO, aided in diminishing this discomfort.

In Denver, the portfolio manager sought to balance all three mechanisms—oversight, autonomy, and support—without clearly highlighting some and minimizing the focus on others. Here, shifts in the central office allowed schools in all sectors to access support and expertise there, and charter school leaders, in particular, accessed these supports based on their perceived value rather than on mandates. Supports were differentiated between traditional, innovation, and charter schools, but they were available to all the sectors. In exchange for these commonly available supports, the central office in Denver set consistent expectations and processes around oversight while limiting the range of autonomy across the sectors. For all sectors, Denver Public Schools (DPS) strongly emphasized supporting school leaders; for charter schools, support for leaders was one of two primary strategies used by the portfolio manager in an effort to balance autonomy with support.

In the previous chapters and in the sections that follow, we highlight other examples of the many intersections between the PMM mechanisms that show how these interactions can unfold in ways that are consistent with but also challenge the overall theory of action. As discussed below, we also saw tensions around core educational values and distinct interpretation of those values.

PMMS AND COMPETING VALUES OF EDUCATION

Taken as a whole, the PMM idea is a reform that prioritizes liberty—in the sense that parents have greater control over the decisions about where their children attend school, and educators have increased autonomy over core educational decisions related to budget, human capital, curriculum and teaching, and student services. These freedoms are assumed to bring about innovation, efficiency, and improvements in the quality of education. Yet, rather than complete autonomy, the PMM idea asserts that some centralized control may be needed to balance competing values of school quality and equitable treatment for students, schools, and educators. In practice, however, tensions between PMM mechanisms and competing understandings of quality and equity challenged the PMM idea altogether. When these tensions were resolved, the resolutions often involved leaders in all three systems recentralizing particular domains of decision-making in order to address the competing pressures between equity and quality.

PMMs and Tension Between Autonomy and Equity

Those who favor the PMM idea and its underlying theory of action often discuss equity in terms of equitable access to higher-quality schools for students. However, for students, schools, and educators, other issues of equity arose that largely focused on potential disparities resulting from school-based autonomy. In essence, granting greater freedom to educators could infringe on the liberties of these other stakeholders, thus requiring a recentralizing of control.[5]

Equitable Treatment for Students

Across the three cities, the core PMM tenet of freedom or autonomy for school leaders came into conflict with the broader goal of equity and access for students. In some cases, the tension between leader autonomy and student equity led to a recentralization of control at the system level. One area where we saw this occurring was in student discipline. In New Orleans, individual schools' disciplinary practices were challenged, causing a recentralization of expulsion practices. A similar recentralization of procedures for suspensions occurred within Los Angeles for all district-run schools following civil rights concerns.

Friction surrounding schools' autonomy over enrollment processes also highlighted the tension between autonomy and equity. In both Denver and New Orleans, enrollment systems were seen as an important strategy to enhance equity through student access. School-level educators did not always welcome these shifts, and such disapproval created ongoing tensions within these systems. For instance, concerns about inequitable access to schools in Denver led to a number of targeted strategies intended to enhance equity through limiting enrollment autonomy, such as requiring charter schools to accept late arrivals and to accept new students when students chose to leave. Conversely, the lack of a centralized enrollment system in Los Angeles generated significant concerns about students' inequitable access to high-quality school options. As these two examples make clear, balancing autonomy with competing priorities remains an ongoing challenge within these systems.

Equitable Opportunities for Schools

School leaders also felt the ramifications of this autonomy-equity trade-off. In particular, decentralized systems made it difficult at times for all schools to access necessary supports. For instance, in New Orleans, the robust ecosystem of nonprofits in the city enhanced the capacity of many individual schools. However, the fact that these organizations were decentralized raised questions about equitable access to these resources, including whether or not schools operated by charter management organizations (CMOs) were receiving more of these nonprofit benefits than were stand-alone charters. In Los Angeles, on the one hand, the charters had access neither to portfolio manager supports (as in Denver) nor to the depth and breadth of the well-funded ecosystem of support that served the much smaller number of schools in New Orleans. Los Angeles' district-run sector, on the other hand, had access to the substantial supports of the Los Angeles Unified School District (LAUSD), but school leaders were more limited in their ability to identify and select the sources of support that they felt would be most valuable. By contrast, DPS focused most explicitly on "equity of opportunity" for schools as well as students and had multiple strategies in place to support all school sectors.

Equitable Treatment for Educators

Our work also disclosed a third type of tension between autonomy and equity, related to schools' flexibility around human capital management. Under the idealized PMM, school leaders were intended to have autonomy around hiring, retaining, and compensating their staff; often, this is tied to diminishing or altogether excising the influence of collective bargaining agreements (CBAs) and their focus on standardizing human capital management processes. In New Orleans and in the charter sectors of the Denver and Los Angeles systems, these human capital autonomies generally resulted in a lack of protections for teachers in terms of job stability, due process, and other central tenets of collective bargaining agreements, which in turn dramatically shifted the working conditions of teachers in schools (or entire systems) in which contracts are diminished or removed. Without the specific regulations found within CBAs, some educators and educator associations worried about unfair treatment in schools or systems without bargained protections for teachers. High turnover rates in New Orleans and Denver, relative to Los Angeles, may be linked to the increasing number of teachers working outside of collective bargaining agreements.[6] As we discuss further below, these tensions led to significant political strife in two of the three cities in the years following our data collection.

PMMs and Competing Conceptions of Quality

Fundamental to the PMM is the idea that the decentralization of decision-making to school-level actors, coupled with choice and strong performance-based accountability, will lead to high-quality service delivery, education, and outcomes. In the PMM, quality is, in theory, to be defined by local audiences and should go beyond simply achievement on standardized tests. However, expansive and varied definitions of quality came into conflict with systems' commitments to the PMM mechanisms of oversight and school-based autonomy.

Diverse Options Versus High Scores

The PMM's melding of market-based accountability via parental choice and test-based accountability in portfolio management created significant tensions in the ultimate makeup of the portfolio of schools in these systems. Was the ultimate goal to achieve a portfolio of schools that reflected diverse school options, or simply one that had high performing schools even if the schools were all quite similar? While rhetoric around school choice often emphasizes the potential for innovation and a diverse array of school options that allow parents to identify the right fit for their child, performance-based high-stakes oversight and planning in Denver and New Orleans pushed schools to pursue a common and narrow set of goals defined primarily by student achievement. In response, school leaders implemented school-based strategies that were designed specifically to improve test scores. This attention to testing became central to the understanding of "quality" schooling in these cities. School leaders in lower performing schools vulnerable to negative consequences were particularly likely to report more narrow practices focused on improving test scores.

To some of those we interviewed, performance-based oversight and the emphasis on student outcomes stifled support and approval for schools with features not measured by accountability frameworks, such as music or mentoring. An important rationale for closure or school reorganization was that it would provide opportunities for different operators and/or schools to replace lower performing schools. The emphasis on selecting "proven" school operators with a "track record of success"—justified by portfolio managers as a means to ensure equitable access to quality education, particularly for underserved students—also favored particular educational models promoted by veteran CMOs.

Community Priorities and System Definitions of Quality

As described in chapter 2, an underlying assumption of the PMM is that this structure can better align those who set the goals of a system (principals) and those who work toward those goals (agents). In the case of PMMs, portfolio managers serve as the primary principal, and they set the system goals for all schools. In theory, portfolio managers should design frameworks that reflect the goals of the community as a whole as well as respond to state requirements. Although parent demand can serve as an alternative means of signaling priorities, some stakeholders questioned the extent to which parent and community goals—which might suggest different understandings of school quality—were adequately valued and promoted by the portfolio manager.

One important instantiation of this tension was the concern expressed in all three cities, but particularly New Orleans and Denver, over the broken bonds of local neighborhoods resulting from expanded parental choice. While choice was a central tenet of both PMM systems, many in the local communities noted that the inability of students to attend schools with neighborhood peers and of families to establish relationships with neighbors was a significant trade-off associated with these reforms. This trade-off undercut ideas of school quality associated with schools as valued community institutions.

Not only was the choice mechanism in tension with community values, but community voice was also at times pushed to the side by the need for centralized planning and oversight. As noted in chapter 4, individuals with close ties to communities—particularly in New Orleans and Denver— sometimes felt left out of planning decisions about what schools would be located where, an issue exacerbated by the limited availability of facilities. One concrete example discussed in that chapter was the case of a Black mother questioning why DPS was placing an additional "no excuses" school in an area already rife with similar schools. Once again, the community's definition of a quality school did not match that of the portfolio manager.

Concerns around community voice were amplified even further in decisions surrounding school closure. School closure became a flashpoint for families and communities in both Denver and New Orleans, where PMM system leaders in their oversight roles touted closure as a potential solution to persistent challenges with student performance. We found that leaders in both cities became less focused on closure over the course of PMM implementation, diminishing this approach in order to mitigate community backlash. In these cases, closure based on the portfolio manager's definition of school quality—designed to separate school oversight from questions of politics and power—became instead a focus for those very questions. While the politics of Los Angeles were, in many ways, the most contentious in our three cities, closure was never central to reform efforts, and thus the particular tension between oversight resulting in closure and community support was not a prominent concern.

The combination of school choice and performance-based oversight could lead to a portfolio of schools that balanced the preferences of families and the oversight system. Our findings, however, suggest that this balancing often tipped heavily in the direction of the portfolio manager's preferences in providing centralized oversight and facilitating choice. This carried down to the school level, where (as discussed in chapter 4) school leaders were far more concerned about pressures from the school board and/or authorizer than about pressures from parents.

Quality Schooling and School Autonomy

At a system level, district and CMO leaders noted the difficulties of ensuring quality instruction across multiple schools when there was too much autonomy. In all three cities, leaders of CMOs (especially larger ones) limited some school-level autonomy around educational programs—for example, by adopting common special education processes and uniform curricula, frameworks, or assessments. Leaders often justified these shifts promoting uniformity based on variation in site capacity and a need to ensure quality instruction across their network of schools. As one CMO leader explained, they needed to "systematize" more in "areas of risk" to ensure equal access to quality schooling. These shifts at times created significant tension for school-level actors, who longed for greater freedom and questioned the commitments of system and CMO leaders amid concerns about "creeping" recentralization occurring within the system.

Quality at What Cost?

In the pursuit of high-quality education, the PMM may be imposing new burdens on local actors in ways that could undermine the goals reformers seek to achieve. Allowing greater flexibility at the school level to choose support providers and establish educational programs aligned with local needs at times imposed significant costs on teachers and administrators. No longer bolstered by a central office able to provide support for the development of curriculum, assessments or professional development, some newly autonomous schools struggled to ensure the well-being and retention of teachers. Potential burnout and turnover clearly challenges a school's ability to provide high-quality instruction to students. The move among CMOs to recentralize some of these tasks was often promoted as a solution to this problem, but once again raises questions about whether such a move simply reverts the system back to the status quo.

Similarly, school choice and the complex enrollment systems in place in all three cities placed considerable burdens on parents. While portfolio managers worked hard to improve the quality of information and access to it, parents nonetheless expressed deep frustrations with these processes. Limited transportation created additional stressors for families who faced difficult trade-offs with traveling far to attain quality choices.

In sum, the enactment of PMM in all three cities involved significant tensions and trade-offs regarding values of equity and quality. We return to these issues later in the chapter when considering next steps for system reform and practice.

UNDERSTANDING THE "WHY" OF PMM VARIATION

Up until now, we have focused on how the three systems interpreted the PMM model and to what effect, but have spent less time examining why these variations and patterns of outcomes have occurred. In this section, we consider several interrelated conditions shaping these systems, including institutional and political pressures as well as local conditions such as capacity, size, and policy. We also consider how these conditions may help us to understand the unexpected patterns of intermediate outcomes discussed above and in chapter 9.

The idealized PMM is intended to be a system of continuous improvement, in which schools (or school operators) are opened or closed based on meeting system goals, so that, over time, the set of schools currently operating becomes higher performing than the set that operated previously. Under this reasoning, the technocratic process of assessing schools using clear and unambiguous metrics will disrupt existing norms both by offering incentives to schools to meet those expectations and by using a fair means of closing schools or changing operators when schools do not. The varied ways in which the PMM mechanisms can be enacted—such as different criteria for school quality and attention to building capacity—enable a portfolio manager to adapt to context while still holding on to a coherent theory of action. At the system level, this focus on well-structured incentives ideally separates decisions about schools from the problematic realms of individual relationships and politics. For schools, the clear focus on outcomes is anticipated to center efforts on the technical aspects of educating students rather than on long-standing school norms. However, in all three systems, we saw the challenges of the PMM approach in practice and how these varied pressures could shape organizational behavior.

Institutional Pressures in a PMM

As discussed in chapter 2, institutional pressures linked to taken-for-granted norms can result in resistance to change and the re-creation of existing practices.[7] In contexts where the processes that are needed to reach desired goals are uncertain, for example, such pressures can result in organizations (often unconsciously) seeking to act in ways that are perceived as "legitimate" by other organizations in the same field or aligned with professional norms.[8] The analysis touched on a number of ways in which institutional pressures, rather than incentives and structures, may be shaping these three systems. In particular, two different and sometimes competing sets of institutional pressures repeatedly emerged as sources of legitimacy: those from traditional public schools and districts, and those from a set of reform-oriented organizations including CMOs, educator preparation organizations such as Teach for America and the Relay Graduate School of Education, and foundations.

Efforts to recentralize and the common practices and tensions observed across school systems and sites might suggest that there are broader institutional forces pushing against efforts to use autonomy as a lever of change. The study's finding that CMOs across all three cities, particularly larger CMOs, may be limiting site-level autonomies and adopting centralized practices similar to those in traditional school districts is consistent with these ideas and arguments made by other scholars—that organizations within the same field tend to look more similar over time as they conform to expected ways of behaving.[9] Concerns expressed in Los Angeles and Denver about school district "creep" and an inability to be "open" and embrace change further support these arguments. Ultimately, more than a conscious effort to advance other system goals, the recentralization and limits on autonomy may reflect broader field-level expectations and norms favoring centralized models of schooling.

Chapter 5 described another seemingly contradictory pattern around the reports of marketing practices. Based on market-based assumptions of choice, we predicted that low demand from families would lead to increased school marketing efforts. Yet we found that the efforts in low-demand schools were comparable to those seen in high-demand schools in New Orleans and Denver and were generally high in CMO schools regardless of demand. These patterns are perhaps not surprising given broader institutional forces at play in all three cities. Schools might be driven to engage in marketing and recruitment activities not as a direct result of market pressure, but rather as a response to an assumed expectation that schools should recruit students and engage in marketing efforts to sustain their image as high-demand organizations. In this sense, recruitment activities may serve to maintain a school's legitimacy in a context of institutionalized choice.

How might considering these institutional pressures relate to the intermediate outcome patterns? One of the two puzzling patterns we found involved the similarities between outcomes in the district-run and charter systems in Los Angeles. Based on alignment with the PMM theory of action, we anticipated both that these two systems would be distinct from one another and that educators in the charter sector would report stronger intermediate outcomes. It may be that these similarities were shaped in part by schools operating under similar institutional pressures. For example, professional norms about school leadership may have been shared across sectors; anecdotally, the interviewed charter school leaders in Los Angeles all had experience working in district-run schools. In a related paper drawing on this data, we found substantial shared commitments in Los Angeles schools, regardless of school sector, to values such as academics, whole child support, community, and professionalism.[10] We also found, in chapter 4, that school leaders' strategies for increasing student achievement

were often quite similar across sectors in Los Angeles, including more attention to adopting new curricular or instructional methods than was seen
in either Denver or New Orleans.

Local Conditions in a PMM

As described in chapter 3, the local conditions in New Orleans, Denver,
and Los Angeles differ in many ways. Here, we highlight a small number
of those that appear to be of particular importance in understanding the
trajectory and intermediate outcomes of the PMMs in each location.[11]

Capacity and Capital

Three critical types of local capacity repeatedly emerged in our analysis
as essential to schools and systems: physical and fiscal capital, leadership
capacity, and social capital. Variation in the availability of these shaped all
three systems and schools.

Physical and fiscal capital   As a reform strategy focused on structures, the PMM
idea attends less directly to overall availability of financial resources and
more to how those resources are distributed. However, money does matter.[12] Although funding was not an explicit focus of our analysis, New Orleans schools both had more public funding per student than in the other
two systems (despite the city having a lower cost of living) and benefited
from substantial private funding that fueled not only the schools directly
but also the extensive ecosystem of nonprofit support organizations. Denver teachers, on the other hand, reported higher levels of dissatisfaction
with their overall compensation than in the other cities and raised concerns about inequities in light of the city's ProComp compensation system,
which was only available to teachers in district-run schools (discussed in
chapter 7). These resource differences may be as important as or more important than enactment of the PMM mechanisms for understanding why
educators reported more positive intermediate outcomes in New Orleans
than in Denver.

   In Los Angeles, on the other hand, shrinking enrollment in district-run
schools and strong budgetary concerns enhanced political opposition to
charter schools and challenged efforts to support schools. Among district-
operated schools in Los Angeles, for example, principals reported that
district support was inconsistent and limited in focus. Concerns about

efficiency and economies of scale often led to district support only for particular curricular, assessment, and professional development programs, rather than the more differentiated approach observed in DPS. These fiscal concerns, coupled with a climate of mistrust (see discussion below), likely contributed to ongoing resistance to a more unified system that would bring the two systems of charters and noncharters under one umbrella. Increasing enrollment in Denver in the early phases of the PMM, in contrast, made the expansion of nontraditional schools and the enactment of a coherent PMM structure less threatening at the time of our study.

Leadership capacity   The stability and capacity of leaders (or lack thereof) played important roles at the system and school levels. At the system level, in Denver, the consistency from 2005 to 2018 of two superintendents with very similar orientations toward change may have contributed to sustaining the centralized control systems of its PMM. In contrast, leadership turnover in Los Angeles echoed the patterns of reform: a period of portfolio-like reforms flourished under Superintendent Deasy during a period of weak union power, but these reforms were quickly dismantled by his successors.

Leadership also mattered at the intermediate and school levels. As noted in chapter 6, leadership greatly affected the realization of school-level autonomy. Notably, leaders with limited experience or who were uninformed about the details of their school plan helped explain why some schools did not enact the autonomies spelled out in their charters or autonomous school plans. Turnover at the supervisory level was especially salient to the support (or lack thereof) provided to semiautonomous schools in LAUSD.

Social capital   Creating and sustaining change not only involves structures; it also requires constructive relationships that enable trust. This is especially true when some of the participants in charge may have historically had either minimal or problematic relationships. In our analysis of intermediate outcomes, we included consideration of trust within schools, both among teachers and between teachers and school leaders.[13] However, we also saw trust and relationships as an important contextual condition at the system level—affecting the level of centralization in core PMM policies.

In Denver, participants generally described a high level of trust at the system level—translating into high levels of centralization in core mechanisms, such as enrollment systems. The high levels of trust were likely owing to the combination of consistent leadership that supported the portfolio idea within the portfolio manager and the creation of structures for shared decision-making between the district and charter sectors. The joint DPS-charter Collaborative Council and its work toward shared decisions about enrollment processes, in particular, were referenced by multiple participants as important to building trust. So, too, was the inclusion of charter schools in a 2012 bond initiative that brought additional resources across the district. Trust was not universally felt, however; for example, one stand-alone leader suggested that the trust at the system level was largely between DPS and CMOs, with stand-alone charters less favored.

A persistent and long-standing lack of trust at the system level between charter schools and the portfolio manager in Los Angeles, however, was a critical barrier to bringing the different systems together around potentially shared interests such as a common enrollment system or intentional planning of school locations and operators to address community needs and preferences. The polarized political climate fueled by millions of dollars spent on board elections (some from actors living outside of the state) contributed to a deep divide between charter and noncharter supporters. In 2015, a leaked plan written by foundation leaders and spearheaded by the Broad Foundation to expand the number of charter schools in Los Angeles heightened these tensions. Historical crises within the central office (for example, the malfunctioning of student information systems on the opening day of school) also contributed to charter leaders' concerns about LAUSD's ability to effectively manage more centralized processes.

In New Orleans, trust and relationships took on a somewhat different shape.[14] Being formed in post-hurricane New Orleans, the reforms were initially chaotic and brought together many people who did not know one another. The policies had been put in place, but without a clear end goal. The term *portfolio model* was not part of the conversation. Over time, however, as the reforms began to take shape, the leadership of the Recovery School District (RSD) began to recognize the centrality of the school and CMO leaders in the PMM, began meeting with them regularly, and actively engaged them in the policy process. As a result, New Orleans did not have the level of animosity found in Los Angeles among educators working in the schools and system leaders.

The other side of this dynamic, however, involved substantial tension between those within the system and the broader community. The key decisions creating the New Orleans PMM in the immediate aftermath of Hurricane Katrina were made in a top-down fashion by a small group of mostly White leaders from outside the city—decisions that affected the livelihoods of the city's mostly Black students, parents, and teachers. The pre-Katrina teacher workforce, three-quarters of whom were Black, was fired en masse. The community had little input over either the design of the system or the types of schools that were opened to serve their children. The tensions and mistrust lingering from this initial process continue to shape the system.

State Policy

State policies—including charter school and labor laws—were another critical local condition that shaped system change in myriad ways in each city. For example, differences in state charter school laws shaped the implementation of portfolio strategies in the three cities. Under Colorado law, DPS was the sole authorizer of charter schools, giving it considerable control as a portfolio manager. Additionally, Colorado charter schools were not their own local education agencies, as they were in the other two states. Therefore, DPS had greater legal responsibility for compliance issues regarding charter schools, which likely contributed to the greater centralization of practices regarding charters compared to the other cities and gave the charter schools a powerful incentive to collaborate with the district over time.

In California, however, state law allowed for multiple authorizers, which may have contributed to the less coherent portfolio approach. If the LAUSD school board rejected a charter petition, the school operator could go to the county or state for approval, leaving the board with less control over deciding which schools would operate within their geographic boundaries. This diminished authority might help explain why we saw considerably less involvement of district leaders in shaping the portfolio to meet the needs of particular local communities and in making planning decisions around which schools operate and where. The option for charter schools closed by LAUSD to seek an alternative authorizer may also have limited the willingness of the central office and board to proceed down the politically fraught path of school closure. If this is the case, it would help explain the reasons that charter leaders in Los Angeles were less concerned about high-stakes consequences than charter leaders in the other cities.

The strength of teachers' associations, along with state labor laws, also established very different policy landscapes in each city. Research consistently ranks California's teachers' union as one of the strongest in the country, particularly when compared to that of Louisiana (one of the weakest, and in a right-to-work state) and that of Colorado (stronger than in Louisiana but still weak).[15] The weak union in Louisiana clearly enabled post-Katrina reform leaders to terminate the teachers' contract and shift to school choice without effective, organized opposition. The same is true for Denver's early evolution to a centralized portfolio. In contrast, the strength of the California Teachers Association contributed greatly to the polarization of education politics around charter schools and the competing systems in Los Angeles. Some advocates also believed that strong state labor laws drove charter expansion throughout California and the desire for less restrictive options for school operations, particularly around staffing.

These union contexts continued to play a role in ongoing implementation. In Los Angeles, human capital strategies and levels of autonomy over staffing varied significantly across the competing systems because the union had a stronger role in district-managed schools than in charter schools. Strong union resistance to charter growth also placed tremendous pressure on school board members and local elections. Many observers linked increasing constraints on local charter school autonomy to the growing strength of pro-union board members. In contrast, since New Orleans is in a Southern state with typically weak union control, it was more difficult for union power to reemerge there, where charter schools continue to experience considerable autonomy. Finally, the more collaborative relationship between the union and district leaders in DPS contributed to principals' perceived autonomy over personnel decisions such as dismissal of ineffective teachers.

System Size

The vast difference in system size also contributed to the evolution and implementation of portfolio systems in the three cities. Throughout our study, interviewees described LAUSD as a "behemoth" of a bureaucracy protecting the status quo and resisting deep changes. The vast geographic terrain also contributed to explicit problems of trust that shaped the emergence of competing systems. The large size also made it difficult for LAUSD to establish the common understandings and capacity needed to support implementation of PMM strategies. As discussed in chapter 6, complaints that principal supervisors often did not understand the autonomies afforded by the various governance models (such as pilot schools) are but one example. The relatively smaller size of the other two cities and systems may have made it easier to enact more cohesive approaches to change. In many cases, school leaders in New Orleans and Denver had a personal relationship with key system leaders, and they could regularly meet as a group to discuss issues and ways forward, leading to better coordination.

Politics and Power in a PMM

The evolution of the three school systems at the center of this book and the implementation of PMM strategies are deeply political—adding yet another set of pressures that help explain the variation and tensions we observed. As discussed in chapter 3, powerful actors helped facilitate these changes, affecting both the pace of change and the characteristics of these new systems. These actors included civic and education leaders, foundations, and business leaders—indicating that an increasingly diverse set of local, state, and national actors are shaping local public education.[16] In the end, the shift to these various forms of the PMM resulted in a powerful set of new actors, including the leaders of influential private organizations such as CMOs or NSNO, invested in sustaining and institutionalizing these changes. Old political actors have also taken on new roles. For example, rather than directing the nature of internal school programs, elected board members are expected to operate at a higher level, directing which schools should and should not operate in the system.

Much like the adoption of PMM reforms, the ongoing enactment of PMM core mechanisms is a highly political process. In all three cities we heard common critiques that, in practice, these new school systems did not always elevate community voices, and that at times the systems perpetuated long-standing societal inequities, including racism. These latter critiques came from charter advocates, union leaders, and members of community-based organizations. In Denver and New Orleans, we heard concerns about new elite policy actors from privileged social groups—White men leading CMOs, for example—excluding the voices of communities of color and local leaders from decision-making. Building on lingering concerns about the power imbalance and racial dynamics of the immediate post-Katrina reforms, community members in New Orleans were particularly vocal about their lack of voice and the displacement of Black educators. As one Black community advocate noted, "One of the most aggravating elements of a post-Katrina environment is this notion that we have no history, and if we do, it's all bad." Individuals questioned the underlying values of a system run by leaders who they believed did not represent the true interests of the diverse community.

In all three districts, we also heard that the structure of the new system and its values inadequately served students of color and low-income students. For example, in Denver and elsewhere, several community leaders worried that the prioritization of large CMOs limited the variety of school options in low-income neighborhoods and communities of color. In several cities, critics believed PMM-oriented change unfairly burdened low-income communities of color and the educators serving them—this was particularly true in the case of school closures, where families felt their communities were under attack, but also pertained to the burdens related to limited transportation, access to information, and language barriers affecting school choice.

The political dynamics of system change and implementation of PMM strategies continue to evolve in all three cities. In fact, when we were preparing this book, political battles directly implicating PMM reforms heated up in all three cities, leading to some adjustments in the overall structure and mechanisms of the school systems.

In Denver, in October 2018, Superintendent Boasberg resigned over what some characterized as significant concerns that he had not done enough to eradicate student achievement gaps, or more starkly from opponents, that he "destroyed public education."[17] At this time, the teachers' association gained considerable strength, and in February 2019 organized its first strike in twenty-five years. One major impetus for the strike was growing concern about the fairness of the ProComp compensation system and about the uncertainty it generated for teachers. Building on the momentum of the strike and a desire to "flip the board," leaders secured a pro-union majority on the school board in the November 2019 elections. At the time of the elections, one media outlet asked in a headline, "Is Denver's era of education reform coming to an end?"[18] Since the election, the new DPS board has taken a noticeably "softer tone with low-performing schools,"[19] opting for less punitive interventions in schools that fail to meet performance goals, such as requiring improvement planning instead of closure.

In New Orleans, the Louisiana legislature passed a "reunification" policy requiring all New Orleans RSD schools to return to oversight by the Orleans Parish School Board (OPSB) by 2018. Now that the local board has power again, citizens are starting to reengage in board elections and public meetings. School closure and takeover decisions, a mainstay of the portfolio model, are once again being met with public resistance. The national teachers' unions are also funding efforts to re-unionize individual charter schools and CMOs. While these efforts have met with limited success so far, reform leaders are feeling the pressure to move back toward more traditional public schools.

In January 2019, Los Angeles experienced its first teacher strike in thirty years—one that included teachers across the district and at two independent charter schools. Among the demands for higher salaries, smaller class sizes, and more support staff, the striking teachers called for limits on charter schools, whose growth the union blamed for the district's declining enrollment. In an op-ed published in the *Los Angeles Times* prior to the strike, the head of the United Teachers of Los Angeles explicitly connected the strike to the PMM, noting that teachers "may have to strike" in large part to fight against the superintendent's "agenda to dismantle the district": "Through an outside foundation, he has brought on firms that have led to public school closures and charter expansion in some districts where they have worked, from New Orleans to Washington, D.C. This approach, drawn from Wall Street, is called the 'portfolio' model, and it has been criticized for having a negative effect on student equity and parent inclusion."[20]

The negotiations ultimately led to a 6 percent teacher pay raise and promises of additional school staff and smaller class sizes. The negotiations also included an agreement to put a resolution before the school board calling for the state to enact a cap on charter schools. In response to pressure from Los Angeles, other districts, and advocates, the state enacted several changes to state charter law—including some that were intended to limit growth, such as a provision that district authorizers could deny new charter schools if their creation would hurt the finances of the district.

Since the strike, LAUSD school board politics have also shifted. A special election for a vacant school board seat in May 2019 resulted in a landslide victory for a candidate backed by the union, and more elections are on the horizon that could dramatically affect the district's direction with regard to charter schools.

These recent developments highlight the evolving, contentious, and political nature of school system reform and suggest the story is far from over.

NOW WHAT? IMPLICATIONS FOR SYSTEMS, SCHOOLS, AND RESEARCH

Neither understanding nor studying large-scale system change is an easy task, and the story told in this book is one of substantial variation both across and within the educational systems of Denver, New Orleans, and Los Angeles. As each system moved down a path aligned at least in part with the idea of portfolio management, each faced significant tensions and implementation challenges. Ultimately our research suggests that leaders and policy makers face significant trade-offs when engaging in portfolio-style reform. For those interested in adopting, adapting, or providing support for the reforms we investigate herein, we offer a set of considerations and questions derived from the experiences of these three cities.

Centralization and Decentralization

As portfolio managers, leaders must consider how to weigh their responsibility to ensure schools are meeting performance targets (*oversight*) and experiencing the discretion authorized by their governance arrangement (*autonomy, human capital*), with a possible complementary responsibility to provide support to ensure they are meeting targets (*school supports*). For the portfolio manager to remain uninvolved in direct support means that schools need to have access to a broader ecosystem of supports to step in when help is needed. Leaders engaged in portfolio reforms must explicitly investigate this assumption. Unfettered autonomy also brings potential risks when the capacity to take advantage of the autonomy does not exist, or when unlimited autonomy threatens the realization of higher-level goals and values related to equity. Thus, is it enough to maintain distance when a lack of direct support or control might lead to inequitable access or treatment of students or teachers? Or what if it leads to decisions to close schools? Leaders should also consider the ripple effects of such decisions: not only the specific effects on families directly involved in these consequences but the broader effects on community trust and well-being.

Preferencing Community Voice

Performance-based oversight of schools places a premium on system-level definitions and expectations of high-quality schools. Yet community stakeholders may hold other values and expectations worthy of consideration. The mechanisms of high-stakes accountability, closure, and choice do not always align with parents' interests in having their students attend local schools with neighborhood peers or keeping open a school symbolizing their community's history. Much of the political tension within the three cities hinged on perceptions of community members not having a voice in the process—for example, ranging from those wanting models other than "no excuses" approaches to discipline, or wanting more offerings with arts programs, to others opposing decisions to close their community schools. Leaders should push for enhanced communication that includes community voices, and, especially, elevates the voices of those who are traditionally excluded from important spaces and conversations about schooling and students' well-being.

Diversity and Quality of School Options

As noted, the combination of market-based accountability and performance-based accountability in the PMM raises important questions about how much diversity is desired in a system. If leaders define high quality by performance frameworks and preference operators who have proven track records of meeting achievement-based criteria, there is the potential to drive out diversity in the types of schools present in a system's portfolio. Yet the underlying assumption of choice and market-based reform is that such competition will lead to innovation and diversity of options so that families can find the right match for their needs. Leaders in portfolio systems must confront this trade-off. If quality outweighs diversity, leaders should ask whether choice mechanisms—and the significant resources they require and the potential challenges they bring with them—are even needed in such a system. If more diversity is desired, leaders might examine whether planning and oversight processes or limits placed on autonomy may be stifling opportunities for innovation, or whether a more intentional approach is needed to shape the diversity of schools across the city.

Capacity and Support

Among the many forces shaping the enactment of PMM reforms, issues of capacity are the most malleable. Leaders considering structural reforms such as PMM should anticipate the significant resources—human, fiscal, and social—required to enact sweeping change in system and school management and operations. Beyond the relational dimensions discussed above, the sheer funding of systems, not just how those resources are distributed, matters. And the promise of improvement via local discretion may not be realized without greater attention to building the knowledge, skills, and dispositions allowing for individuals at all levels to support and use various flexibilities.

Technical and Human Demands

System leaders should not underestimate the technical demands of designing and implementing the PMM mechanisms. In all three cities, administrators worked hard to develop performance frameworks, enrollment processes, algorithms, and associated information to create choice systems that are fair and transparent. Redesigning human capital systems and outlining the parameters of new autonomous school models are also no small endeavor. Yet, at the same time, one must not overlook the corresponding demands and consequences of these changes on the end users and recipients of these new systems. Leaders in all three cities recognized the burdens of choice on families (as shown by attempts to ameliorate this burden by providing human "navigators" to help parents with choice in New Orleans) and the similar burdens of a less regulated market for teachers (efforts to unionize teachers in some schools are but one sign of this).

Moreover, the ability to enact reforms relies heavily on the relationships of trust between and among actors at all levels of the system. Leaders must invest in these relationships and in ensuring the well-being of educators and families—and ultimately consider whether, after all is said and done, the benefits of this new system outweigh the real costs to individuals in the system. As discussed further below, leaders should consider ways to ensure opportunities for input and collaboration (like Denver's Collaborative Council), particularly in designing mechanisms of change. However, we cannot deny that for some stakeholders, no level of inclusion or strategy would lessen the resistance to portfolio reforms, which they view as a market-based threat to the institution of public education.

Anticipating Competing Pressures

Although institutional and political pressures are not as malleable as fiscal or human inputs, they are nonetheless important to keep in mind when enacting reforms. As the experiences of the three cases illustrated, PMM-like system change is context dependent and subject to ongoing pressures resulting from the shifting political winds, including particularly fierce resistance from well-organized interests, such as teachers' unions. In addition, system and school change will inevitably be shaped by substantial taken-for-granted norms and institutional pressures of the field and profession. While structural change may disrupt some of those norms, they can either return or be replaced by new norms that are also based on an idea of legitimacy rather than educational benefit.

Future Research

We see many opportunities for future research to build on what we have started here in our investigation of system change.

What to Study

As noted, portfolio reforms are one of many approaches to system change occurring in the United States and beyond. Future studies comparing the various approaches (networked systems, state takeover, mayoral control, among others) would advance our understanding of district change—perhaps shedding light on the relative importance of key mechanisms. Comparisons to nonstructural reforms (that is, curricular and pedagogical reforms) might also provide insight into the impacts of system-level change on classroom-level practices. To understand the deeper effects of system change on schools, and whether there are important differences in the nature of teaching and learning, scholars might investigate classroom-level practices in greater depth.

Where to Study

While generative to our research, the three cities we examine are not representative of all cities and systems engaged in portfolio and other system-level reforms. Future studies might examine settings that vary in their location and demographics (suburban districts, or environments with higher-income populations), as well as political context (places with fewer political interest groups, for instance), to see how these conditions influence implementation and practice. Research might also investigate why other districts—some quite similar to New Orleans, Denver, and Los Angeles—have not opted for portfolio reforms, and what the intermediate and long-term outcomes of students look like in those settings. How else is the one best system fraying, and how, where, and why is it holding strong?

How to Study

Given the political nature of PMM reform and the tensions observed particularly with low-income communities of color, it behooves researchers to elevate the voices of all stakeholders in research on systems. To achieve this goal and attend to the impact of reforms on traditionally underserved families, scholars might consider incorporating social movement theory and other critical frameworks into future studies of system change. In addition, while challenging, approaching the study of systems using multiple methods and forms of analysis, as well as gathering data from different levels of the system, allows for a view of systems from multiple angles.

In addition, our study is naturally limited by the fact that we focus on whole systems, and as such we are unable to isolate the effects of the PMM model on longer term outcomes such as student achievement, graduation rates, and labor market opportunities. Although there is some extant work that examines the impact of New Orleans' shift to a PMM model, it is impossible to isolate the effect Denver's and Los Angeles' more gradual adoption of the PMM model on relevant outcomes.[21] Future work on PMM systems located in districts within states with inclusive longitudinal datasets may be better able to capture the comparative effect of PMMs on outcomes relative to other similar cities and systems.

RETURNING TO SYSTEM AND SCHOOL CHANGE

At the beginning of this volume, we pointed to David Tyack's notion that school districts have historically adopted and sustained a common form or "one best system," and we described how this relatively stable structure is increasingly fraying at the edges.[22] In light of those changes, we asked: Are systems incrementally evolving or fundamentally restructuring? And are these system changes leading to meaningful changes in school practice? While we neither advocate nor oppose the PMM idea, we hope that our findings can inform the work of leaders in these and other educational systems, as well as policy makers and scholars interested in PMMs specifically or governance change more broadly.

Overall, we do see fundamental change away from the one best system, with emerging—and distinct—norms and expectations around the nature of a school system in each of the three cities. In none of the cities do we see a central office that oversees a bureaucracy that incorporates all publicly funded schools with common rules, procedures, and educational practices. Moreover, families are not explicitly limited to attending an assigned neighborhood school and now face some choices (albeit with clear constraints). As well, we see important changes in educational elites, as new actors have increasingly gained power, often alongside diminished power for associations of professional educators, including teachers' unions.

However, while we do see significant system change aligned with many of the PMM mechanisms, we also uncover critical limitations of the PMM idea specifically and, by extension, reforms centered on structures and incentives more broadly. Ultimately, the pieces on the outside of the PMM theory of action seen in figures 2.1 and 9.1—pieces that concern the complicated contexts of systems and the intervening influences of institutional and political pressures—are central to these changes rather than parts of the periphery.

The PMM idea explicitly does not seek to address the proverbial black box of schooling. In other words, it does not seek to identify pedagogical, curricular, or organizational practices within schools that can lead to improvement. Instead, it relies on structures, incentives, and alignment to drive those in schools to figure out the best educational practices, and it discounts forces such as institutional pressures that may result in schools focusing on legitimacy in a climate of uncertainty. Ultimately, we find that the PMM idea offers some helpful insights into the use of the core policy mechanisms and their interactions. However, our work also raises critical questions about the potential for reforms to lead to real and persistent educational improvement in classrooms without serious and sustained attention to institutional and political pressures as well as critical issues of local educational capacity, context, and policy.

STUDY DATA
AND METHODS

QUALITATIVE DATA AND ANALYSIS

TABLE A.1   Qualitative data sources

	DENVER	LOS ANGELES	NEW ORLEANS
System-level interviews (N=76)	N=27	N=31	N=18
School-level interviews (N=210)	8 schools: 17 leaders, 30 teachers, 20 parents, 5 principal-supervisors	6 schools: 10 leaders, 30 teachers, 27 parents, 4 principal-supervisors	7 schools: 14 leaders, 33 teachers, 15 parents, 5 principal-supervisors
Documents	Media accounts; district and school websites; existing research	Media accounts; district and school websites; existing research	Media accounts; district and school websites; existing research

Notes on Qualitative Data Analysis

Interviews ranged from 30 to 107 minutes, and all but one were audio-recorded and transcribed. Interview transcripts were uploaded to NVivo and were coded using a provisional list of codes derived from extant literature on PMMs, including codes for PMM mechanisms; local history, politics, and context; and the influence of state and federal policy.[1] Team members then reviewed the coded data to write detailed system case profiles, ranging from 120 to 190 single-spaced pages, as well as school profiles, ranging from approximately 30 to 60 pages.[2] These system and school profiles presented analysis of key themes and data around the PMM mechanisms and issues of system and school context. For each mechanism, a team of researchers analyzed data across systems and schools to identify themes, using memos and matrices to identify cross-case patterns.[3] For validation of our findings, we triangulated across multiple sources of data and participated in peer debriefing sessions.[4] Throughout data analysis, we searched for disconfirming evidence that might challenge our claims, and adjusted findings accordingly.

SURVEY DATA

Extensive detail about the survey items and constructs can be found at challengingtheonebestsystem.net.

TABLE A.2   Survey data

	DENVER	LOS ANGELES	NEW ORLEANS
Teacher surveys (N=1927)	N=686 from 1,307 teachers in 48 schools (RR= 52.5%)	N=633 from 1,296 teachers in 52 schools (RR= 48.8%)	N=608 from 987 across 24 schools (RR=61.6%)
Leader surveys (N=628)	N=104 out of 216 school leaders (RR= 48.1%)	N=493 out of 991 school leaders (RR= 49.8%)	N=39 out of 79 school leaders (RR=49.4%)

SURVEY RESPONSES BY SECTOR

TABLE A.3   Principal surveys—schools by sector

	TRADITIONAL PUBLIC SCHOOLS	AUTONOMOUS DISTRICT-RUN SCHOOLS	STAND-ALONE CHARTER SCHOOLS	CMO CHARTER SCHOOLS
Denver	46/95	36/68	14/24	11/32
Los Angeles	295/570	103/155	20/43	74/176
New Orleans	–	–	9	14

# of schools responded / # of schools sampled

Note: Autonomous district-run schools include magnets, pilots, ESBMM, network partnership and LIS schools in Los Angeles, and innovation and magnets in Denver.

TABLE A.4   Teacher surveys—schools by sector

	TRADITIONAL PUBLIC SCHOOLS	AUTONOMOUS DISTRICT-RUN SCHOOLS	STAND-ALONE CHARTER SCHOOLS	CMO CHARTER SCHOOLS
Denver	17 (262) / 17 (488)	17 (267) / 17 (464)	6 (65) / 6 (137)	8 (92) / 8 (218)
Los Angeles	15 (219) / 15 (434)	30 (336) / 30 (708)	3 (34) / 3 (78)	4 (44) / 4 (76)
New Orleans	1 (22) Not used	–	9 (260)/ 9 (376)	14 (336)/ 14 (565)

# of schools (# of teacher responses) / # of schools sampled (# of teachers sampled)

Note: Autonomous district-run schools include magnets, pilots, ESBMM, network partnership, and LIS schools in Los Angeles, and innovation and magnets in Denver.

Notes on Survey Data Analysis

We compare responses on survey items and scales across a number of dimensions including school governance model, city, school performance level, and student demographics. In cases where we report statistical significance, we compare responses using t-tests and an alpha level of 0.05. We do not make adjustments for multiple t-tests. All survey results are weighted by school governance model and school performance level to account for sampling procedures and low response rates to the survey. We also imputed missing teacher survey data using multiple imputation with a series of chained equations. Multiple imputation uses an iterative algorithm to generate predicted values for missing values based on, among other things, variables that are associated with patterns of missing data.[5]

INTERMEDIATE OUTCOMES WITHIN AND ACROSS SYSTEMS

TABLE B.1 Comparing school sectors within cities on intermediate outcomes

| | LOS ANGELES | | DENVER | | NEW ORLEANS |
	Traditional vs. Others	CMO vs. Standalone Charter	Traditional vs. Others	CMO vs. Standalone Charter	CMO vs. Standalone Charter
Teacher collaboration & trust	+St charter		+CMO* +St Charter	−St charter	
Principal instructional leadership	−Aut −CMO +St charter	+St charter	+Aut −St charter		−St charter*
School climate	+St charter*	+St charter			
Parent engagement	+Aut +St charter*	+St charter	+St charter*		+St charter
School program coherence	+St charter			−St charter	
Teacher professional development	+Aut −CMO +St charter	+St charter	−Aut +CMO +St charter	−St charter	−St charter
Teacher data use	−Aut −CMO −St charter	+St charter	−Aut −CMO +St charter	+St charter	−St charter

(continues)

TABLE B.1 **Comparing school sectors within cities on intermediate outcomes,** *continued*

| | LOS ANGELES | | DENVER | | NEW ORLEANS |
	Traditional vs. Others	CMO vs. Standalone Charter	Traditional vs. Others	CMO vs. Standalone Charter	CMO vs. Standalone Charter
Teacher-principal trust	+Aut −CMO +St charter*	+St charter	+Aut +CMO* −St charter	−St charter	−St charter

Aut = autonomous school, CMO = charter school belonging to a CMO, St charter = stand-alone charter school

Note: This table compares intermediate outcomes between traditional public schools and all other school model types and between CMO and stand-alone charter schools. We observe the first five outcomes (teacher collaboration and trust to school program coherence) in our school leader and teacher survey data and only report findings that are consistent between both datasets. The last three outcomes (teacher professional development to teacher-principal trust) are only observed in our teacher survey data. Blank cells indicate no consistent findings between our data sources.

− indicates that school model values are lower than the school model in the column header. + indicates the school model values are higher than the school model in the column header.

* indicates that differences are statistically significant at p<0.05 or lower in at least one of our survey datasets.

TABLE B.2: **Comparing systems across intermediate outcomes**

	NEW ORLEANS	DENVER
Teacher collaboration & trust	−DPS −LA*	−LA
Principal instructional leadership	−DPS* −LA*	
School climate	−DPS* −LA	
Parent engagement	−LA	+LA*
School program coherence	−DPS −LA*	
Teacher professional development	−DPS* −LA	+LA
Teacher data use	−DPS −LA*	−LA*
Teacher-principal trust	−DPS* −LA*	−LA*

Note: This table compares intermediate outcomes between our three case school systems. We observe the first five outcomes (teacher collaboration and trust to school program coherence) in both our school leader and teacher survey data and only report findings that are consistent between both datasets. The last three outcomes (teacher professional development to teacher-principal trust) are only observed in our teacher survey data. Blank cells indicate no consistent findings between our data sources.

− indicates that system values are lower than the system in the column header. + indicates the system values are higher than the system in the column header.

* indicates that differences are statistically significant at p<0.05 or lower in at least one of our survey datasets.

NOTES

Chapter 1

1. Katrina E. Bulkley, Jeffrey R. Henig, and Henry M. Levin, eds., *Between Public and Private: Politics, Governance, and the New Portfolio Models for Urban School Reform* (Cambridge, MA: Harvard Education Press, 2010); Paul T. Hill, Christine Campbell, and Betheny Gross, *Strife and Progress: Portfolio Strategies for Managing Urban Schools* (Washington, DC: Brookings Institution Press, 2012).
2. Paul T. Hill, Lawrence Pierce, and James Guthrie, *Reinventing Public Education: How Contracting Can Transform America's Schools*, RAND Research Study (Chicago: University of Chicago Press, 1997).
3. Deborah Stone, *Policy Paradox: The Art of Political Decision Making*, 3rd ed. (New York: W.W. Norton & Company, 2012); David Labaree, "Public Goods, Private Goods: The American Struggle over Educational Goals," *American Educational Research Journal* 34 (2012): 39–81, doi: 10.3102/00028312034001039.
4. Adrienne D. Dixson and Celia K. Rousseau, "And We Still Are Not Saved: Critical Race Theory in Education Ten Years Later," *Race Ethnicity and Education* 8 (2005): 7–27, doi: 10.1080/1361332052000340971.
5. Erica O. Turner, *Suddenly Diverse: How School Districts Manage Race in Inequality* (Chicago: University of Chicago Press, 2020).
6. Council of the Great City Schools, *Urban School Superintendents: Characteristics, Tenure, and Salary; Eighth Survey and Report*, Urban Indicator (Washington, DC: Council of the Great City Schools, 2014), https://www.cgcs.org/cms/lib/DC00001581/Centricity /Domain/87/Urban%20Indicator_Superintendent%20Summary%2011514.pdf; Kristin Blagg, *Making the Grade in America's Cities: Assessing Student Achievement in Urban Districts* (Washington, DC: Urban Institute, 2016), https://www.urban.org/sites/default /files/publication/81621/2000821-making-the-grade-in-americas-cities-assessing -student-achievement-in-urban-districts_4.pdf; Bruce D. Baker, Matthew Di Carlo, and Mark Weber, *The Adequacy and Fairness of State School Finance Systems: Findings from the School Finance Indicators Database, School Year 2015–2016* (Washington, DC: Albert Shanker Institute, 2019), http://schoolfinancedata.org/wp-content/uploads /2019/03/SFID_AnnualReport_2019.pdf; and Sean F. Reardon, "The Widening Academic Achievement Gap Between the Rich and the Poor: New Evidence and Possible Explanations," in *Whither Opportunity? Rising Inequality, Schools, and Children's Life Chances*, ed. Greg J. Duncan and Richard J. Murnane (New York: Russell Sage Foundation, 2011), 91–116.

7. Eric A. Hanushek and Alfred A. Lindseth, *Schoolhouses, Courthouses, and Statehouses: Solving the Funding-Achievement Puzzle in America's Public Schools* (Princeton, NJ: Princeton University Press, 2009); National Commission on Excellence in Education, *A Nation at Risk* (Washington, DC: US Government Printing Office, 1983).

8. See, for example, "75 Examples of How Bureaucracy Stands in the Way of America's Students and Teachers" (Los Angeles: Eli and Edythe Broad Foundation, 2012), http://blogs.edweek.org/edweek/rick_hess_straight_up/2013/02/busting_bureaucracy_and_the_beginners_mind.html; Chester E. Finn Jr. and Michael J. Petrilli, "The Failures of U.S. Education Governance Today," in *Education Governance for the Twenty-First Century: Overcoming the Structural Barriers to School Reform*, ed. Paul Manna and Patrick McGuinn (Washington, DC: Brookings Institution Press, 2013), 21–35; and Hill, Pierce, and Guthrie, *Reinventing Public Education*.

9. Patrick McGuinn and Paul Manna, "Education Governance in America: Who Leads?," in Manna and McGuinn, *Education Governance for the Twenty-First Century*, 9; see also, National Commission on Governing America's Schools, *Governing America's Schools: Changing the Rules* (Denver: NCGAS, 1999), http://files.eric.ed.gov/fulltext/ED439513.pdf.

10. David K. Cohen, James P. Spillane, and Donald J. Peurach, "The Dilemmas of Educational Reform," *Educational Researcher* 47 (2018): 204–12, doi:10.3102/0013189X17743488; Donald J. Peurach, David K. Cohen, and Maxwell M. Yurkosky, "From Mass Schooling to Education Systems: Changing Patterns in the Organization and Management of Instruction," *Review of Research in Education* 43 (2019): 32–67, doi: 10.3102/0091732X18821131; Ron W. Zimmer, Gary T. Henry, and Adam Kho, "The Effects of School Turnaround in Tennessee's Achievement School District and Innovation Zones," *Educational Evaluation and Policy Analysis* 39 (2017): 670–96, doi: 10.3102/0162373717705729; and Domingo Morel, *Takeover: Race, Education, and American Democracy* (Oxford: Oxford University Press, 2018).

11. John E. Chubb and Terry M. Moe, *Politics, Markets, and America's Schools* (Washington, DC: Brookings Institution Press, 1990); W. G. Ouchi, "Power to the Principals: Decentralization in Three Large School Districts," *Organization Science* 17 (2006): 298–307, doi: 10.1287/orsc.1050.0172.

12. Matt Barnum, "With Big Names and $200 Million, a New Group Is Forming to Push for the 'Portfolio Model,'" Chalkbeat, last updated August 21, 2018, https://chalkbeat.org/posts/us/2018/07/31/the-city-fund-portfolio-model-200-million.

13. McGuinn and Manna, "Education Governance in America."

14. Hill, Campbell, and Gross, *Strife and Progress*, 3.

15. Center on Reinventing Public Education, *The 7 Components of a Portfolio Strategy*, rev. ed. (Seattle: Center on Reinventing Public Education, 2013), https://www.crpe.org/sites/default/files/brief_Portfolio_comprehensive_all_components.pdf.

16. Jeffrey R. Henig, "Portfolio Management Models and the Political Economy of Contracting Regimes," in Bulkley, Henig, and Levin, *Between Public and Private*.

17. Chubb and Moe, *Politics, Markets, and America's Schools*.

18. Hill, Campbell, and Gross, *Strife and Progress*.

19. Chubb and Moe, *Politics, Markets, and America's Schools*; Joseph Murphy and Lynn G. Beck, *School-Based Management as School Reform: Taking Stock* (Thousand Oaks, CA: Corwin Press, 1995); Ouchi, "Power to the Principals"; and Meredith I. Honig and Lydia R. Rainey, "Autonomy and School Improvement: What Do We

Know and Where Do We Go from Here?," *Educational Policy* 26 (2011): 465–95, doi: 10.1177/0895904811417590.

20. Chubb and Moe, *Politics, Markets, and America's Schools*; Priscilla Wohlstetter and Allan Odden, "Rethinking School-Based Management Policy and Research," *Educational Administration Quarterly* 28 (1992): 529–49, doi: 10.1177/0013161X92028004005; Honig and Rainey, "Autonomy and School Improvement"; and Ouchi, "Power to the Principals."

21. "75 Examples of How Bureaucracy Stands in the Way."

22. Center on Reinventing Public Education, *7 Components of a Portfolio Strategy*.

23. Matthew P. Steinberg, "Does Greater Autonomy Improve School Performance? Evidence from a Regression Discontinuity Analysis in Chicago," *Education Finance and Policy* 9 (2014), doi:10.1162/EDFP_a_00118: 1–35; Katharine O. Strunk et al., "The Impact of Turnaround Reform on Student Outcomes: Evidence and Insights from the Los Angeles Unified School District," *Education Finance and Policy* 11 (2016): 251–82, doi:10.1162/EDFP_a_00188; Ayesha K. Hashim, Katharine O. Strunk, and Julie A. Marsh, "The New School Advantage? Examining the Effects of Strategic New School Openings on Student Achievement," *Economics of Education Review* 62 (2018): 254–66, doi: 10.1016/j.econedurev.2017.12.002; David Menefee-Libey, "Neoliberal School Reform in Chicago? Renaissance 2010, Portfolios of Schools, and Diverse Providers," in Bulkley, Henig, and Levin, *Between Public and Private*, 55–90; Douglas N. Harris and Matthew F. Larsen, *The Effects of the New Orleans Post-Katrina Market-Based School Reforms on Student Achievement, High School Graduation, and College Outcomes* (New Orleans: Education Research Alliance for New Orleans, 2018), https://educationresearchalliancenola.org/files/publications/Harris-Larsen-Reform-Effects-2019-08-01.pdf; and Jonathan Gyurko and Jeffrey R. Henig, "Strong Vision, Learning by Doing, or the Politics of Muddling Through?," in Bulkley, Henig, and Levin, *Between Public and Private*, 91–126.

24. Susan Aud Pendergrass, Kevin Hesla, and Rebecca David, *A Growing Movement: America's Largest Public Charter School Communities*, 12th ed. (Washington, DC: National Alliance for Public Charter Schools, 2017), https://www.publiccharters.org/sites/default/files/documents/2017-10/Enrollment_Share_Report_Web_0.pdf.

25. Sean Gailmard, "Accountability and Principal-Agent Theory," in *The Oxford Handbook of Public Accountability*, ed. Robert E. Goodin and Thomas Schillemans (Oxford: Oxford University Press, 2014); Susanna Loeb and Patrick J. McEwan, "An Economic Approach to Education Policy Implementation," in *New Directions in Education Policy Implementation: Confronting Complexity*, ed. Meredith I. Honig (Albany: State University of New York Press, 2006).

26. Luis A. Huerta and Andrew Zuckerman, "An Institutional Theory Analysis of Charter Schools: Addressing Institutional Challenges to Scale," *Peabody Journal of Education* 84 (2009): 414–31, doi:10.1080/01619560902973621; Katrina E. Bulkley and Eva Travers, "Variations on a Theme: The Shift from Distinction to Commonality in Philadelphia's Diverse Provider Model, 2002–2008," *Journal of School Choice* 7 (2013): 532–59, doi: 10.1080/15582159.2013.837767; Paul DiMaggio and Walter Powell, "The Iron Cage Revisited: Institutional Isomorphism and Collective Rationality in Organizational Fields," *American Sociological Review* 48 (1983): 147–60; and Katrina E. Bulkley, "Charter School Authorizers: A New Governance Mechanism?," *Educational Policy* 13 (1999): 674–97, doi: 10.1177/0895904899013005004.

Chapter 2

1. Heather Lewis, *New York City Public Schools from Brownsville to Bloomberg: Community Control and its Legacy* (New York: Teachers College Press, 2015); Paul Peterson, "Monopoly and Competition in American Education," in *Choice and Control in American Education, Volume 1: The Theory of Choice and Control in Education,* ed. William H. Clune and John F. Witte (New York: Falmer Press, 1990).

2. Jeffrey R. Henig and Wilbur C. Rich, *Mayors in the Middle: Politics, Race, and Mayoral Control of Urban Schools* (Princeton, NJ: Princeton University Press, 2004); Dorothy Shipps, "Regime Change: Mayoral Takeover of the Chicago Public Schools," in *A Race Against Time: The Crisis in Urban Schooling,* ed. James G. Cibulka and William L. Boyd (Westport, CT: Praeger, 2003); Priscilla Wohlstetter and Allan Odden, "Rethinking School-Based Management Policy and Research," *Educational Administration Quarterly* 28 (1992): 529–49, doi: 10.1177/0013161X92028004005; and Marshall Smith and Jennifer O'Day, "Putting the Pieces Together: Systems for School Reform," (New Brunswick, NJ: Consortium for Policy Research in Education, 1991), https://repository.upenn.edu/cgi/viewcontent.cgi?article=1060&context=cpre_policybriefs.

3. John E. Chubb and Terry M. Moe, *Politics, Markets, and America's Schools* (Washington, DC: Brookings Institution Press, 1990); David Osborne and Ted Gaebler, *Reinventing Government: How the Entrepreneurial Spirit Is Transforming the Public Sector,* (Reading, MA: Addison-Wesley, 1992); and Paul T. Hill, Lawrence Pierce, and James Guthrie, *Reinventing Public Education: How Contracting Can Transform America's Schools,* RAND Research Study (Chicago: University of Chicago Press, 1997).

4. David Tyack, *The One Best System: A History of American Urban Education* (Cambridge, MA: Harvard University Press, 1974).

5. David A. Gamson and Emily M. Hodge, "Education Research and the Shifting Landscape of the American School District, 1816–2016," *Review of Research in Education* 40 (2016): 216–49, doi: 10.3102/0091732X16670323.

6. Chester E. Finn Jr. and Michael J. Petrilli, "The Failures of U.S. Education Governance Today," in *Education Governance for the Twenty-First Century: Overcoming the Structural Barriers to School Reform,* ed. Paul Manna and Patrick McGuinn (Washington, DC: Brookings Institution Press, 2013); Tyack, *One Best System*; Amy M. Hightower et al., eds., *School Districts and Instructional Renewal* (New York: Teachers College Press, 2002).

7. Cynthia E. Coburn, Judith Toure, and Mika Yamashita, "Evidence, Interpretation, and Persuasion: Instructional Decision Making at the District Central Office," *Teachers College Record* 111 (2009): 1115–61, https://www.tcrecord.org ID Number: 15232.

8. Meredith I. Honig, Nitya Venkateswaran, and Patricia McNeil, "Research Use as Learning: The Case of Fundamental Change in School District Central Offices," *American Educational Research Journal* 54 (2017): 938–71, doi: 10.3102/0002831217712466.

9. Gamson and Hodge, "Education Research and the Shifting Landscape"; Tina Trujillo, "Learning from the Past to Chart New Directions in the Study of School District Effectiveness," in *Thinking and Acting Systemically: Improving School Districts Under Pressure,* ed. Alan J. Daly and Kara S. Finnigan (Washington, DC: American Educational Research Association, 2016).

10. Katrina E. Bulkley, "Introduction: Portfolio Management Models in Urban School Reform," in *Between Public and Private: Politics, Governance, and the New Portfolio Models for Urban School Reform,* ed. Katrina E. Bulkley, Jeffrey R. Henig, and Henry M. Levin (Cambridge, MA: Harvard Education Press, 2010).

11. Trujillo, "Learning from the Past," 11.
12. Chubb and Moe, *Politics, Markets, and America's Schools*; Finn and Petrilli, "Failures of U.S. Education Governance"; Frederick M. Hess and Olivia M. Meeks, "Rethinking District Governance," in Manna and McGuinn, *Education Governance for the Twenty-First Century*; and Hill, Pierce, and Guthrie, *Reinventing Public Education*.
13. Trujillo, "Learning from the Past," 12.
14. Hill, Pierce, and Guthrie, *Reinventing Public Education*; Jeffrey R. Henig, "Portfolio Management Models and the Political Economy of Contracting Regimes," in Bulkley, Henig, and Levin, *Between Public and Private*, 27–52.
15. Katrina E. Bulkley and Jeffrey R. Henig, "Local Politics and Portfolio Management Models: National Reform Ideas and Local Control," *Peabody Journal of Education* 90 (2015): 54.
16. Meredith I. Honig and Michael DeArmond, "Where's the Management in Portfolio Management?," in Bulkley, Henig, and Levin, *Between Public and Private*, 195–216, doi: 10.1080/0161956X.2015.988528.
17. Sean Gailmard, "Accountability and Principal-Agent Theory," in *The Oxford Handbook of Public Accountability*, ed. Mark Bovens, Robert E. Goodin, and Thomas Schillemans (Oxford: Oxford University Press, 2014); Susanna Loeb and Patrick J. McEwan, "An Economic Approach to Education Policy Implementation," in *New Directions in Education Policy Implementation: Confronting Complexity*, ed. Meredith I. Honig (Albany: State University of New York Press, 2006).
18. Henig, "Portfolio Management Models"; Hill, Pierce, and Guthrie, *Reinventing Public Education*.
19. Julian R. Betts, "The Impact of Educational Standards on the Level and Distribution of Earnings," *American Economic Review* 88 (1998): 266–75, https://www.jstor.org/stable/i300820.
20. Robin J. Lake and Paul T. Hill, *Performance Management in Portfolio School Districts* (Seattle: Center on Reinventing Public Education, 2009), https://www.crpe.org/sites/default/files/pub_dscr_portfperf_aug09_0.pdf.
21. Paul T. Hill, Christine Campbell, and Betheny Gross, *Strife and Progress: Portfolio Strategies for Managing Urban Schools* (Washington, DC: Brookings Institution Press, 2012); Hess and Meeks, "Rethinking District Governance."
22. Paula Arce-Trigatti et al., *Is There Choice in School Choice?*, (New Orleans: Education Research Alliance for New Orleans, 2016); Betheny Gross et al., *Are City Schools Becoming Monolithic? Analyzing the Diversity of Options in Denver, New Orleans, and Washington, DC* (Seattle: Center on Reinventing Public Education, 2017).
23. Patrick Denice and Betheny Gross, "Choice, Preferences, and Constraints: Evidence from Public School Applications in Denver," *Sociology of Education* 89 (2016): 300–320, doi: 10.1177/0038040716664395; A+ Colorado, *Unequal Choices: School Model Diversity in Denver Public Schools* (Denver: A+ Colorado, 2018), http://apluscolorado.org/wp-content/uploads/2018/05/Unequal-Choices-School-Model-Diversity-in-Denver-Public-Schools.pdf.
24. Matthew P. Steinberg, "Does Greater Autonomy Improve School Performance? Evidence from a Regression Discontinuity Analysis in Chicago," *Education Finance and Policy* 9 (2014): 1–35, doi: 10.1162/EDFP_a_00118; Julie A. Marsh, Katharine O. Strunk, and Susan Bush, "Portfolio District Reform Meets School Turnaround: Early Implementation Findings from the Los Angeles Public School Choice Initiative," *Journal of Educational Administration* 51 (2013): 498–527, https://eric.ed.gov/?id=EJ1014254.

25. Robin J. Lake et al., *Sticking Points: How School Districts Experience Implementing the Portfolio Strategy* (Seattle: Center on Reinventing Public Education, 2016), https://www.crpe.org/sites/default/files/crpe-sticking-points.pdf; Christian Buerger and Douglas N. Harris, *How Did the New Orleans School Reforms Influence School Spending?* (New Orleans: Educational Research Alliance for New Orleans, 2017), https://educationresearchalliancenola.org/files/publications/020717-Buerger-Harris-How-Did-the-New-Orleans-School-Reforms-Influence-School-Spending.pdf.

26. Bulkley and Henig, "Local Politics and Portfolio Management Models."

27. Clarence N. Stone et al., *Building Civic Capacity: The Politics of Reforming Urban Schools* (Lawrence: University Press of Kansas, 2001).

28. David Osborne, "Denver Expands Choice and Charters," *Education Next* 16, no. 3 (Summer 2016), https://www.educationnext.org/denver-expands-choice-and-charters; Richard Welsh and Michelle Hall, "The Point of No Return? Interest Groups, School Board Elections and the Sustainment of the Portfolio Management Model in Post-Katrina New Orleans," *Teachers College Record* 120, no. 7 (2018): 1–38, https://www.tcrecord.org ID Number: 22116; and Jeffrey R. Henig, Rebecca Jacobsen, and Sarah Reckhow, *Outside Money in Local School Board Elections: The Nationalization of Education Politics* (Cambridge, MA: Harvard Education Press, 2019).

29. Sarah Reckhow, "Disseminating and Legitimating a New Approach: The Role of Foundations," in Bulkley, Henig, and Levin, *Between Public and Private*, 277–304; Sarah Reckhow, *Follow the Money: How Foundation Dollars Change Public School Politics* (New York: Oxford University Press, 2012); Janelle T. Scott, "The Politics of Venture Philanthropy in Charter School Policy and Advocacy," *Educational Policy* 23 (2009): 106–36, doi: 10.1177/0895904808328531; and Elizabeth H. DeBray et al., "Intermediary Organizations in Charter School Policy Coalitions: Evidence from New Orleans," *Educational Policy* 28 (2014): 175–206, doi: 10.1177/0895904813514132.

30. Matt Barnum, "With Big Names and $200 Million, a New Group Is Forming to Push for the 'Portfolio Model,'" Chalkbeat, last updated August 21, 2018, https://chalkbeat.org/posts/us/2018/07/31/the-city-fund-portfolio-model-200-million.

31. Marsh, J., Allbright, T., Bulkley, K., Brown, D., Strunk, K., & Harris, D. (In press). The process and politics of educational governance change in New Orleans, Los Angeles, and Denver. *American Educational Research Journal*, https://doi.org/10.3102/0002831220921475

32. Adrienne D. Dixson, Kristen L. Buras, and Elizabeth K. Jeffers, "The Color of Reform: Race, Education Reform, and Charter Schools in Post-Katrina New Orleans," *Qualitative Inquiry* 21 (2015): 288–99, doi: 10.1177/1077800414557826.

33. Wayne Au and Joseph J. Ferrare, eds., *Mapping Corporate Education Reform: Power and Policy Networks in the Neoliberal State* (New York: Routledge, 2015); Stephen J. Ball, "Neoliberal Education? Confronting the Slouching Beast," *Policy Futures in Education* 14 (2016): 1046–59, doi: 10.1177/1478210316664259; Pauline Lipman, *The New Political Economy of Urban Education: Neoliberalism, Race, and the Right to the City* (New York: Routledge, 2013); and Janelle T. Scott, "School Choice and the Empowerment Imperative," *Peabody Journal of Education* 88 (2013): 60–73, doi: 10.1080/0161956X.2013.752635.

34. Kevin Hesla, Jamison White, and Adam Gerstenfeld, *A Growing Movement: America's Largest Charter Public School Communities*, 13th ed. (Washington, DC: National Alliance for Public Charter Schools, 2019), https://www.publiccharters.org/sites/default

/files/documents/2019-03/rd1_napcs_enrollment_share_report%2003112019.pdf; Todd Ziebarth, *Top 10 Charter Communities by Market Share* (Washington, DC: National Alliance for Public Charter Schools, 2006), https://www.publiccharters.org /sites/default/files/migrated/wp-content/uploads/2014/01/marketsharepiecefinal914 _20110402T222333.pdf.

35. Mary L. Mason and Sarah Reckhow, "Rootless Reforms? State Takeovers and School Governance in Detroit and Memphis," *Peabody Journal of Education* 92 (2017): 64–75, doi: 10.1080/0161956X.2016.1264813.

36. Judith Kafka, "Institutional Theory and the History of District-Led School Reform: A Reintroduction," in *The Shifting Landscape of the American School District: Race, Class, Geography, and the Perpetual Reform of Local Control, 1935–2015*, ed. David A. Gamson and Emily M. Hodge (New York: Peter Lang, 2018).

37. W. Richard Scott, *Institutions and Organizations: Ideas and Interests* (Thousand Oaks, CA: Sage Publications, 2008).

38. Heinz-Dieter Meyer and Brian Rowan, eds., *The New Institutionalism in Education* (Albany: State University of New York Press, 2006); Meyer and Rowan, "Institutionalized Organizations: Formal Structure as Myth and Ceremony," *American Journal of Sociology* 83 (1977): 340–63, doi: 10.1086/226550.

39. Meyer and Rowan, "Institutionalized Organizations"; John W. Meyer, W. Richard Scott, and Terence E. Deal, "Institutional and Technical Sources of Organizational Structure: Explaining the Structure of Educational Organizations," in *Organizational Environments: Ritual and Rationality*, ed. John W. Meyer and W. Richard Scott (Thousand Oaks, CA: Sage Publications, 1983).

40. Luis A. Huerta and Andrew Zuckerman, "An Institutional Theory Analysis of Charter Schools: Addressing Institutional Challenges to Scale," *Peabody Journal of Education* 84 (2009): 414–31, doi: 10.1080/01619560902973621.

41. Katrina E. Bulkley and Eva Travers, "Variations on a Theme: The Shift from Distinction to Commonality in Philadelphia's Diverse Provider Model, 2002–2008," *Journal of School Choice* 7 (2013): 532–59, doi: 10.1080/15582159.2013.837767; Paul DiMaggio and Walter Powell, "The Iron Cage Revisited: Institutional Isomorphism and Collective Rationality in Organizational Fields," *American Sociological Review* 48 (1983): 147–60.

42. Karl E. Weick, "Educational Organizations as Loosely Coupled Systems," *Administrative Science Quarterly* 21 (1976): 1–19; Cynthia E. Coburn, "Beyond Decoupling: Rethinking the Relationship Between the Institutional Environment and the Classroom," *Sociology of Education* 77 (2004): 211–44, doi: 10.1177/003804070407700302.

43. Chubb and Moe, *Politics, Markets, and America's Schools*; Terry M. Moe, "Political Control and the Power of the Agent," *Journal of Law, Economics, and Organization* 22 (2006): 1–29, doi: 10.1093/jleo/ewj011; and Charles E. Bidwell, "Varieties of Institutional Theory: Traditions and Prospects for Educational Research," in *The New Institutionalism in Education*, ed. Heinz-Dieter Meyer and Brian Rowan (Albany: State University of New York Press, 2006).

44. Chubb and Moe, *Politics, Markets, and America's Schools*; Terry M. Moe, *Special Interest: Teachers Unions and America's Public Schools* (Washington, DC: Brookings Institution Press, 2011).

45. David Tyack and William Tobin, "The 'Grammar' of Schooling: Why Has It Been So Hard to Change?," *American Educational Research Journal* 31 (1994): 453–79, doi: 10.3102/00028312031003453.

46. Jennifer L. Bartlett et al., "Prologue: Stability and Change," *Journal of Management and Organization* 17 (2011): 522–33, doi: 10.1017/S1833367200001425; Scott, *Institutions and Organizations*.

47. Scott Davies, Linda Quirke, and Janice Aurini, "The New Institutionalism Goes to the Market: The Challenge of Rapid Growth in Private K–12 Education," in Meyer and Rowan, *New Institutionalism in Education*, 103–122; Huerta and Zuckerman, "Institutional Theory Analysis."

48. Scott, *Institutions and Organizations*.

49. Reckhow, *Follow the Money*.

50. Steinberg, "Does Greater Autonomy Improve School Performance?"; Katharine O. Strunk et al., "The Impact of Turnaround Reform on Student Outcomes: Evidence and Insights from the Los Angeles Unified School District," *Education Finance and Policy* 11 (2016): 251–82, doi: 10.1162/EDFP_a_00188; Ayesha K. Hashim, Katharine O. Strunk, and Julie A. Marsh, "The New School Advantage? Examining the Effects of Strategic New School Openings on Student Achievement," *Economics of Education Review* 62 (2018): 254–66, doi: 10.1016/j.econedurev.2017.12.002; and Douglas N. Harris and Matthew F. Larsen, *The Effects of the New Orleans Post-Katrina Market-Based School Reforms on Student Achievement, High School Graduation, and College Outcomes* (New Orleans: Education Research Alliance for New Orleans, 2018), https://educationresearchalliancenola.org/files/publications/Harris-Larsen-Reform-Effects-2019-08-01.pdf.

51. Andrew J. McEachin, Richard Osbourne Welsh, and Dominic James Brewer, "The Variation in Student Achievement and Behavior Within a Portfolio Management Model: Early Results from New Orleans," *Educational Evaluation and Policy Analysis* 38 (2016): 669–91, doi: 10.3102/0162373716659928; Strunk et al., "Impact of Turnaround Reform."

52. Ron W. Zimmer and Cassandra M. Guarino, "Is There Empirical Evidence That Charter Schools 'Push Out' Low-Performing Students?," *Educational Evaluation and Policy Analysis* 35 (2013): 461–80, doi: 10.3102/0162373713498465; Kevin Booker, Ron Zimmer, and Richard Buddin, *The Effects of Charter Schools on School Peer Composition* (Santa Monica, CA: RAND Corporation, 2005), https://www.rand.org/content/dam/rand/pubs/working_papers/2005/RAND_WR306.pdf.

53. E. Christine Baker-Smith, "Suspensions Suspended: Do Changes to High School Suspension Policies Change Suspension Rates?," *Peabody Journal of Education* 93 (2018): 190–206, doi: 10.1080/0161956X.2018.1435043; Johanna Lacoe and Matthew P. Steinberg, "Rolling Back Zero Tolerance: The Effect of Discipline Policy Reform on Suspension Usage and Student Outcomes," *Peabody Journal of Education* 93 (2018): 207–27, doi: 10.1080/0161956X.2018.1435047; and Ayesha K. Hashim, Katharine O. Strunk, and Tasminda K. Dhaliwal, "Justice for All? Suspension Bans and Restorative Justice Programs in the Los Angeles Unified School District," *Peabody Journal of Education* 93, no. 2 (2018): 174–89, doi: 10.1080/0161956X.2018.1435040.

54. Baker-Smith, "Suspensions Suspended," 202.

55. Denice and Gross, "Choice, Preferences, and Constraints"; Sean Corcoran and Henry M. Levin, "School Choice and Competition in the New York City Schools," in *Education Reform in New York City: An Ambitious Change in the Nation's Most Complex School System*, ed. Jennifer A. O'Day, Catherine S. Bitter, and Louis M. Gomez (Cambridge, MA: Harvard University Press, 2011).

Chapter 3

1. For more on the history and evolution of these three systems, see Julie A. Marsh et al., "The Process and Politics of Educational Governance Change in New Orleans, Los Angeles, and Denver," *American Educational Research Journal* (forthcoming, published online May 2020), doi: 10.3102/0002831220921475, on which this section of the chapter is based.

2. David D. Tyack, *The One Best System: A History of American Urban Education* (Cambridge, MA: Harvard University Press, 1974).

3. For more on these reforms, see Charles Taylor Kerchner et al., *Learning from L.A.: Institutional Change in American Public Education* (Cambridge, MA: Harvard Education Press, 2008).

4. David Osborne, *Reinventing America's Schools: Creating a 21st Century Education System* (New York: Bloomsbury, 2017).

5. Douglas Harris and Carolyn Herrington, "Accountability, Standards, and the Growing Achievement Gap: Lessons from the Past Half-Century," *American Journal of Education* 112, no. 2 (February 2006): 209-238, doi: 10.1086/498995.

6. Bruce Fuller, *When Schools Work: Pluralistic Politics and Institutional Reform in Los Angeles* (unpublished manuscript).

7. Jim Griffin, "Colorado's Charter Schools: Their History and Their Future," *Denver Post*, May 17, 2013, https://www.denverpost.com/2013/05/17/colorados-charter-schools-their-history-and-their-future.

8. Gary Sernovitz, "What New Orleans Tells Us About the Perils of Putting Schools on the Free Market," *New Yorker*, July 30, 2018, https://www.newyorker.com/business/currency/what-new-orleans-tells-us-about-the-perils-of-putting-schools-on-the-free-market; Erik W. Robelen, "New Orleans Eyed as Clean Educational Slate," *Education Week*, September 21, 2005, 22–23.

9. Peter F. Burns and Matthew O. Thomas, *Reforming New Orleans: The Contentious Politics of Change in the Big Easy* (Ithaca, NY: Cornell University Press, 2015).

10. Gordon Russell, "Mose Jefferson Is Indicted in School Bribe," Nola.com, April 3, 2008, https://www.nola.com/news/article_3b50209e-02bc-500f-90ba-93259ffcdfc2.html.

11. Douglas Harris, *Charter School City: What the End of Traditional Public Schools in New Orleans Means for American Education* (Chicago: University of Chicago Press, 2020).

12. Andre Perry et al., *The Transformation of New Orleans Public Schools: Addressing System-Level Problems Without a System* (New Orleans: The Data Center, 2015), https://s3.amazonaws.com/gnocdc/reports/TheDataCenter_PublicEducation.pdf.

13. Perry et al., *Transformation of New Orleans Public Schools*.

14. Debra Vaughan et al., *Transforming Public Education in New Orleans: The Recovery School District 2003–2011* (New Orleans: Cowen Institute, 2011).

15. Jane Arnold Lincove, Nathan Barrett, and Katharine O. Strunk, "Lessons from Hurricane Katrina: The Employment Effects of the Mass Dismissal of New Orleans Teachers," *Educational Researcher* 47, no. 3 (April 2018): 192; Perry et al., *Transformation of New Orleans Public Schools*.

16. Harris, *Charter School City*.

17. "Ten Years After Katrina," *New York Times*, August 28, 2015, https://www.nytimes.com/interactive/2015/08/26/us/ten-years-after-katrina.html.

18. Center on Reinventing Public Education, "The 7 Components of a Portfolio Strategy," 2013, https://www.crpe.org/publications/7-components-portfolio-strategy.

19. New Orleans Equity Index, *Equity Matters: A Look at Educational Equity in New Orleans Public Schools* (New Orleans: Converge, 2017), http://neworleansequityindex.org /files/downloads/New-Orleans-Education-Equity-Index-Report-2017.pdf.

20. Harris, *Charter School City*.

21. Whitney Bross and Douglas N. Harris, *How (and How Well) Do Charter School Authorizers Choose Schools? Evidence from the Recovery School District in New Orleans* (New Orleans: Education Research Alliance for New Orleans, 2016), https://education researchalliancenola.org/files/publications/Bross-Harris-How-Do-Charter-Authorizers -Choose-Schools.pdf.

22. Kristen L. Buras, *Charter Schools, Race, and Urban Space: Where the Market Meets Grassroots Resistance* (New York: Routledge, 2015); Burns and Thomas, *Reforming New Orleans*; Harris, *Charter School City*.

23. At the time of this study, a small number of the highest performing schools did not participate in EnrollNOLA.

24. Vincent Rossmeier, *A Primer on Differentiated Funding* (New Orleans: Cowen Institute, 2016), http://www.thecoweninstitute.com.php56-17.dfw3-1.websitetestlink.com /uploads/CI-DIfferentiated-Funding-Draft-1505855257.pdf.

25. Kate Babineau, Dave Hand, and Vincent Rossmeier, *The State of Public Education in New Orleans 2016–17* (New Orleans: Cowen Institute, 2017), https://tulane.app.box .com/s/ddngdxbtar9kkn21szyzi6gsplslwqn3.
Due to the hurricane, no administrative data are available for 2005–6. Although not depicted in figure 3.1, the years prior to 2003 reflect a similar pre-Katrina pattern of majority traditional schools with a few charter schools.

26. *Public School Governance in New Orleans: 2016–17 School Year* (New Orleans: Cowen Institute, 2016), http://www.thecoweninstitute.com.php56-17.dfw3-1.websitetestlink .com/uploads/governance-poster-16-17FINAL-1505855054.pdf.

27. See "Philly School Exec Headed to New Orleans," *Oklahoman*, May 4, 2007, https:// newsok.com/article/2827139/philly-school-exec-headed-to-new-orleans; "Meet John White," Louisiana Department of Education, https://www.louisianabelieves.com /resources/about-us/meet-john-white (page since removed from website); and Dawn Ruth Wilson, "The Way to Recovery," MyNewOrleans.com, January 2, 2015, https:// www.myneworleans.com/the-way-to-recovery.

28. "City and Town Postcensal Tables: 1990–2000, Denver City, Colorado," US Census Bureau website, https://www.census.gov/data/tables/time-series/demo/popest/2000- subcounties-eval-estimates.html; "City and Town Population Totals: 2010–2018, Denver City, Colorado," US Census Bureau website, https://www.census.gov/data/tables /time-series/demo/popest/2010s-total-cities-and-towns.html.

29. See, e.g., "U.S. News & World Report Unveils the 2017 Best Places to Live," *U.S. News & World Report*, February 7, 2017, https://www.usnews.com/info/blogs/press-room /articles/2017-02-07/us-news-unveils-the-2017-best-places-to-live.

30. David Osborne, "Denver Expands Choice and Charters," *Education Next*, 16, no. 3 (Summer 2016).

31. Osborne "Denver Expands Choice," 37.

32. Osborne, "Denver Expands Choice."

33. Melanie Asmar, "Split Decision: Two Incumbents Losing in Denver School Board Elections, Two Supporters of District Policies Prevail," Chalkbeat.org, November 7, 2017, https://www.chalkbeat.org/posts/co/2017/11/07/control-of-the-denver-school-board -in-play-in-tuesdays-contentious-election.

34. Hereafter, schools that exercised the options granted under the Innovation Schools Act will be referred to as "innovation schools."
35. Osborne, *Reinventing America's Schools*.
36. "2017 Public Elementary-Secondary Education Finance Data, Individual Unit Tables, Denver School District 1," US Census Bureau website, https://www.census.gov/data /tables/2017/econ/school-finances/secondary-education-finance.html.
37. *Understanding Colorado School Finance and Categorical Program Funding* (Denver: Colorado Department of Education, October 2018), https://www.cde.state.co.us /cdefinance/fy2018-19brochure.
38. Kerchner et al., *Learning from L.A.*
39. Fuller, *When Schools Work*, first page of chapter 3.
40. Julie A. Marsh, "The Political Dynamics of District Reform: The Form and Fate of the Los Angeles Public School Choice Initiative," *Teachers College Record* 118, no. 9 (2016), https://www.tcrecord.org ID Number: 21519.
41. Fuller, *When Schools Work*, page 25 of chapter 3.
42. Kerchner et al., *Learning from L.A.*
43. To deny a charter petition, school boards were required to submit "written factual findings" that the charter included an "unsound educational program," that petitioners were "demonstrably unlikely" to succeed in implementing their plan, and that the petition lacked the requisite signatures and description of required elements. See California Education Code, Sections 47601–47615, https://leginfo.legislature.ca.gov/faces /codes_displayText.xhtml?lawCode=EDC&division=4.&title=2.&part=26.8.&chapter =1.&article=.
44. Passed by voters in 2000, Proposition 39 lowered the threshold for votes required to pass local bonds from two-thirds to 55 percent of the votes cast. It also included a provision requiring school districts to make classroom and nonclassroom facilities available to charter schools serving students residing in the district.
45. Fuller, *When Schools Work*.
46. For details on this reform see Julie Marsh, Katharine Strunk, and Susan Bush, "Portfolio District Reform Meets School Turnaround: Early Implementation Findings from the Los Angeles Public School Choice Initiative," *Journal of Educational Administration* 51, no. 4 (2013), doi: 10.1108/09578231311325677; and Katharine Strunk et al., "The Impact of Turnaround Reform on Student Achievement: Evidence and Insights from the Los Angeles Unified School District," *Education Finance and Policy* 11, no. 3 (Summer 2016), doi: 10.1162/EDFP_a_00188.
47. Patrick Murphy and Jennifer Paluch, *Financing California's Public Schools* (San Francisco: Public Policy Institute of California, 2018), https://www.ppic.org/wp-content /uploads/jtf-financing-californias-public-schools.pdf.
48. "2017 Public Elementary-Secondary Education Finance Data, Individual Unit Tables, Los Angeles Unified School District," US Census Bureau website, https://www.census .gov/data/tables/2017/econ/school-finances/secondary-education-finance.html.
49. "K–12 Public School Enrollment: 1964733-Los Angeles Unified," Data Reporting Office, California Department of Education, https://dq.cde.ca.gov/dataquest/DQ/Enr TimeRpt.aspx?Level=District&cYear=2010-11&cname=LOS%20ANGELES%20 UNIFIED&cCode=1964733.
50. Jeffrey R. Henig, Rebecca Jacobsen, and Sarah Reckhow, *Outside Money in Local School Board Elections: The Nationalization of Education Politics* (Cambridge, MA: Harvard Education Press, 2019).

51. For more on this history, see Michelle Maltais and Sonali Kohli, "See How LAUSD Has Wavered Between Picking Leaders from the Outside and Within," *Los Angeles Times*, January 13, 2016, http://www.latimes.com/local/education/lausd/la-me-edu-la-unified -superintendents-20160112-htmlstory.html.

52. Howard Blume and Anna M. Phillips, "Charter Backers Win Their First L.A. School Board Majority," *Los Angeles Times*, May 17, 2017, http://www.latimes.com/local /lanow/la-me-edu-school-election-20170516-story.html. See also Henig, Jacobsen, and Reckhow, *Outside Money*.

53. Christian Buerger and Douglas Harris, *How Did the New Orleans School Reforms Influence School Spending?* (New Orleans: Educational Research Alliance for New Orleans, 2017), https://educationresearchalliancenola.org/files/publications/020717 -Buerger-Harris-How-Did-the-New-Orleans-School-Reforms-Influence-School -Spending.pdf.

54. "Supporters," A+ Colorado, retrieved June 4, 2018, http://apluscolorado.org/supporters; "The A+ Story," A+ Colorado, retrieved June 4, 2018, http://apluscolorado.org/about -us/the-a-story; and Osborne, "Denver Expands Choice."

55. Adrienne D. Dixson, Kristen L. Buras, and Elizabeth K. Jeffers, "The Color of Reform: Race, Education Reform, and Charter Schools in Post-Katrina New Orleans," *Qualitative Inquiry* 21, no. 3 (2015), doi: 10.1177/1077800414557826; Harris, *Charter School City*.

56. For more on these tensions, see Marsh et al., "The Process and Politics of Educational Governance Change."

Chapter 4

1. Whitney Bross and Douglas N. Harris, *How (and How Well) Do Charter Authorizers Choose Schools? Evidence from the Recovery School District in New Orleans* (New Orleans: Education Research Alliance for New Orleans, 2016), https://educationresearch alliancenola.org/files/publications/Bross-Harris-How-Do-Charter-Authorizers -Choose-Schools.pdf.

2. Regarding the effect of school closures on students whose schools are closed, see Whitney Bross, Douglas N. Harris, and Lihan Liu, *The Effects of Performance-Based School Closure and Charter Takeover on Student Performance* (New Orleans: Education Research Alliance for New Orleans, 2016), https://educationresearchalliancenola. org/files/publications/Bross-Harris-Liu-The-Effects-of-Performance-Based-School-Closure-and-Charter-Takeover-on-Student-Performance.pdf; and Julia Gwynne and Marisa de la Torre, *When Schools Close: Effects on Displaced Students in Chicago Public Schools* (Chicago: Consortium on Chicago School Research at the University of Chicago, 2009), https://consortium.uchicago.edu/sites/default/files/2018-10/CCSRSchool Closings-Final.pdf. On performance of students improving when they move from a closed school to a higher performing school, see Deven Carlson and Stéphane Lavertu, "Charter School Closure and Student Achievement: Evidence from Ohio," *Journal of Urban Economics* 95 (2016): 31–48, doi: 10.1016/j.jue.2016.07.001.

3. Jennifer A. O'Day, "Complexity, Accountability, and School Improvement," *Harvard Educational Review* 72, no. 3 (2002): 293–329; Brian M. Stecher et al., *Organizational Improvement and Accountability: Lessons for Education from Other Sectors* (Santa Monica, CA: Rand Corporation, 2004), https://www.rand.org/content/dam/rand/pubs /monographs/2004/RAND_MG136.pdf.

4. Orleans Parish School Board, "Request for Proposal No. 18-0019," February 13, 2020, https://www.documentcloud.org/documents/4374158-REQUEST-for-PROPOSAL -NO-18-0019-McDonogh-35-Long.html, 9.

5. See Kristen L. Buras, *Charter Schools, Race, and Urban Space: Where the Market Meets Grassroots Resistance* (New York: Routledge, 2015); Adrienne D. Dixson, Kristen L. Buras, and Elizabeth K. Jeffers, "The Color of Reform: Race, Education Reform, and Charter Schools in Post-Katrina New Orleans," *Qualitative Inquiry* 21, no. 3 (2015): 288–99, doi: 10.1177/1077800414557826.

6. "2015–16 School Report Card Technical Guide: High School Metrics," Los Angeles Unified School District, accessed February 15, 2020, https://achieve.lausd.net/site /handlers/filedownload.ashx?moduleinstanceid=29205&dataid=44190&FileName =Technical%20Guide_High_2015-16.docx.

7. See Jennifer Booher-Jennings, "Below the Bubble: 'Educational Triage' and the Texas Accountability System," *American Education Research Journal* 42, no. 2 (2005): 231–68.

8. Booher-Jennings, "Below the Bubble."

9. For example, see Buras, *Charter Schools, Race, and Urban Space*; and Dixson, Buras, and Jeffers, "Color of Reform."

Chapter 5

1. John E. Chubb and Terry M. Moe, *Politics, Markets, and America's Schools* (Washington, DC: Brookings Institution Press, 1990); Milton Friedman, *Capitalism and Freedom* (Chicago: University of Chicago Press, 1962).

2. Jennifer Jennings, "School Choice or Schools' Choice? Managing in an Era of Accountability," *Sociology of Education* 83, no. 3 (2010): 227–47; Kevin Welner, *The Dirty Dozen: How Charter Schools Influence Student Enrollment* (Boulder, CO: National Education Policy Center, 2013); and Douglas N. Harris, *Charter School City: What the End of Traditional Public Schools in New Orleans Means for American Education* (Chicago: University of Chicago Press, 2020).

3. Julian R. Betts and Tom Loveless, eds., *Getting Choice Right: Ensuring Equity and Efficiency in Education Policy* (Washington, DC: Brookings Institution Press, 2005).

4. Douglas S. Massey, Jonathan Rothwell, and Thurston Domina, "The Changing Bases of Segregation in the United States," *Annals of the American Academy of Political and Social Science* 626, no. 1 (2009): 74–90, doi: 10.1177/0002716209343558.

5. Douglas N. Harris, Jon Valant, and Betheny Gross, "The New Orleans OneApp," *Education Next* 15, no. 4 (Fall 2015), https://www.educationnext.org/new-orleans-oneapp.

6. Harris, *Charter School City*.

7. Jennings, "School Choice or Schools' Choice?"

8. "About Zones of Choice | Sobre las Zonas de Opción," Zones of Choice, Los Angeles Unified School District website, February 14, 2020, https://achieve.lausd.net /domain/291.

9. Sonahli Kohli, "Magnet Schools: How to Navigate One of L.A.'s Most Complex Mazes," *Los Angeles Times*, October 9, 2015, https://www.latimes.com/local/education/lausd /la-me-edu-magnet-schools-guide-20151008-htmlstory.html.

10. Harris, *Charter School City*.

11. A t-test of the difference in means shows that New Orleans is statistically higher than Denver, which is statistically higher than Los Angeles.

12. Recall that New Orleans does not have traditional public schools.

13. An enrollment demand measure could not be calculated for Los Angeles because no unified enrollment process or data set was in place at the time of data collection.
14. Harris, Valant, and Gross, "New Orleans OneApp."
15. Jennings, "School Choice or Schools' Choice?"
16. Harris, *Charter School City*.

Chapter 6

1. John E. Chubb and Terry M. Moe, *Politics, Markets, and America's Schools* (Washington, DC: Brookings Institution Press, 1990); J. Murphy and L. G. Beck, *School-Based Management as School Reform: Taking Stock* (Thousand Oaks, CA: Corwin Press, 1995); and W. G. Ouchi, "Power to the Principals: Decentralization in Three Large School Districts," *Organizational Science* 17, no. 2 (2006): 298–307.
2. Center on Reinventing Public Education, *The 7 Components of a Portfolio Strategy*, Education Finance Policy 9 (Seattle: CRPE, 2013).
3. Paul T. Hill, *Defining and Organizing for School Autonomy* (Seattle: CRPE, 2013), https://www.crpe.org/publications/defining-and-organizing-school-autonomy.
4. CRPE, *7 Components*.
5. Atila Abdulkadiroğlu et al., "Accountability and Flexibility in Public Schools: Evidence from Boston's Charters and Pilots," *Quarterly Journal of Economics* 126, no. 2 (2011): 699–748.
6. Matthew P. Steinberg, "Does Greater Autonomy Improve School Performance? Evidence from a Regression Discontinuity Analysis in Chicago," *Education Finance and Policy* 9, no.1 (2014): 1–35; Matthew P. Steinberg and Amanda Barrett Cox, "School Autonomy and District Support: How Principals Respond to a Tiered Autonomy Initiative in Philadelphia Public Schools," *Leadership and Policy in Schools* 16, no. 1 (2017): 130–65, doi: 10.1080/15700763.2016.1197278.
7. CRPE, *7 Components*.
8. Steinberg, "Does Greater Autonomy Improve Performance?"
9. Meredith I. Honig and Lydia R. Rainey, "Autonomy and School Improvement: What Do We Know and Where Do We Go from Here?," *Educational Policy* 26, no. 3 (2012): 465–95.
10. CRPE, *7 Components*.
11. Note that while the survey data suggest lower levels of teacher-reported influence in stand-alone charter schools in Denver relative to other school types, this result is not statistically significant, and the study did not find corroborating evidence to support this finding in the case study schools.
12. Andre Perry et al., "The Transformation of New Orleans Public Schools: Addressing System-Level Problems Without a System," in *The New Orleans Index at Ten: Measuring Greater New Orleans' Progress Toward Prosperity* (New Orleans: The Data Center, 2015), 1–16.
13. Ayesha K. Hashim, Katharine O. Strunk, and Tasminda K. Dhaliwal, "Justice for All? Suspension Bans and Restorative Justice Programs in the Los Angeles Unified School District," *Peabody Journal of Education* 93, no. 2 (2018): 174–89.
14. This finding is consistent with prior research, e.g., Honig and Rainey, "Autonomy and School Improvement."
15. Andrew J. McEachin, Richard O. Welsh, and Dominic J. Brewer, "The Variation in Student Achievement and Behavior Within a Portfolio Management Model: Early

Results from New Orleans," *Educational Evaluation and Policy Analysis* 38, Educational Evaluation and Policy Analysis 38, no.4 (2016): 669–91.

Chapter 7

1. Raj Chetty, John N. Friedman, and Jonah E. Rockoff, "Measuring the Impacts of Teachers II: Teacher Value-Added and Student Outcomes in Adulthood," *American Economic Review* 104, no. 9 (2014): 2633–79; Susan Moore Johnson, Matthew A. Kraft, and John P. Papay, "How Context Matters in High-Need Schools: The Effects of Teachers' Working Conditions on Their Professional Satisfaction and Their Students' Achievement," *Teachers College Record* 114, no. 10 (2012): 1–39.

2. Terry M. Moe, *Special Interest: Teachers Unions and America's Public Schools* (Washington, DC: Brookings Institution Press, 2011).

3. Christine Campbell and Michael De Armond, *Talent Management in Portfolio Districts,* Working Paper No. 2010-4 (Seattle: Center on Reinventing Public Education, 2010).

4. David A. Gamson and Emily M. Hodge, "Education Research and the Shifting Landscape of the American School District, 1816–2016," *Review of Research in Education* 40, no. 1 (2014). (2016): 216–49.

5. Rodney T. Ogawa and Paula A. White, "School-Based Management: An Overview," in *School-Based Management: Organizing for High Performance,* ed. Susan A. Mohrman, Priscilla Wohlstetter, and associates (San Francisco: Jossey-Bass, 1994), 53–80.

6. Kenneth K. Wong, "The Big Stick: School Reform in Chicago Depended on Setting Standards and Promoting Systemwide Improvement," *Education Next* 3, no. 1 (2003): 44–50.

7. See, e.g., Bradley D. Marianno, "Teachers' Unions on the Defensive? How Recent Collective Bargaining Laws Reformed the Rights of Teachers," *Journal of School Choice* 9, no. 4 (2015): 551–77.

8. Meredith I. Honig and Lydia R. Rainey, "Autonomy and School Improvement: What Do We Know and Where Do We Go from Here?," *Educational Policy* 26, no. 3 (2012): 465–95; Matthew P. Steinberg and Amanda Barrett Cox, "School Autonomy and District Support: How Principals Respond to a Tiered Autonomy Initiative in Philadelphia Public Schools, *Leadership and Policy in Schools* 16, no. 1 (2017): 130–65, doi: 10.1080/15700763.2016.1197278.

9. See Moe, *Special Interest.*

10. See Dale Ballou, "Contractual Constraints on School Management: Principals' Perspectives on the Teacher Contract," in *City Schools: Lessons from New York,* ed. Diane Ravitch and Joseph P. Viteritti (Baltimore: John Hopkins University Press, 2000), 89–116; Jennifer Mulhern, Jessica Levin, and Joan Schunck, *Unintended Consequences: The Case for Reforming the Staffing Rules in Urban Teachers Union Contracts* (New York: TNTP, 2005), https://tntp.org/publications/view/unintended-consequences-the -case-for-reforming-staffing-rules; and Terry M. Moe, "Bottom-Up Structure: Collective Bargaining, Transfer Rights, and the Plight of Disadvantaged Schools" (working paper, Stanford University, 2006), http://eric.ed.gov/?id=ED508944.

11. Bradley D. Marianno et al., "Cut from the Same Cloth? Comparing Urban CBAs Within States and Across the United States," *Educational Policy* 32, no. 2 (2018): 334–59.

12. Melanie Asmar, "How a Once-Promising Merit Pay System Led Denver Teachers to the Brink of a Strike," Chalkbeat, February 2019, https://chalkbeat.org/posts/co/2019/02/05 /how-once-promising-merit-pay-system-procomp-led-denver-teachers-brink-strike.

13. Katharine O. Strunk, Edward Cremata, and Julie A. Marsh, "Two Birds, One Policy? Estimating the Impact of a Multiple Measure Teacher Evaluation System on Teacher Effectiveness and Mobility in LAUSD" (paper presented at the annual meeting of the Association for Public Policy Analysis and Management, Chicago, IL, November 2, 2017).

Chapter 8

1. Henry M. Levin, "Some Economic Guidelines for Design of a Charter School District," *Economics of Education Review* 31, no. 2 (2012): 331–43.
2. Christian Buerger and Douglas N. Harris, *How Did the New Orleans School Reforms Influence School Spending?* (New Orleans: Educational Research Alliance for New Orleans, 2017), https://educationresearchalliancenola.org/files/publications/020717-Buerger -Harris-How-Did-the-New-Orleans-School-Reforms-Influence-School-Spending.pdf; Lindsay Bell Weixler, Jane Arnold Lincove, and Alica Gerry, "The Provision of Public Pre-K in the Absence of Centralized School Management," *American Educational Research Journal* 56, no. 6 (2019): 2439–73.
3. David Figlio and Susanna Loeb, "School Accountability," in *Handbook of the Economics of Education*, ed. Eric A. Hanushek, Stephen Machin, and Ludgar Woessmann (Amsterdam: Elsevier, 2011): 383–421.
4. Figlio and Loeb.
5. Denver Public Schools Office of Portfolio Management, *The 2016 Call for New Quality Schools* (January 2016), http://www.schoolrestarts.org/wp-content/uploads/2016/05 /Call_for_New_Quality_Schools_2016.pdf.
6. Homepage, ExED website, https://exed.org.

Chapter 9

1. Paul T. Hill, Christine Campbell, and Betheny Gross, *Strife and Progress: Portfolio Strategies for Managing Urban Schools* (Washington, DC: Brookings Institution Press, 2012).
2. Anthony S. Bryk et al., *Survey Measures, Factors, Composite Variables and Items Used in Organizing Schools for Improvement: Lessons from Chicago* (Chicago: Chicago Consortium for School Research, 2009), https://consortium.uchicago.edu/sites/default/files /2019-02/Survey-Development-Process-Appendix.pdf; *Research Brief: Design, Validity and Reliability of the 2014 North Carolina Teacher Working Conditions Survey* (Santa Cruz, CA: New Teacher Center, 2014), https://ncteachingconditions.org/uploads/File /NC%20val%20rel%20brief%20%205-14.pdf; Katharine O. Strunk et al., "The Best Laid Plans: An Examination of School Plan Quality and Implementation in a School Improvement Initiative," *Educational Administration Quarterly* 52, no. 2 (2016): 259–309, doi: 10.1177%2F0013161X15616864; Susan Moore Johnson, Matthew A. Kraft, and John P. Papay, "How Context Matters in High-Need Schools: The Effects of Teachers' Working Conditions on Their Professional Satisfaction and Their Students' Achievement," *Teachers College Record* 114 (2012): 1–39, https://www.researchgate.net /publication/266336145_How_context_matters_in_high-need_schools_The_effects _of_teachers%27_working_conditions_on_their_professional_satisfaction_and_their _students%27_achievement; Matthew A. Kraft and John P. Papay, "Can Professional Environments in Schools Promote Teacher Development? Explaining Heterogeneity in Returns to Teaching Experience," *Educational Evaluation and Policy Analysis* 36 (2014): 476–500, doi: 10.3102%2F0162373713519496; and Dallas Hambrick Hitt and Pamela D. Tucker, "Systematic Review of Key Leader Practices Found to Influence Student

Achievement: A Unified Framework," *Review of Educational Research* 86, no. 2 (2016): 531–69, doi: 10.3102%2F0034654315614911.

3. More detail about the survey items and constructs can be found in Appendix A and at https:\\challengingtheonebestsystem.net.

4. As our analysis here is focused on cities as a whole, we do not separate out the two parallel systems in Los Angeles.

5. Teacher/leader alternative certification cannot be ruled out as an explanation: based on survey responses, more teachers/leaders in New Orleans are alternatively certified than in the other two cities, and being alternatively certified is sometimes related to the outcomes. However, the presence of fewer URM students and school size can be ruled out as alternative explanations. The study found that New Orleans does not have significantly smaller schools than DPS, and it found that New Orleans educated more URM students than DPS. If school size or URM students were driving our results, we would expect DPS to have the highest intermediate outcomes, which is not the case.

6. This proposition is true to some degree. Indeed, in Los Angeles, stand-alone charters are smaller than traditional schools and have less experienced teachers/leaders, on average. Moreover, these characteristics are related to the intermediate outcomes as described above (teachers at smaller schools and those with less experience report higher intermediate outcomes). Thus, it is possible that charter school size and teacher experience drive some of the positive relationships between school governance type and various intermediate outcomes. However, traditional and stand-alone charters educate similar numbers of URM students, so again, we can rule out enrolling fewer URM students as an explanation of the differences between sectors. No differences were evident in the proportion of alternatively certified teachers between school models in Los Angeles.

Chapter 10

1. David A. Gamson and Emily M. Hodge, "The Relentless Reinvention of the American School District," in *The Shifting Landscape of the American School District: Race, Class, Geography, and the Perpetual Reform of Local Control, 1935–2015*, ed. David A. Gamson and Emily M. Hodge (New York: Peter Lang, 2018); David Tyack, *The One Best System: A History of American Urban Education* (Cambridge, MA: Harvard University Press, 1974).

2. Susanna Loeb and Patrick J. McEwan, "An Economic Approach to Education Policy Implementation," in *New Directions in Education Policy Implementation: Confronting Complexity*, ed. Meredith I. Honig (Albany: State University of New York Press, 2006); Sean Gailmard, "Accountability and Principal-Agent Theory," in *The Oxford Handbook of Public Accountability*, ed. Mark Bovens, Robert E. Goodin, and Thomas Schillemans (Oxford: Oxford University Press, 2014).

3. The idealized PMM also highlights two additional mechanisms: public engagement—focused largely on external communications with the larger community and parents or families—and pupil-based funding, which emphasizes the distribution of funding rather than the overall amount of funding. While these are also central components of the overall PMM, we emphasize the other five because of their centrality to changing systems and the priorities placed on them by advocates. See Paul T. Hill, Christine Campbell, and Betheny Gross, *Strife and Progress: Portfolio Strategies for Managing Urban Schools* (Washington, DC: Brookings Institution Press, 2012).

4. Hill, Campbell, and Gross, *Strife and Progress.*

5. Deborah Stone, *Policy Paradox: The Art of Political Decision Making*, 3rd ed., (New York: W.W. Norton & Company, 2012); Douglas N. Harris, *Charter School City: What the End of Traditional Public Schools in New Orleans Means for American Education* (Chicago: University of Chicago Press, 2020).

6. David A. Stuit and Thomas M. Smith, "Explaining the Gap in Charter and Traditional Public School Teacher Turnover Rates," *Economics of Education Review* 31 (2012): 268–79, https://eric.ed.gov/?id=EJ957641; A. Chris Torres, "Are We Architects or Construction Workers? Re-Examining Teacher Autonomy and Turnover in Charter Schools," *Education Policy Analysis Archives* 22 (2014): 124, doi: 10.14507/epaa.v22.1614.

7. Heinz-Dieter Meyer and Brian Rowan, eds., *The New Institutionalism in Education* (Albany: State University of New York Press, 2006); Heinz-Dieter Meyer and Brian Rowan, "Institutionalized Organizations: Formal Structure as Myth and Ceremony," *American Journal of Sociology* 83 (1977): 340–63, https://www.jstor.org/stable/2778293; and John W. Meyer, W. Richard Scott, and Terence E. Deal, "Institutional and Technical Sources of Organizational Structure: Explaining the Structure of Educational Organizations," in *Organizational Environments: Ritual and Rationality*, ed. John W. Meyer and W. Richard Scott (Beverly Hills, CA: Sage Publications, 1983).

8. Paul DiMaggio and Walter Powell, "The Iron Cage Revisited: Institutional Isomorphism and Collective Rationality in Organizational Fields," *American Sociological Review* 48 (1983): 147–60, doi: 10.2307/2095101.

9. Andrew J. McEachin, Richard Osbourne Welsh, and Dominic James Brewer, "The Variation in Student Achievement and Behavior Within a Portfolio Management Model: Early Results from New Orleans," *Educational Evaluation and Policy Analysis* 38 (2016): 669–91, doi: 10.3102%2F0162373716659928.

10. Julie A. Marsh, et al., (forthcoming) Institutional logics in Los Angeles schools: Do multiple models disrupt the grammar of schooling? American Journal of Education. https://www.journals.uchicago.edu/doi/full/10.1086/709516

11. This discussion of contextual factors influencing PMM design draws heavily on Julie A. Marsh et al., "The Process and Politics of Educational Governance Change in New Orleans, Los Angeles, and Denver," *American Educational Research Journal* (forthcoming, published online May 2020), doi: 10.3102/0002831220921475.

12. C. Kirabo Jackson, Rucker C. Johnson, and Claudia Persico, "The Effects of School Spending on Educational and Economic Outcomes: Evidence from School Finance Reforms," *The Quarterly Journal of Economics* 131, no. 1 (2016): 157–218, doi: 10.1093/qje/qjv036; Julien Lafortune, Jesse Rothstein, and Diane Whitmore Schanzenbach, "School Finance Reform and the Distribution of Student Achievement," *American Economic Journal: Applied Economics* 10, no. 2 (2018): 1–26, doi: 10.1257/app.20160567.

13. Anthony S. Bryk and Barbara Schneider, *Trust in Schools: A Core Resource for Improvement* (New York: Russell Sage Foundation, 2002); Julie Reed Kochanek and Matthew Clifford, "Trust in Districts: The Role of Relationships in Policymaking for School Improvement," in *Trust and School Life: The Role of Trust for Learning, Teaching, Leading, and Bridging*, ed. Dimitri Van Maele, Patrick B. Forsyth, and Mieke Van Houtte (Dordrecht, Netherlands: Springer, 2014), 313–34.

14. Harris, *Charter School City.*

15. Amber M. Winkler, Janie Scull, and Dara Zeehandelaar, *How Strong are U.S. Teacher Unions? A State-by-State Comparison* (Washington, DC: Fordham Institute, 2012).

16. Julie A. Marsh, "The Political Dynamics of District Reform: The Form and Fate of the Los Angeles Public School Choice Initiative," *Teachers College Record* 118, no. 9 (2016): 1–54, https://eric.ed.gov/?id=EJ1108497; Jeffrey R. Henig, *The End of Exceptionalism in American Education: The Changing Politics of School Reform* (Cambridge, MA: Harvard Education Press, 2013); Jeffrey R. Henig, Rebecca Jacobsen, and Sarah Reckhow, *Outside Money in Local School Board Elections: The Nationalization of Education Politics* (Cambridge, MA: Harvard Education Press, 2019); Sarah Reckhow, *Follow the Money: How Foundation Dollars Change Public School Politics* (New York: Oxford University Press, 2013); Janelle T. Scott, "The Politics of Venture Philanthropy in Charter School Policy and Advocacy," *Educational Policy* 23 (2009): 106–36, doi: 10.1177%2F0895904808328531; and Clarence N. Stone et al., *Building Civic Capacity: The Politics of Reforming Urban Schools* (Lawrence: University Press of Kansas, 2001).
17. Parker Baxter, Todd Ely, and Paul Teske, "Redesigning Denver's Schools: The Rise and Fall of Superintendent Tom Boasberg," *Education Next* 19, no. 2 (Spring 2019): 9, https://www.educationnext.org/files/ednext_XIX_2_baxter_et_al.pdf.
18. Kevin Mahnken, "Is Denver's Era of Education Reform Coming to an End? Outsider School Board Candidates Aim to 'Flip the Board' This November," The 74, October 9, 2019, http://www.the74million.org/article/is-denvers-era-of-education-reform -coming-to-an-end-outsider-school-board-candidates-aim-to-flip-the-board-this -november.
19. Melanie Asmar, "A New Denver School Board Takes a Softer Tone with Low-Performing Schools," *Denver Post*, December 27, 2019, https://www.denverpost.com/2019/12/27 /new-denver-school-board-low-performing-schools.
20. Alex Caputo-Pearl, "Why Los Angeles Teachers May Have to Strike," *Los Angeles Times*, January 6, 2019, https://www.latimes.com/opinion/op-ed/la-oe-caputo-pearl-teachers -strike-20190106-story.html.
21. Harris, *Charter School City*.
22. Tyack, *The One Best System*.

Appendixes

1. Matthew B. Miles, A. Michael Huberman, and Johnny Saldaña. *Qualitative Data Analysis* (Thousand Oaks, CA: Sage Publications, 2013).
2. Joseph A. Maxwell, *Qualitative Research Design: An Interactive Approach* (Thousand Oaks, CA: Sage Publications, 2012); Johnny Saldaña, *The Coding Manual for Qualitative Researchers*, 3rd ed. (Thousand Oaks, CA: Sage Publications, 2016).
3. Miles, Huberman, and Saldaña, 2013.
4. John W. Cresswell, *Qualitative Inquiry and Research Design: Choosing Among Five Approaches* (Thousand Oaks, CA: Sage Publications, 2007).
5. See Craig K. Enders, *Applied Missing Data Analysis* (New York: Guilford Press, 2010).

ACKNOWLEDGMENTS

The authors wish to thank the many educators, family members, civic leaders, and others committed to quality education in Denver, Los Angeles, and New Orleans who shared their time and insights with us. We hope this work furthers efforts in their cities and others to improve public education. We also would like to thank the Spencer Foundation for providing the core financial support for this project through a Lyle Spencer Research Grant.

We want to highlight the contributions of three individuals who, while not authors of the book, were absolutely essential to this complex project. Jane Lincove helped in writing the grant proposal that resulted in this book. Both she and Chris Torres contributed in critical ways throughout the project as part of the overall project leadership team, with Chris playing a particularly important role in the qualitative data collection and analysis. Laura Mulfinger was the organizational mastermind behind much of the logistical work, and is that rare combination of an excellent project manager and an outstanding researcher.

At critical stages of the project, we were fortunate to draw on the expertise and insights of our advisory board: Larry Cuban, Betheny Gross, Laura Hamilton, Jeff Henig, and Janelle Scott. Caroline Chauncey at Harvard Education Press guided us through the process of preparing this book, providing us timely, clear, concise, and always on target feedback, and editing by the HEP team, along with Bob Banning, improved the writing in the book. In addition, anonymous reviewers for both the grant proposal to the Spencer Foundation and the book prospectus to Harvard Education Press provided valuable feedback that shaped the project in important ways. We are grateful for this support.

The research represented in this book is the product of a true team effort across multiple institutions, and many people contributed in critical ways. The qualitative work involved extensive interviewing and the drafting of lengthy and detailed system and school profiles that provided the foundation for all of the qualitative analysis presented in this book. In addition to the book's authors, the qualitative team included: Taylor Allbright, Danica Brown, Elaine Chu, Tasminda Dhaliwal, Eupha Jeanne Daramola, Taylor Enoch-Stevens, Kate Kennedy, Tait Kellogg, Laura Mulfinger, Chris Torres, Johaiva Torres-Reyes, Kathryn Wiley, and Sarah Woodward.

The survey development and analysis, a complicated endeavor given the multiple systems and sectors we studied, included valuable contributions from: Cathy Balfe, Tasminda Dhaliwal, Alica Gerry, Taeyeon Kim, Jane Lincove, Laura Mulfinger, Sarah Rabovsky, Chris Torres, and Lindsay Weixler. Logistical and administrative support was provided by: Deanna Allen, Meghan Butler, Briana Diaz, Michelle Huhn, Laura Mulfinger, and April Serfass. Rose Krebill-Prather and Thom Allen at the Social and Economic Sciences Research Center at Washington State University were wonderful to work with on our complex surveys and multipronged survey administration.

Finally, the authors would like to thank their spouses and children, who have been (generally) patient and supportive of our work.

ABOUT THE AUTHORS

KATRINA E. BULKLEY is a professor of educational leadership at Montclair State University. Her research examines school and school district change with a focus on the intersection of policy and leadership in efforts to increase market-linked ideas in education and enhance accountability, equity, and data-driven change. She is the editor of *Between Public and Private: Politics, Governance, and the New Portfolio Models for Urban School Reform* (Harvard Education Press, with Jeffrey Henig and Henry Levin) and *Taking Account of Charter Schools: What's Happened and What's Next* (Teachers College Press, with Priscilla Wohlstetter). Her work has also been published in journals including *Educational Administration Quarterly, Educational Policy, Education Policy Analysis Archives, Education and Urban Society,* and *Phi Delta Kappan.*

JULIE A. MARSH is a professor of education policy at the Rossier School of Education at the University of Southern California and faculty director of Policy Analysis for California Education (PACE). She is also a member of the executive leadership board for the National Center for Research on Education Access and Choice (REACH). Marsh specializes in research on K–12 policy and governance, blending perspectives in education, sociology, and political science. Her work has focused on accountability and instructional policy, with particular attention to the process and politics of adoption and implementation, and the ways in which policies shape practice in urban settings. Marsh is a coeditor of the journal *Educational Evaluation and Policy Analysis,* author of the book *Democratic Dilemmas: Joint Work, Education Politics, and Community* (SUNY Press) and coeditor of the book *School Districts and Instructional Renewal* (Teachers College Press, with Amy Hightower, Michael Knapp, and Milbrey McLaughlin).

KATHARINE O. STRUNK is the Clifford E. Erickson Distinguished Chair in Education and a professor of education policy and by courtesy economics at Michigan State University. She is also the director of the Education Policy Innovation Collaborative (EPIC). Her research focuses on K–12 education governance, including teachers' unions, collective bargaining agreements, and portfolio management models, as well as teacher labor markets, school turnaround, and accountability policies. She works in partnership with district and state policymakers, including with the Los Angeles Unified School District and the Michigan Department of Education to help decision-makers formulate, design, and revise policy. She is the president-elect of the Association for Education Finance and Policy and a member of the executive leadership board for the National Center for Research on Education Access and Choice (REACH), as well as a past associate editor and policy brief editor of the journal *Education Finance and Policy*.

DOUGLAS N. HARRIS is a professor and chair of the Department of Economics, the Schlieder Foundation Chair in Public Education, and director of both the Education Research Alliance for New Orleans (ERA-New Orleans) and the National Center for Research on Education Access and Choice (REACH), all at Tulane University. With nearly 100 journal articles and other publications, his research has influenced policy on a wide variety of K–12 and higher education policy issues. He is author of the book, *Charter School City: What the End of Traditional Public Schools in New Orleans Means for American Education* (University of Chicago Press). His first book, *Value-Added Measures in Education* (Harvard Education Press), was nominated for the national Grawemeyer prize in education. A nonresident senior fellow at the Brookings Institution, he has advised governors in seven states and education ministries in several foreign countries, testified in the US Senate, and advised the US Department of Education and Obama White House on multiple education policies. His work is also widely cited in national media.

AYESHA K. HASHIM is an assistant professor of policy, leadership, and school improvement at the University of North Carolina at Chapel Hill School of

Education. Dr. Hashim's research focuses on district-level school reform aimed at improving student achievement in underserved communities. A mixed-methods researcher, Dr. Hashim draws on theories from economics, sociology, and organizational change to study the impacts of reforms on teacher and student outcomes, as well as leadership, organizational, and implementation conditions that shape these results. Much of her research has focused on the Public School Choice Initiative in the Los Angeles Unified School District, which paved the way for a wide range of autonomous school providers to operate in the district. Her work has been published in *Education Finance and Policy, Economics of Education Review, Educational Evaluation and Policy Analysis, Computers and Education,* and *Peabody Journal of Education.* She received the New Scholar Award in 2017 from the Association for Education Finance and Policy for her dissertation on how instructional coaches coordinate systemic change in a school district aiming to integrate technology with instruction of the Common Core State Standards.

ABOUT THE
CONTRIBUTING AUTHORS

TAYLOR N. ALLBRIGHT is an assistant professor of educational leadership at California State Polytechnic University, Pomona. Her research focuses on efforts to further educational equity in K–12 schools, investigating how leaders design and implement policies with equity goals, the enactment of policies intended to mitigate racial inequity, and the politics and process of educational policy change. Her work has been published in journals including the *American Journal of Education* and *Educational Policy*.

DANICA ROBINSON BROWN is a PhD candidate in sociology in the City, Culture, and Community program at Tulane University. Her research examines how the social organization of schools shapes the outcomes of historically marginalized students. Her current research examines the impact of schools of choice on college attendance of underrepresented students in higher education. Her work seeks to understand the organizational conditions under which choice policies have positive or negative impacts.

EUPHA JEANNE DARAMOLA is an urban education policy PhD candidate at the University of Southern California. Her research examines K–12 policy implementation with particular attention to how systemic racism influences the enactment of policies at the school and district levels. In combination, these areas of research have manifested into studies on community engagement, discipline, and school choice policies.

TASMINDA K. DHALIWAL is a PhD candidate in urban education policy at the University of Southern California. Her research examines in- and out-of-school factors that drive unequal educational outcomes for marginalized students, including those related to housing instability and homelessness, school discipline, and school choice. Her work has been published in *Peabody Journal of Education* and *AERA Open*.

JANE ARNOLD LINCOVE is an associate professor of public policy at the University of Maryland, Baltimore County, and a research affiliate of the Education Research Alliance for New Orleans at Tulane University; the Maryland Longitudinal Data System Center at the University of Maryland, Baltimore; and the Baltimore Education Research Consortium at the Johns Hopkins University. Her research focuses on the equity effects of school choice and other market-based reforms in public education. Her work has been published in *Economics of Education Review, Educational Evaluation and Policy Analysis, Educational Researcher, American Education Research Journal,* and other outlets.

LAURA STEEN MULFINGER, PhD, is a project administrator at the University of California's Rossier School of Education, where she coordinates and conducts K–12 policy research. She also serves as a managing editor of *Educational Evaluation and Policy Analysis,* and is a coauthor of *Learning from L.A.: Institutional Change in American Public Education* (Harvard Education Press).

A. CHRIS TORRES is an associate professor of K–12 educational administration at Michigan State University. He studies how educators and communities are experiencing new policies, systems, and organizations that are increasing their influence in traditionally marginalized spaces, and how educator recruitment, development, and retention affect the viability and sustainability of organizational improvement efforts. He serves on editorial boards of journals such as *Educational Evaluation and Policy Analysis* and is an associate editor for *Educational Administration Quarterly.* His work has also been published in various journals including *Educational Administration Quarterly, Urban Education, Teaching and Teacher Education,* and the *Journal of School Leadership.*

SARAH M. WOODWARD is the programs director for the Arts Council New Orleans, where she directs arts-based youth and community development programs. Sarah earned her PhD in urban studies from the City, Culture, and Community program at Tulane University. Her research focuses on the ways test-based and market accountability shape access to arts education in charter school systems, and the role of arts education in supporting academic, transformative, and professional outcomes for youth.

INDEX